Pine-Tarred and Feathered

Pine-Tarred and Feathered

a year on the baseball beat

jim kaplan

For Josh —
With thanks and appreciation —

Jim
7 May 1998

Algonquin Books of Chapel Hill
Chapel Hill, North Carolina   1985

Algonquin Books of Chapel Hill
Post Office Box 2225
Chapel Hill, North Carolina, 27515–2225
ISBN 0-912697-15-6
Portions of this book appeared in *Sports Illustrated*.
LIBRARY OF CONGRESS CATALOGING IN PUBLICATION DATA
Kaplan, Jim.
    Pine-tarred and feathered.
    1. Kaplan, Jim.   2. Sportswriters—United States—
Biography.   3. Baseball—United States.   I. Title.
GV742.42.K36A36   1985   070.4'49796357'0924 [B]   84-24393
ISBN 0-912697-15-6

to my parents

preface

"What do you do for a living?"

I write for *Sports Illustrated*.

The questions continue: "Do you cover any particular beat?" Yes, baseball. "Any particular team?" No, whichever one is newsworthy. "I bet you get to travel all over." Well, to baseball cities. "Which players are you friendliest with?" And so on.

The answers always satisfy the questioner more than me. How do I explain my work to outsiders? They think it's glamorous and fun, and in certain respects they're right. But the real enjoyment isn't what they expect it to be. It's certainly not travel, which consists almost entirely of airports and hotels and clubhouses. Nor is it watching ballgames and getting my name in print—transitory pleasures both. The joy is establishing friendships with baseball people and writing stories I find satisfying—both of which are difficult to convey conversationally. And is there any way to flesh out the really hard work I do: the week-long preoccupation with my subject matter (I earn my paycheck as much for what comes before the writing as for the writing itself), the all-night sessions at the computer, the endless visions and revisions before the taking of sleep?

Late in 1982, it occurred to me: If I kept a record of one calendar year, I could explain once and for all what I do—and perhaps learn something about myself in the process. Noting that writers have been getting ideas and inspirations from

preface

their journals since the days of Pepys, my girlfriend Audrey McGinn suggested that I take daily peeps at myself. "The life of every man," wrote Sir Matthew Barrie, "is a diary in which he means to write one story, and writes another; and his humblest hour is when he compares the volume as it is with what he vowed to make it."

I vowed to make my diary personal as well as professional. By recording everything of importance—and thereby forgetting nothing—I could retain the events in my life that too often had proved elusive. So many things had happened to me, so many thoughts had occurred, so many many feelings had arisen. Unrecorded and forgotten, they'd vanished in utter silence.

As I outlined the project in my mind, other potential benefits began to appear. The diary might be useful to aspiring journalists. As a former graduate student in j-school and occasional contributor to professional publications, I'd long felt that journalism students were getting too much theoretical and too little practical advice. But every time I began to write down useful pointers, I came across as too pedantic: You *will* do this, you *won't* do that. The journal could have a different tone. If I simply described the rules I followed while writing stories, the advice would come across painlessly, almost subliminally.

Then I thought about baseball readers. Baseball is more than our national pastime: It's our national obsession. After more than a dozen years on the beat, I still found the sport endlessly fascinating. I had learned that if I concentrated and asked questions, I could discover something unique and surprising about almost every game I attended. Postgame conversations with players, managers, coaches, scouts and sportswriters were always revealing. *The Boston Globe*'s Bob Ryan, one of the most deliciously opinionated columnists I know, recently put it this way: "Whether you believe Jim Rice is a man who delivers big hits in late innings, just consider that nobody ever had a debate over whether O. J. Simpson, Gale Sayers, Hugh McElhenny or anybody else was a big third-down runner. As a talking game, baseball beats all the rest put together." Alas, because of space limitations, I was unable to give my readers every conversational tidbit they might have enjoyed. The trivia and gossip and, I fear, some of the insight remained in my mind and my notebooks. Until the Kaplan diaries. Nothing was too trivial for *this* pursuit.

Perhaps too, there were significant statements to make about the sport. Away from the pressbox, I could record thoughts about the private lives of the players: how they lived on the road; how they felt about being public figures; how their wives and kids were affected by their celebrity status and constant travel.

I'm writing with the benefit of hindsight: The journal is complete. I thought it would be a simple but time-consuming process. I was half right. In the beginning, I'd take whatever free moments I had—before bed, in the subway, on a plane— and jot down the day's entries in a record book. Every month or so, I'd type the notes into my computer—rewriting, editing, adding thoughts along the way. And that's when it grew complicated. As I reread a month's entries, I'd find associations, contradictions, ironies. Making connections—and sense—of them was the real challenge. The difficulty wasn't noting or quoting but emoting. At times the process was painful and dislocating; so is the moment of birth.

In the end I was left with a narrative mural of game notes, conversations, editorial thoughts—and one of the most satisfying professional experiences of my life. The journal helped me to understand my business, my beat and myself. And I will never again have to explain what I do for a living.

Jim Kaplan
Chilmark, Mass.
July 28, 1984

list of illustrations

Pine-Tarred and Feathered

january 1, 1983

My New Year's resolutions are as follows:

1. Improve my writing for *Sports Illustrated*, the magazine I've been associated with the last 12½ years. As a baseball writer, I'm going to read all the baseball stories in *SI*, the papers and *The Sporting News*, not to mention the considerable variety of schlock written about the game.

2. Write a book. On what? Baseball, journalism and myself. Forewarned is forearmed.

3. Spend more time with my sons, Benjamin, 14, and Matthew, 13, who live half a dozen subway stops from me. In New York, travel is measured by transit.

4. Write a *good* book.

5. Get in shape again.

6. Be more assertive.

7. Write a *great* book.

8. Loosen up; generally, relax.

I made some progress in the last category over New Year's Eve. Come midnight and I was chucking streamers and yelling "wuh-ho!" with my girlfriend, Audrey McGinn. We took the subway to another party, with streamers and confetti on our coats, and people were pointing at us and laughing. I loved it. Very much out of character.

I tend to hang back and wait for things to happen—for someone else to initiate conversation or make plans, for the

january

story I'm writing to appear before me on the field, for the guy I'm interviewing to begin speaking reams of copy into my tape recorder. So I'm not only going to read more stories, but speak with more people—"visit" with them, in baseball parlance. That way I'll initiate rather than react.

I'm also aware that I tend to follow baseball to the exclusion of all else. I do write about other sports from time to time, and I'd better start backgrounding myself. But the main reason to read more nonbaseball stories in *SI* is that it's a hell of a magazine. By secluding myself in a baseball shack, I'm missing a wider world.

In addition to my magazine work I'd like to write a weekly newspaper column for average chess players. As far as I can see, the typical column is either written for experts (results of tournaments, etc.) or novices ("white mates in two moves")—not ordinary players trying to improve their games. Another project I'm hoping to do is a baseball book with Doug DeCinces, the California Angels third baseman. Tomorrow I'll send a written proposal to my agent, Dominick Abel. If we get a contract, Doug will write and I will edit a diary of the 1983 season.

2 Wrote the final copy of the DeCinces proposal. I don't ever want to use a typewriter again. After dealing with paper, drafts, whiteouts and penned-in insertions, I'm exhausted. For my *SI* stories I've been using a Portabubble word processor, and it's the greatest invention since moveable type. What a pleasure it is to move paragraphs, make insertions and type corrections on the screen—to write, in effect, one long draft. No paper, no pens, no muss, no fuss. I figure the machine cuts my writing time in half. It's also as much fun as playing Scrabble or Anagrams.

Unfortunately, the machine doesn't come equipped with a print-out mechanism, at least not one that produces neat 8" ×

11" pages suitable for freelance submissions. To get print-outs I have to call a special number at Time Inc., stick the phone in the computer and transmit. I can't use the company for freelance assignments. However, Associate Editor John Papanek tells me I can buy a good printer for about $600. As soon as Doug and I get the advance, I'll buy the printer and be in business.

I've been assigned to cover Saturday's NFL playoff between the New England Patriots and Miami Dolphins. I haven't covered football all season. What's a guy to do? **3**

At the magazine a lot is done for you. Football Editor Joe Marshall told me whom to call for press credentials and briefed me on Miami. Writer-reporter Bob Sullivan gave me some New England background. The Time Inc. travel department routinely makes airline, rent-a-car and hotel reservations for writers. All that remains for me to do is to fill up a couple of notebooks and write several hundred lines of informative, incisive, entertaining, witty, clever, immortally phrased copy.

I'm going to Miami Wednesday night, expecting to spend a day with the Dolphins and a day with the Patriots. Getting copy on the Dolphins won't be so tough, but the Patriots aren't arriving until Friday night. They'll have dinner and meetings lasting almost until their curfew. The assistant public relations man said he'd try to rush in a couple of guys for interviews during the breaks. The operative word here is "try." **4**

The game figures to attract a horde of media. It's in Miami and features two old American Football Conference rivals. Fortunately, our Miami correspondent, Charlie Nobles, says he thinks Dolphins coach Don Shula will be available for a private interview. That's a break. But most of the star players will be mobbed. In a situation like this, I usually go for a peripheral player who is known for his insights. My Patriots choice is Mark van Eeghen, a Colgate grad who played for some excellent teams in Oakland.

The tendency of sportswriters to choose "articulate" players is at once understandable and hazardous. It's understandable because we're looking for someone who is agreeable, quotable and incisive. It's hazardous because, let's face it, we're also looking for someone who is like us—or like the way we perceive ourselves to be. One problem with this approach is that we're only getting one perspective. Another is that we're not using the opportunity to meet people unlike us—people who, admittedly, may be difficult interviews. Finally, by discovering athletes who like the things in our world, we frustrated jocks feel reassured in our masculinity (for the record, I was a willing athletic participant not known for his speed; my high school teammates called me "Snowshoes"). Our choice of sportswriting as a career can't be bad, we tell ourselves, if intelligent people make sports their career. At the same time we can feel at least equal to noncultivated athletes; they may have what we're missing, but we have what their lives lack.

Having said all this, my Patriot choice for an interview is Mark van Eeghen.

Actually, most of the preparation could be moot. Playoff stories center on the game rather than the pregame; it's assumed people know a lot about the teams and the seasons they've had. If favored Miami wins, I'll compile a background report of 150–200 lines (an *SI* line is 38 characters across). Staff Writer Alex Wolff will use about 60 of my lines in a roundup story on six of the eight NFL playoff games. My job will be to do a nuts-and-bolts job, with an angle that holds up for the roundup. If New England wins, Gil Rogin may want me to write a separate story on the game. That would be a major challenge.

Fortunately, I'll have all night to write because the game's being played on Saturday and the story won't close until Sunday. If the game were on Sunday afternoon, I'd be under the gun.

There are certain rituals I follow on a trip. **5**

● Before leaving, I double-check what I'm bringing. I don't check everything, just the essentials—tickets, money, tape recorder, computer, research material. If I'm missing any of these, I'm in trouble. Anything else I can buy.

● I always use the same car service to go from my Brooklyn apartment to the airport. I'm not superstitious—I just think that if the drivers get used to me, they'll give me courteous service.

● I arrive at the airport an hour before the flight is scheduled to leave; at 38 I'm too old to be rushing for gates.

● I'm among the last to board and leave the plane. No use waiting in line.

Normally I believe in checking everything I have with the porter at curbside. Unfortunately, I can't risk losing the word processor or my briefcase, so I wheel them on board with my luggage carrier. It took me a long time to buy a carrier; I had a macho hangup about wheeling my bags. Then I had a hernia scare; and comfort became more important than appearance, *The Preppy Handbook* notwithstanding. Just call me Words on Wheels.

For vacations I'm perfectly happy traveling coach class. As a business passenger I have real problems in coach. The aisles are so narrow that it's difficult to wheel the carrier back to my seat, and the three-across seats are so cramped that it's difficult to get any work done.

Once airborne, I'll immediately bury myself in my reading. That's because I find almost nothing enjoyable about planes. Airports are often light years from the hotel, the captain talks too much and the movie's lousy. Incredibly, *An American in*

january

Paris was playing on this flight, but in first class where I couldn't watch it. That's my definition of frustration.

All wasn't lost. My life is made up of what I call "existential moments"—the instants when we face decisions that will bring us immediate comfort or distress. Today's existential moment came at 7:45 P.M., when I checked in and found that the flight wouldn't be leaving until 9 o'clock. Decision: wait for the free dinner on board or eat now. A sign for "Steak House" made up my mind. There followed a feast of soup, salad, baked potato and steak. And after takeoff the meal—a snack—wasn't served until 11.

Once in Miami, I checked into the Airport Marriott Hotel and was given a package from Charlie Nobles. He left me press credentials, parking pass and a note confirming the Shula interview. Later, I called Nobles to thank him. He covered pro football for nine years and wants nothing more to do with it. Nonetheless, he told me that if I needed someone to do a locker room interview, he'd be available. Despite my insecurity about the assignment, I politely refused. He has done enough.

6 Swam at the hotel's heated pool. That's three days of exercise out of six. I'm right on schedule for one resolution. I also think I'll swim more often. It's the only sport I know in which it's virtually impossible to get hurt.

I always go to a team practice at least an hour early because I tend to get lost on the way. (I'm in distinguished company. Explaining how he took the subway to Brooklyn for the World Series, Yogi Berra said, "I knew I was going to take the wrong train, so I left early.") Today I assumed the Dolphins would practice at the Orange Bowl, the site of the game. I arrived and was told they were working out at Biscayne College. A cop gave me directions and I arrived on time.

In baseball you can watch a practice from close-up. Here

the writers were allowed to sit on benches about 100 yards from where the Dolphins were practicing; Shula wouldn't let the New England writers watch practice at all. I guess war games are supposed to be secret. In baseball you can march right into the clubhouse and talk to the players. Here the locker room is closed and I had to grab players on the way in and out. All I got was a lineman. Shula, on the other hand, was pleasant and engaging. We sat in his office, amid his crowded desk and playbook and memorabilia, and chatted for twenty minutes. Not as hostile as many football coaches.

Returning to the hotel, I ran into Don Mitchell and Bob Ryan from Boston's Channel 5, and we had a splendid dinner at a Miami Beach restaurant called Joe's Stone Crabs. Mitchell, a very classy fellow, is a Jamaica-born cameraman, a jogger and a chess buff like me. Ryan, a reporter, is an energetic, amusing guy, full of anecdote and opinion. He used to work at *The Boston Globe*, where he was one of the country's best pro basketball writers.*

Having caught three more Dolphins by morning and three **7** Patriots by night, I feel modestly prepared for a Dolphin victory and poorly prepared for a Patriot win. Shamefacedly, I'm rooting for Miami—that is to say, for a background file instead of a by-lined story. "Ridiculous!" Audrey thundered over the phone. "Get mad! Show them! I want the Patriots to crush them!"

As an English teacher at Scarsdale High School who has taught kids at every level, Audrey has a built-in B.S. detector. That's why she jumped all over me. And she was right: Already I'm shrinking from challenges.

I had dinner tonight with Byron Day of NBC.** I have much

---

*In 1984 Ryan returned to *The Globe* to write columns and features.
**He is now at Sports Time, a cable network.

more respect than a lot of print people do for network sports reporters (local TV sports is, for the most part, a disaster). They're constantly in a position to embarrass themselves. If they make a mistake, all America hears or sees it; if we make one, we can always delete it by press time. I was impressed by Day's preparation and general good cheer. Electronic people seem less neurotic than print people. What other glib generalizations am I prepared to make about them? That they wink at you and shake hands a lot.

8   The Dolphins won 28–13. Befitting my mixed feelings about my ability to handle the assignment, I felt simultaneously relieved and guilty. I never said I was normal.

In any case, I wrote a file stressing the similarities between the 1983 team and the glory clubs of the 1970s—another No-Name Defense, a hard-charging fullback like Larry Csonka and a precision passer like Bob Griese. Alex Wolff will have plenty to use.

Football is a tough beat. It's not enough that all the writing invariably comes after the game: The Dolphins were elusive interviewees who cleared out the locker room half an hour after the game. No lingering over beers, as in baseball. My postgame quotes were sketchy indeed. Fortunately, one of the game's stars was fullback Andra Franklin, whom I'd interviewed yesterday. Another postgame break: Shula had an especially eye-catching criticism to make of his own owner, Joe Robbie, who had taken a cheap shot at New England by ordering ice shavings dumped near the end zone. A pleasantry that didn't figure in my file was a nice conversation I had with tight end Joe Rose, another of the game's heroes. He went on at some length about how much he admired *Sports Illustrated*. I don't think it was just a put-on.

Sometimes people will go out of their way for us. After one Super Bowl, Steve Wulf got word in the locker room that he was supposed to do a sidebar on the Raiders' Rod Martin.

Wulfie found Martin amid a gaggle of reporters. "Rod, I'm
Steve Wulf from *Sports Illustrated*," he said. "Steve," said Rod,
"let's talk."

Swimming is not an injury-free sport after all. Following **9**
four days in the pool, my right knee—the patella tendon, to
be exact—is hurting. I've had every manner of injury and
ailment: a broken ankle; a badly sprained ankle; acute chon-
dromalacia of the selfsame patella tendon; hernia and ulcer
scares and a chronic soreness of some sort in the neck. When
you get to be my age (hah), you're always playing in pain.
   Meanwhile, I'm suffering from a disease that will be with
me for the rest of my life. It's called hypochondria.

In the front and back of the magazine are "regional" **10**
stories. They're called regionals because they run in tandem
with regional advertising. If there's a two-thirds ad that runs
in the Southern editions of the magazine, then one-third of a
page is available for edit copy. Even when there's room
around national advertising, the edit space is called regional.
Regional stories vary from book reviews to first-person ac-
counts to sports medicine to editorial "Viewpoints." Almost
any story that has merit but doesn't fit into some category in
the bulk of the magazine has a chance to run as a regional.
   I've written a potential regional on the appeal of golf. One
reason I like the sport is that it has so much in common with
baseball. Both are leisurely, chummy sports with much time
for conversation and reflection. Both use similar muscle
groups (especially the brain). Both have intricate rulebooks,
bizarre situations and long traditions. And both, I find, have
congenial people. My story features the raffish gang I hang
out with at Dyker Beach Golf Club in Brooklyn: Marty Rosenmertz, a stock-market whiz and retired clothing-store manager; Vince Scilla, an artist who lives in Little Italy; Artie Cola,

a semiretired dye maker and Art Carney look-alike who sings as he swings, and Artie Hersh, an infectiously enthusiastic physical education teacher in the Bedford-Stuyvesant neighborhood of Brooklyn.

Unfortunately, the editors weren't interested in the story. Too obvious for a sports magazine, Gil said. No problem. With Gil's permission, I'm sending the story to Pucci Meyer at the *New York News Sunday Magazine.* No reason not to. If a story deserves to be told, it deserves to be sold.

11   A friend of mine who works in Rockefeller Center has just received a demotion. "I learned that you get ahead two ways," he told me, "politics and family connections."

There's some truth to what he's saying, but I'm not as outraged as he is. I used to take pride in doing the "right" thing. I'd quietly work away in my office and then act outraged and self-righteous when a more sociable person got rewarded. No more. If life were simply a process of telling right from wrong, we could submit all our problems to computers. I don't view politics as a dirty word. It comes from a Greek word meaning citizen; at heart politics is nothing more than dealing with people. And there are better ways of dealing with people, I've discovered, than being arrogant and self-righteous. That just gets the other guy's back up.

I'm not advocating servility. An abject yes-man is just as helpless as an arrogant dissenter. I know of one fellow who was afraid to go on strike with us in 1976; he felt his position with the magazine was too tenuous. So he walked through the picket line—and got fired a few years later.

What I'm getting at is the idea of making oneself "visible"—something I've been very poor at. I think there's just as much to be gained from well-intended dissent as silent agreement. Someone with the company's best interests in mind will dissent freely; the exchange of ideas is part of the creative process. Unfortunately, there's too little dissent at the magazine.

Musing on the subject, I'm determined to speak again with Gil. Something he said about the golf story bothered me, and I didn't pick up on it during our last conversation. When I asked if I could freelance the piece, he said, "Did you spend a lot of money on it?" I said I hadn't. "Then it's O.K. to sell," he replied.

What I'm thinking now is, what difference does it make how much money was spent? If Time Inc. didn't want the story, they shouldn't prevent me from selling it elsewhere. I see the issue as a First Amendment question: the right to expression. Besides, when a Time Inc. employee publishes a story elsewhere, the company looks good.

I have the week to write my Baseball Issue story—why the **12** National League has won 19 of the last 20 All-Star Games and the last four World Series—and I did some good work today. First, I finished the research by attending the Hall of Fame press conference and interviewing Chub Feeney and Monte Irvin. Feeney's the president of the National League. When I wrote a pro–player strike story two years ago, he walked up to me, shook his head and said, "Bad, Jim, bad." We hadn't exchanged ten words since, and I wasn't sure he'd talk now. Feeney was brusque but polite, and he answered all my questions. Irvin's an assistant to the Commissioner. A Hall of Famer and veteran of the old Negro Leagues, Monte is also one of the most decent people in the game. He was most helpful when I asked him about the NL's superior recruiting of blacks and Hispanics.

Then I started writing. Baseball Editor Larry Keith and I have decided to attack the story by considering the differences between the leagues—in rules, personnel, ballparks and traditions—to determine how these differences might help the National League. The story is going to be a monster, and it needs a catchy, anecdotal lead. The World Series just happened to supply one. The first run in the Series finale came when Milwaukee's Pete Vuckovich threw a perfect pitch. The Cardinals' Lonnie Smith hit a weak grounder, but reached first when the ball took moon hops off the artificial turf at Busch Memorial Stadium. Here, encapsulated, was one of the major AL problems—adjusting to turf fields—and how costly it became. Only 4 of the 14 AL parks—as opposed to 6 of the 12 NL stadiums—have artificial turf. Invariably, AL fielders can't adjust to high and skipping bounces; nor are AL baserunners speed-oriented enough to take advantage of the fast infields. By contrast, it's easier for NL teams to switch from a carpeted field to a slower grassy one, because their reflexes have been sharpened.

Here are some other differences I'm going to present in the story:

• The NL's superior farm systems and head start on recruiting black and Hispanic players.

• The preponderance of home-run parks in the AL. Six of the 14 AL parks are considered home-run heavens, and only three are considered pitchers' parks. Only three NL fields are considered slugger-oriented; most of the rest favor the pitchers. As a result, AL hitters tend to swing for the fences, while their NL brethren try to make contact. Contact-hitting teams tend to have an advantage over otherwise equal homer-oriented clubs because they have so many more ways to score.

• Speed. Even before artificial turf encouraged base-stealing, the NL was a runner's league and the AL wasn't.

• The designated hitter. The DH hits in place of the AL pitcher; the NL doesn't have a DH, so the pitcher bats for himself. Because they don't have to make a decision about pinch-hitting for pitchers, AL managers tend to overwork their rotations and underwork their bullpens. With that extra bat in the lineup, the AL waits for big innings; the NL manufactures runs by using the sacrifice bunt and the stolen base.

• The NL is considered a fastball pitchers' league with a low strike zone, the AL a breaking-ball league with a high strike zone. Advantage to the NL for two reasons. First, it's easier to adjust from fastballs to breaking balls than vice-versa. Second, relying on the high strike zone is costly in interleague play because most homers are hit on high pitches.

13 Lead completed, I'm sitting here with mounds of information—files from our correspondents, data gathered by the Elias Sports Bureau and interview notes. How to proceed? I've scribbled down the sketchiest of outlines, but basically I'm writing the story out of my head and consulting notes when I need to fill in something. For me, the important thing is to get the draft down on paper—er, screen. Once I'm done, I can go over my copy and make insertions and corrections.

In this case, the final product doesn't have to be especially smooth. What I'm giving Larry is a run-through of a complicated story that won't be edited for almost a month. We'll go over what I've done to see if I'm on the right track, and then I'll write the final copy.

14 I spent the entire day at the screen and wound up with my draft about three-quarters complete at 750 lines. In the process I relearned two old lessons. First, I can't overload my trusty Portabubble with so many words. Some of the corrections I typed in didn't take—FUL and OPN kept flashing on the screen. I finally calmed the thing down by killing a previous story I'd been saving in the memory. That opened up some space.

Second, I remembered that transitions are overrated. The more tired I got, the more difficult I found it to make transitions, so I stopped making them altogether. The story scans well nonetheless. In journalism, I think, it's often acceptable to go from one subject to another without transitions. Anyway, a lot of obvious transitional words and phrases—"and," "but," "speaking of which"—look forced.

15   I transmitted the 750-line segment, then wrote and transmitted a 250-line conclusion. It's Saturday, but I won't be speaking with Larry until Monday. He's the college basketball editor as well as the baseball editor, and he'll be busy all weekend. Most stories close Sunday night, and the editors routinely work so late that they have to sleep in midtown hotels—or their offices. I was a researcher closing stories for ten years. It was not uncommon to come home as the sun was rising Monday morning. Waiting for copy to be edited and processed, I would grow deathly tired—too tired to read, too tired to sleep, sometimes too tired even to watch TV. It was a long night's journey into day.

The magazine's official work week runs from Thursday through Monday so that weekend results can be included in the issue. I suppose the schedule is fine for single people, who can just as easily go skiing on a Tuesday as a Saturday, but it's difficult for married people with school-age children. I've missed a lot of time I could have spent with my sons. I can't say the job ended my marriage, but it didn't help. One of the best things about being promoted to staff writer three years ago is that I'm no longer tied to the Thursday-Monday week. Unless I'm writing a news story on a late deadline, I usually get weekends off. Sometimes I think I'm spending more time with the kids during the separation than I did during the marriage.

16   I didn't get up until 1 P.M. Last night Audrey and I went over to some friends' apartment for pizza, beer and movies on the cassette machine. Just Dick and Jane at the Olde Town Theater. Only Dick and Jane never saw the original episode of "Amos 'n Andy," a big scene from "Casablanca," the last half of "The Blues Brothers" and all of "Mommy Dearest" in one night. Counting a session with my computer earlier in the day, I figure I spent ten hours in front of a screen. No wonder I needed so much sleep.

Indeed, the only thing that kept me awake for the movies was an afternoon nap. Many people who lived or are living to a ripe old age—Winston Churchill, George Halas, my father Ben, my uncle Moe—have been daily nappers. A doctor once gave me an explanation for long-lived dozers—something about regenerating the system just as it's slowing down. Unfortunately, I can't nap every day, only when I'm exhausted.

17

Not a good day. Pucci Meyer at the *News* hasn't received the golf story, though I mailed it last week. I'm sending another copy over by messenger. My agent, Dominick Abel, hasn't heard from Doug DeCinces' agent, and time is running short if we hope to get a contract by spring training. Finally, Larry Keith wasn't crazy about my National League runthrough. He felt I was too evenhanded and insufficiently polemical. I can see his point. The magazine wants to take a stand about NL superiority, arouse people, get them mad. Why am I always trying to be a "nice guy"?

With this in mind, I had stomach flu half the night.

18

I spoke with DeCinces. He has just received a copy of the proposal and hasn't had time to read it. He'll have an answer by tomorrow, but he did drop a hint. He wasn't sure he wanted to devote so much time to the project, much less say some things that will anger baseball officials several years before his career is over. For some reason, I'm not worried.

january

Maybe I don't have as much invested in the project as I thought I did.

19   Doug decided against the project, at least for now. "I plan on being around the game for quite a while," he said. I'm disappointed but not crushed. Much as I would have liked to do a ballplayer's diary, I'd have been a secondary character—a Boswell instead of a Johnson. Now I'm free to concentrate on my own story.

   I try not to get stuck by setbacks. Each one should be a beginning, not an end. As it happened, I learned today that my best friend, Jim Fesler, is moving from New York to Boston. I'll miss him, and I won't have the advantage of his company and counsel. Maybe I'll compensate by adding other friendships and become more self-sufficient.

20   The word around the office is that Gil isn't pleased with the writing of late. (He can't mean my writing because I haven't been doing any that he's seen—the NL story went right to Larry Keith.) Editors are being urged to have conferences with writers. Some of us began talking about the late Andre Laguerre, who was managing editor when I arrived in 1970. The quintessential "writer's editor," Andre had story conferences every day—at the nearby Ho Ho bar. Holding court, he'd entertain ideas from writers who drank with him. "It was important to stand at his right elbow," Herm Weiskopf was saying, "because he liked to lean on his left."

21   The *News* accepted my golf story! They're paying me $500 or $600, which means I'll be able to buy the printer. I feel great.

I saw "Gandhi" today with Audrey and my son Benjamin. **22** Great figures like Gandhi used to make me question what I do for a living. I couldn't guiltlessly write a sports story unless it dealt with some "issue" like race or unionism. No more. If I get pleasure writing something, that's enough. And I get more pleasure out of writing sports stories than anything I've ever done. My pulse rate doubles when I'm typing. The moment I get over the crisis that accompanies most stories and hear the words start to sing—that's satisfaction enough.

I think Gandhi would have agreed with me. He didn't proclaim himself a great leader: the man with the answer. He enjoyed simple things and appreciated diversity in people. "I think you'll find there's room for all of us," he told South African racists in the movie.

I know there's room for sportswriters.

The baseball season doesn't begin with the first pitch of **23** spring training or even the first pitch of Opening Day. It begins with the annual New York Baseball Writers dinner, the first big baseball event of the year. It's a watershed in which the season past is celebrated and the season future anticipated.

For eating or entertainment, the dinner isn't much. It consists of endless awards presentations and acceptance speeches, some short films, a few laughs and a lot of nostalgia. Furthermore, it's militantly, even offensively all-male; the word stag fairly leaps out of the invitation. In 1973 the *San Francisco Examiner*'s Stephanie Salter, then a reporter with us, tried to attend. They threw her out. Roy Blount, Jr., and I left the dinner in protest, but nobody else did. The incident was news for about two days. Later a couple of officers in the baseball writers association tried unsuccessfully to deny me clubhouse credentials to the World Series. "The only time I see you, you're with some broad," one of them said.

So why do I attend a dinner supported by such antediluvian people? Because in a strange way, they're my heroes. These cigar-chomping traditionalists represent some of baseball's best instincts. There's nothing about baseball they ever wanted to change. Oh, sure, some things, such as segregation and low salaries, cried out for change. But baseball rules and traditions were by and large perfect as they stood in, say, 1950. In one of the game's great ironies, the "progressives" gave us the DH, artificial turf, indoor stadiums, night Series games, expansion and most everything else that over the past two decades or so has dulled the spectacle.

The dinner maintains a sense of tradition. The night's activities are printed in a scorebook, and the national anthem is sung. This year the guest speaker was Joe Piscopo, the hilarious sportscaster on "Saturday Night Live." A lot of people in the audience didn't get his barbed jokes or laugh much. The dinner attracts countless old-timers, and I got the impression that these ruddy fellows had never seen "Saturday Night Live." Much as I like Piscopo, I found myself reassured by his less than total acceptance. I don't want baseball to become too upscale too fast.

A couple of sobering events occurred at the dinner. Moss Klein, the emcee, had us observe a moment of silence to honor the "friends of baseball" who died since last year's dinner. The list was very, very long.

Later came my initiation to another side of journalism. I sat next to a freelancer named Doug Garr. I asked him what he tells young people who are interested in careers as freelancers.

"I ask them to think back to when they were 12 years old," he said. "I say, 'Was your hero Mickey Mantle? If so, you're in trouble. If it was Hemingway, you've got a chance.'"

That rules me out.

Freelance writers have to be extremely aggressive, Garr told me. A successful high-tech writer, he said he clears a profit of about $20,000 a year. From what I've heard, that probably puts him in the top 5 percent. He told me he works best when he chooses a few editors he likes. He's always on the lookout for new ideas and is a tough bargainer when it comes to fees. Editors respect him for holding out, as long as he does it tactfully. "It's a negotiating process," he said. "They offer you one figure, you ask for another, and you settle in between. I'll never work on spec, unless it's for *Esquire* or some other place I'm dying to get in."

Despite all the pressure he's under, he said he'd never work exclusively for money. "I edited a magazine for a month on a freelance basis and made $4,000. It wasn't worth it. I didn't enjoy the work."

Without being asked, he concluded, "The best jobs are staff positions, and they're very hard to come by."

I'll remind myself of that the next time I feel discouraged.

I finally spoke with Gil about freelancing and his question **24** about how much money I spent on the golf story. "If you'd gone to Jamaica and spent $10,000 of our money, the company might want 50 percent of your fee," he said. He added that as managing editor he has to rule on every prospective sale of a piece originally commissioned by the magazine. "Someone might be doing a story for us with the idea of selling it elsewhere," he said. I said that would be unethical. "Not everyone is brought up as well as you or I were," he said.

I'm relieved that I spoke with him, and even more relieved that the freelance policy isn't as restrictive as I'd feared. The known is less frightening than the unknown.

january

26   I picked up the magazine today and read three stories that made me proud to be associated with *SI*. The first was an expose of PBS' hurry-up schlock job on the NFL. What gladdened me wasn't so much the splendid research by Wilmer Ames and Bill (Double A, Double F) Taaffe, the best by-line on the staff. It was the fact that we held off printing the story for a week in order to get all the facts. The scoop syndrome has done incalculable harm to journalism. Better to get it right, than first.

Second was John Papanek's story on the Miami Dolphins' defense. On the theory that the Dolphins would beat the Jets, John spent the week researching the idea. *Voilà:* the Dolphs win and we have double coverage—Paul Zimmerman's game story and John's feature. We weren't waiting for the news to direct us; we were anticipating it. Sure, some of those ideas don't pan out—the wrong team wins, or whatever—but they're worth trying.

Finally, Bil Gilbert and Lisa Twyman wrote the definitive story on fan violence. The story undoubtedly involved dozens of interviews, extensive use of correspondents' files and weeks of research. I love to see us use our resources like that, and it doesn't bother me that I don't get in on many of those long-range assignments. Singles-hitters can be just as valuable as sluggers.

I do get to hit the long ball in my Baseball Issue story. Tonight I made the final cuts, reducing the piece from 1,000 to 700 lines. It wasn't easy because I had plenty of good material. In cutting situations I adopt the following motto: Talk is cheap. There are very few reasons to use quotes: if they're controversial or funny, if they bring out a subject's personality, or if they convey information in ways that wouldn't work without quotes. If I have to cut something other than a quote, I ask myself: "What's really important for a reader to know?" Frequently I've written a nice one-liner or a nifty phrase, but the information just isn't important. Out it goes.

Notice that I've cut to 700 lines. I was asked to do 600. Shame on me. Too many times I've written long on one of two theories: 1) There's so much good stuff here; I can't decide what to cut, so I'll let them do it; or, 2) This is too good a story for the space I've been given; once they see what I've done, they'll change their minds and give me more. Inevitably, I'm confronted by one of two realities: 1) I rarely like the cuts they make as much as the ones I make myself; and, 2) Getting extra space is the exception rather than the rule. It's true that editors sometimes see cuts where writers can't, but most of the time writers should take responsibility. Discipline, young man!

I had lunch with Larry at a Thai restaurant. "Let's Thai one   **27**
on," he said.

We discussed spring training and the first few weeks of the season. The Baseball Issue is expected to include my NL story, scouting reports on the 26 teams, a profile of Montreal catcher Gary Carter, a feature on box scores, and a back-of-the-book "bonus piece" on the old Troy, New York, team. Quite a package. And early-season stories have been planned on Steve Garvey, Tom Seaver and Gorman Thomas.

I felt this would be a good time to discuss any problems I had covering baseball last year. One of my problems was that I was too rigid about following orders. If I was asked to do a story one way on Monday, I was still covering it the same way on Friday, even if the conditions had changed. That shows how little confidence I have. The irony is that Larry is always open to new approaches when we speak during the week.

I felt good about bringing up the problem myself. Larry ended the meal by saying that I've been doing an excellent job. I live off compliments; I need that verbal bag of oats.

january

29   My plans are complete for spring training. I'll be arriving in
the Tampa–St. Pete area March 3 and staying until March 27.
Audrey will spend the first three days with me, and my kids
will be down for the last ten or so.

In some respects my career parallels that of a ballplayer. I
got my early training writing a few stories for the Milton
Academy *Orange and Blue*. Later I covered sports for the *Yale
Daily News* during the school year and wrote sports and some
news for *The Boston Globe* during two college summers. When
I graduated in 1966, I wasn't ready for a major-league job, so I
reported to an instructional league—Northwestern's Medill
School of Journalism—where I earned a Masters in 1967.
Then I got a kind of Triple-A job covering high-school sports
for *The Minneapolis Star* (the *Star* itself wasn't minor-league—
it was ranked among the top 20 papers in the country—but
the high-school beat was). I added some other beats (golf,
pro basketball, book reviewing) and in 1970 I talked my way
onto the magazine—surely a major-league job—as a utility
player. I had received an offer to write sports for Newspaper
Enterprise Association, a feature syndicate based in New
York. I called Merv Hyman, *SI*'s chief of research. "I have an
offer at NEA," I told him, "and I don't want to reply until I
know my standing with you." He offered me a job on the
spot.

Let's stop right here. What was a 23-year-old kid doing
working for an outstanding paper like *The Minneapolis Star*?
And what qualifications did I have for *SI* at 26 that others
lacked?

In retrospect it's easy to say that I proved at both places I
was qualified. But there was surely something else involved,
too. Let's be honest about it: I attended one of the leading
colleges in the country. People are told that these schools will
"open some doors." Did they? When employment interviewers came to Medill, they invariably said they were impressed
with my education (even though I hadn't been an outstand-

ing student at either Yale or Medill). The *Chicago Tribune* said there were no current openings in sports, but that I should be sure to get back to them. I had a personal interview with *Chicago Sun-Times* editor James Hoge, a Yale graduate, and he said the same thing. O.K., let's look at it from the employer's perspective: "This guy went to Yale; we can probably feel safe hiring him." And in most cases they probably could. But how would I feel about a Jim Kaplan if I'd gone to Duluth Central High School and St. Cloud State, then worked ten years for small dailies before *The Minneapolis Star* even considered me? Resentful, to say the least. Moreover, the magazine has always hired an extraordinary number of Ivy Leaguers, especially from Princeton. Talented and qualified people, to be sure. But still.

In any case, I paid my dues after being hired by *Sports Illustrated.* My masthead position was "reporter." My Guild category was "researcher." Actually, while I might do some research or reporting or write an occasional story, my major assignment was the far less glamorous job of fact-checking. Each week I was given a story written by someone else and asked to confirm all the facts, spellings, dates and numbers. In short, I was responsible for the story's accuracy. There were various checking devices at my disposal—the Time Inc. library, statistical services, team and school publicists, my own calculator and the sources mentioned in the story. Above all, the job requires great care and concentration. Any inaccuracy that runs in the magazine is considered the checker's fault.

Why can't writers be responsible for the accuracy of their own stories? For one thing, the editors are always making changes that have to be checked or are asking for additional information. Meanwhile, the writer may be on the plane coming home. Of more importance, a writer—almost any writer—will let things slip by that an independent checker won't. A *New York Post* writer did a story on a basketball player at St. Ann's Episcopal School in Brooklyn. On first reference the writer called the school "St. Ann's." On second reference he wrote, "St. Ann's, an Episcopal school." What's wrong with that? As it happens, St. Ann's is not an Episcopal school; a local Episcopalian church lent its facilities and support when the school was founded, so the school called itself St. Ann's Episcopal School. But it's a progressive, nonparochial, nongrading school; few of the students or faculty think of the place as saintly or Episcopalian. A writer lets the mistake slip by; a literal-minded checker would have caught it. An unimportant error? Maybe so. But when little mistakes—not to mention big ones—build up, a publication gets a bad reputation.

Like all utility players, I felt I deserved to be a starter (staff writer). As I look back over the stories I wrote before my promotion, I can see why I wasn't moved up. My style was anything but natural; I was always restraining my rhetorical impulses to write what I thought the editors wanted. I did get a lesser promotion, to writer-reporter—a position in which checkers are also guaranteed "regular" writing assignments—and I was eventually publishing 15–20 stories a year. But my major duty was still fact-checking. And working weekends. And seething inside.

The outlook improved for me when Gil Rogin became managing editor in 1979. I had always felt Gil was in my corner. Maybe that's why I relaxed. It also helped that I got the opportunity to bring out the best and most natural in my writing. My friend Jeannette Bruce, a regionals specialist, had just died of cancer. I volunteered to cover regionals in addition to checking and occasionally writing baseball stories. Gil readily agreed.

In the last half of 1979 I probably published twenty regionals. I found the job not unlike that of a newspaper columnist, and the opportunity to use the first person brought out my best. Some of the stories were marvelous fun: a little historical digging to uncover Ben Franklin's incisive and erudite views of sport; a visit to the Games Museum in Waterloo, Ontario; a nice splat shot at the racquetball establishment.

Gil eventually took me off regionals, but he had enough confidence in me to give me more freedom on the baseball beat. In June of 1980 the Phillies' silent pitcher, Steve Carlton, was en route to another Cy Young Award–winning season, one in which he would contribute to Philadelphia's first world championship. Carlton hadn't spoken to the press in years, but Larry Keith got the idea that we could get inside Carlton's head through his good friend Tim McCarver, a Phillies broadcaster who had once been Carlton's personal catcher. I was assigned to co-author McCarver's first-person story. McCarver was jovial and anecdotal, no problem to probe. I got additional background from Phillies players and officials. Knowing that McCarver and I were likely to write a positive story, they opened up. The story was well received, and a few months later I was promoted to staff writer. I'm always happy to run into Tim McCarver.

There's another, somewhat less felicitous matchup between writers and ballplayers. Some of our editors equate the two, at least implicitly. If we've written a few good stories in a row, we're "hot." If we've written a few they haven't liked, we're "cold" or "slumping." This drives me crazy. For one thing, we're much more consistent performers than ballplayers. Our writing will invariably fall within certain well-defined perimeters, not between .200 and .350. For another, our careers should last much longer. And finally, the last thing we need is to operate under the same kind of pressure that athletes do: We're already under enough stress.

I'll grant, though, that *SI* writers and ballplayers have this much in common: We tend to be busier in some seasons than others, we have desirable jobs, and we bitch and moan a lot.

Audrey and I watched the first half of the Super Bowl in a **30** crowded, noisy bar, and the second half on my black-and-

january

white TV. It hit me that the visual segment of televised games coverage is much more important than the oral, even though we print people base our reviews inordinately on the announcing. What's more important—an instant replay, or what Merlin Olsen had to say about it? We not only overanalyze the analysis, we expect too much from it. The networks and sports organizations have contractual agreements. Therefore, it's pointless for independent print people to expect consistently critical commentary from network announcers. Better we should grade what we see on the screen. Based on NBC's visual coverage at Pasadena, I'd say that at their best the networks are certainly as good as we are.

31   My back is killing me. Is it my disc or my hypochondria?

february

Today I spoke with Gina DaVito, a senior at Poly Prep **1**
Country Day School in Brooklyn, about attending Yale.
Gina's a three-sport star who can pitch a softball like the
King—as in King and His Court, the famous four-man team.
Someday you'll be reading about her on the sports pages.

I've had terrific fun writing about female athletes. My kids'
former babysitter, Penn sophomore Alicia McConnell, is the
country's best female squash player. As a sophomore at The
Loyola School of Manhattan, she was voted best athlete. Her
sports were basketball, volleyball and softball because the
school had no squash team. Her record at Penn is just about
as spectacular, and I've got the magazine interested in a story
(I won't do it because she's a friend—conflict of interest).
And the best athlete of either sex I've ever written about was
Heather McKay of Australia. A good enough teen tennis
player to be compared with Margaret Court, McKay later became an all-Aussie field hockey player and a squash star who
lost two matches in 20 years. At age 38 she began playing
tournament racquetball—and immediately moved to the top
of the sport.

A spectacular female athlete may stand out because she
probably has less competition than men do. So what? The
women's sports movement is still a-borning. We should enjoy
it while it's young.

february

2 I bought some pills yesterday to ease my back pains and felt better after taking some. Then I woke up this morning feeling as if I could swallow the Nile. My stomach was queasy and my head foggy. It wasn't until I'd taken another pill that I realized they were to blame.

At times like this I identify strongly with athletes. Something is wrong, and I don't know if I'll ever feel right again. Of course, the problem's undoubtedly minor—or in my head—but the fear persists. How would you like to wake up one morning and wonder if your career's shot? Happens all the time to athletes: That's why they're so insecure.

4 I thought I'd crossed every "t" and dotted every "i" in my National League story. Larry keeps finding things.

What's wrong with this sentence, which introduces a reason for NL success?

"BUM LUCK. If Cardinal Reliever Bruce Sutter instead of his Brewer rival Rollie Fingers had missed the 1982 Series; if Fernando Valenzuela hadn't barely survived the fifth inning of the 1981 Series' third game; if the Royals' George Brett had cleanly fielded that smash by Philadelphia's Mike Schmidt in the ninth inning of the fifth game a year earlier; if the Orioles hadn't grooved one pitch too many to Pittsburgh's Willie Stargell in 1979; we might be lecturing you on another matter of import, say ballpark hot dogs."

The problem, Larry pointed out, is that only the Sutter-Fingers clause involves luck. The rest was skill, or at least happenstance. I'd convinced myself that happenstance and luck were identical. Actually, I had some doubts in the back of my mind but didn't act on them. A good rule is that if something isn't clear or correct to me, it won't work for my readers. It certainly didn't work for Larry.

Another case in point: "Success with Blacks and Hispanics." Not "success"—that doesn't mean anything. Larry made it "Prominence of Blacks and Hispanics." More clear, more precise.

Today was pivotal in several respects. My role in the Na- **7** tional League story is pretty well over, and Larry is taking the final copy home to edit over the Tuesday-Wednesday weekend. I had a back X-ray; maybe I'll be able to get this thing resolved. And Gil Rogin began a nine-month leave of absence from the magazine to work for the corporate types upstairs in the Time-Life Building.

I find the Rogin business disquieting. Every once in a while editors take furloughs at other Time Inc. divisions; but a managing editor? Some people on the magazine think the whole thing's innocent; others feel the biggies are testing out eventual successors for Gil. During his absence Peter Carry, Ken Rudeen and Mark Mulvoy will edit the magazine for three months apiece.*

This, of course, means adapting to three different styles. I have no trouble understanding what Peter will ask of me: better writing. My strength is hard work, professionalism, sound reporting; he's asking for more flair. Fair enough.

While attending a negotiating session of Time Inc. and the **8** Newspaper Guild local I belong to, I thought of the baseball players union. I find it interesting that the players and their brethren in the AFL-CIO feel they have little in common. On one level, that's understandable. Steelworkers negotiate all benefits collectively. A ballplayer negotiates his own salary (beyond the minimum of $40,000) and considers himself by and large an independent contractor.

But the two groups have something very important in com-

*In 1984 Rogin became managing editor of *Discover* and Mulvoy succeeded him at *Sports Illustrated*.

mon—a history of exploitation that was overcome only through collective action.

Until 1976 every player was subject to the reserve clause, a contractual stipulation that bound him to his team until he was traded or released. (By definition, the clause was a one-year contract extension, but in practice it was applied every year.) A player had no freedom of movement or bargaining leverage, and his salary more than reflected that grim reality. In 1967 a player representative named Russ Nixon told me that he had been in the game eight years before he made $10,000. (At the time, the minimum salary was $6,000.) Players had poor benefits and weren't encouraged to plan for the future. In addition, they were hurt by the Supreme Court, which had ruled in 1922 and reaffirmed in 1953 that baseball was exempt from the antitrust laws. In one of his lesser decisions, Mr. Justice Holmes had ruled that baseball was not interstate commerce.

Things began to change in 1966, when the previously weak players union hired Marvin Miller, a former economist for the steelworkers, as executive director. Miller unified the players and began winning concessions in collective bargaining: higher minimum salaries, improved pension benefits (the players successfully struck over the issue in 1972) and a system of salary arbitrations for players with two years of service. In arbitrations, the player would submit one figure and the owner another; arguments would be heard, and an arbitrator would decide which of the two figures he preferred. The system forced both sides to submit reasonable-sounding numbers but, notably, required the owner to offer more than he would have paid without arbitrations. So in a sense, even when the players lost, they won.

But players still had no freedon of movement. In 1972 a Cardinal outfielder, Curt Flood, had gone to the Supreme Court to challenge the reserve clause. The Court, which by this time had made rulings that assured football, basketball, boxing and horse racing were interstate commerce, ruled against Flood. However, the Court was also frank about admitting some confusion. In Miller's words, "The Court's decision in effect said, 'We don't know what the answer is. Our ruling is an anomaly and an aberration. Perhaps Congress or someone else can solve the problem.'"

The solver was baseball's impartial arbiter, the late Peter Seitz. In November of 1975 he ruled that the reserve clauses in the contracts of pitchers Dave McNally and Andy Messersmith had restricted them for only one year. Since their contracts had expired, McNally and Messersmith were given the freedom to sell their services on the open market. Seitz' decision,* subsequently upheld in federal and circuit court, threatened to make free agents of all players whose contracts expired at the conclusion of the 1976 season. And that included all but a very few players.

The owners, who had previously refused even to modify the reserve system, were now forced to abolish it. At the 1976 All-Star Game they agreed to institute the now-famous re-entry draft. To qualify, a player needs an expired contract and six years of major-league service. He goes through a November draft and is free to negotiate with teams other than his own. (Why didn't the players insist on total free agency for everyone? Because the owners convinced them that the bidding and player movement would be too chaotic.)

The result was that some players became free agents and began changing teams on their own. Other players were content to remain with their own clubs when they were offered lucrative, long-term contracts. And salaries increased dramatically for virtually everyone. When the 1976 agreement was signed, the average salary was about $50,000. In 1983, it was more than $290,000.

Many fans resent today's high salaries. Even as they break down the gates to see the new millionaires, fans complain that the players are overpaid. But by and large, big money

---

*It resulted in his immediate firing by the owners.

has been good for baseball. There has been more parity in the standings since the advent of free agency. Attendence records have been set almost every year. And for all their complaints about finishing in the red, the owners (who won't open their books) seem to be doing very well. They recently signed a six-year, $1 billion national television contract that will net each team an additional $6 million a year. Clubs are selling for many times their purchase prices (recently a pizza magnate bought the Tigers for an estimated $50 million). And ticket prices are holding firm as the lowest in major sport.

When people accuse them of being overpaid, the players usually resort to one of several arguments. The most common is, "No one's put a gun to the owners' heads. They're paying us high salaries because they think it's a good investment." Then there's the challenging, "Would *you* turn down this kind of money?" And finally, "We're no different from other entertainers, and no one objects to *their* salaries."

But I think the best argument is a simple description of baseball's current economic reality. The old system amounted to little more than socialism for the rich. The new order is insidious, subversive and Machiavellian. It's called free enterprise.

9   My son Matthew and I spent the day at Gina DaVito's school, Poly Prep, where Matthew is applying for admission as a ninth grader. Poly provides the rarest of things educational—private-school education for a diversified student body. I call it "the private school for the people." After attending classes for the day, Matthew and I agreed that the teaching was excellent and the pupils agreeable.

Later we returned to my apartment to set up the printer. Matthew absorbed the complex directions in about fifteen minutes—not for nothing is he known as Matt the Mechanic. We hoped to print up the first 15 days of this diary. Unfortunately, I seem to have purchased the wrong kind of cable to connect the printer with the word processor. Fortunately, John Papanek agreed to print up the entries. I hooked up the computer to the phone, called him and transmitted the entries to his computer. He then attached his computer to his own, working cable and printer, and produced a document in about thirty minutes. I'll have the copy tomorrow.

Staff Writer Dan Levin, a learned ecologist and nutrition **10** buff, approached me in the company cafeteria. "That stuff you're eating is terrible," he said with a smile.

I looked at my tray. On it were chicken with gravy; white rice; jello, and a cup of spring water with ice.

"First place, you're probably going to eat the skin of the chicken," said Levin. "Awful. That yellow sauce is primarily animal fat. You shouldn't eat white rice. And the jello's pure sugar."

He paused. "The spring water is great." I brightened. "But you shouldn't have put ice in it. That comes from natural water."

Larry completed his editing of the National League story **11** and it looks good. I don't think I'll have to do any more work on it, other than help the checker. I started a Viewpoint about chess. Based on the games I've played, I consider the knight a more important piece than the bishop. This is a revolutionary theory comparable to Columbus' assertion that the world is round. I seem to remember a life master getting caught by a knight fork, and I called an official at the United States Chess Federation to verify. He'll check with his library and call me after the weekend. I'm also going to research the history of the knight. I remember something the curator of the Games Museum told me: that the knight is chess' universal piece, the only one used throughout history in all forms the game has taken.

february

At times like this I realize how good my job is. Where else would I be given the opportunity to free-associate over some esoteric subject like the knight in chess? Even when we write about some mainstream sport, we aren't tied down to such hardline journalism practices as inverted-pyramid style. We give you the facts—that's still the bottom line—but beyond that we can fantasize, free-associate, have some chuckles. I don't know many other publications that grant such freedom.

New York finally got a major snowfall. It came down so hard and cold and blowy that the kids couldn't come over, and one of my golf partners, Marty Rosenmertz (the retired clothing-store manager), had to cancel tomorrow's dinner date.

Well, O.K., so there are safety problems to keep the younger and older indoors, but why were people my age huddled in their homes like hobos in a hut? I found snow-covered cars looking like Oldenburg sculptures, snowplows churning, dogs romping, snowballs flying. Too bad people were indoors playing it safe. Life is risk. Unless we take chances, we can't expect to grow and change.

Talk about free-associating.

12   The weather was milder today and people were out. Audrey and I had lunch at Charlie's restaurant on Flatbush Avenue, and then walked to the Brooklyn Museum. I live in Park Slope, the borough's most conveniently located neighborhood. My apartment is within easy reach of the Brooklyn Library, the Brooklyn Museum, the Brooklyn Botanic Garden and Prospect Park. Today the walk was especially pleasant. We shared the streets not with cars and trucks but cross-country skiers. Unfortunately, the museum was closed— Lincoln's birthday.

I was wearing only a cotton burgundy T-shirt and a regular buttondown shirt beneath my sheepskin coat. Three winters in Minnesota taught me the rules of dressing for cold weather:

1. Wear something warm next to the skin.

2. Layer up, but don't wear one heavy layer on top of another. If you do, you'll sweat, and the sweat will freeze.

3. Relax. Much of the discomfort comes not from the cold, but from tense and cramped muscles.

4. Cover the extremities.

5. Walk vigorously, run, throw snowballs—in short, get those molecules moving. When was the last time you saw a bundled-up athlete or construction worker?

13 My existential moment came when my express from Brooklyn reached Chambers Street in Manhattan. I was headed for the local stop at 86th Street, and along came the local, with plenty of seats available. My choice: transfer now and sit, or wait until 72nd Street and transfer there. I gambled and took the express to 72nd, where I had to wait five minutes, leaning against a post. It would have been much more pleasant to have transferred earlier and be sitting the whole time. Time-saving isn't important. Comfort is. If there's a philosophy I've lived by, it's this: Never stand when you can sit, and never sit when you can lie down.

I haven't been doing very well with my reading resolution, though of late I've been pouring over Bill Russell's *Second Wind* and the magazine's annual bathing-suit issue. "I can't wait until baseball season starts," Matthew said over the phone. "Then I'll have a reason to read the papers."

So will I.

15 I had lunch with two old friends, Bob and Marian Wernick. Meeting them was a watershed in my life. When they got my parents hooked on golf in 1956, I trailed along after the foursome and eventually picked up the game myself. Ever since, I've had an off-again, on-again affair with golf. I was diverted by tennis for about ten years, and then I came back with a bang. I realize now that golf is a game to grow old with, and a game that makes me feel young.

But back to the Wernicks. Bob's a freelancer who works primarily for *The Smithsonian.* Marian's a very successful artist (under the name McClanahan). They divide their time between Sea Island, Georgia, and Paris. Not a bad life. Bob has just published an article on Roquefort cheese; naturally, he made Roquefort omelettes. He co-authored *Dr. Creff's 1-2-3 Sports Diet.* The key to an athlete's diet, he said, is balance. If you eat two desserts, you must eat two steaks. In addition to the omelette, we had rolls, a salad and borscht. I felt well-fed, if no more athletic.

16   Boston, Boston, my home town. What is it about the place that makes me feel so good—the easy ride from the airport, the splendid view of the Charles River, the omnipresent sense of history (George Washington took command of the troops on Cambridge Common, just half a mile from my parents' house), or, as they say, the feeling that it's so "livable"?

I flew up here primarily to visit my mother, who has just undergone her second total hip replacement. She was woozy after a bad night, but the operation appears to have been a total success.

Working under her maiden name, Felicia Lamport, my mother has turned out scores of poems and essays, published several collections of them and appeared on the pages of such publications as *The New Yorker, Harper's* and *The Atlantic Monthly.* Her specialty is satiric light verse, and some critics have called her the master of the art. She also teaches expository writing at Harvard.

My father, Benjamin Kaplan, was a Harvard law professor

for twenty-five years and a justice on the Massachusetts Supreme Judicial Court for nine. He retired from the court in 1981 and has since been teaching part-time at Harvard and Boston University and judging at the appellate level.

I've been asked a thousand times, "What was it like having such gifted parents?" I usually answer something noncommittal like, "Oh, O.K.," or "They're just plain folks." A truthful response would have been far more complicated.

Without a doubt I was given the best education and advice available. I've taken lessons in everything from swimming to trumpet; spent a summer in France with the Experiment in International Living; gone to a creative, coed work camp, and cleared trails up mountains in Grand Teton National park— none of which would have been possible without my parents' involvement and encouragement. And God knows, I've met some pretty interesting people. It was nothing for me to come home and find John Kenneth Galbraith, Al Capp, Tom Lehrer, Julia Child, John Updike, Anthony Lewis or Lillian Hellman in the living room.

But there was a down side, too. An awful lot was done for me, and I never became much of a self-starter. I've been unduly deferential toward authority figures, having had two of them to solve my needs. And I don't negotiate or compromise very well, because I was always within reach of The Answer.

I didn't have to be this way. Surrounded by so many accomplished people, I could have questioned these great men and women, grown and thrived. Instead, I became intimidated. I can remember the charades games we played on New Year's Eve. There would be quotations to act out that I'd never heard of, books I'd never read. I got by with "sounds like," but when it came to acquiring knowledge I was, well, a charade. Oh, I read the requisite books and got decent enough grades, but I can remember my marks more easily than the knowledge. I was a pretty good student but a lousy

february

scholar. Viewing my parents' august friends, I thought, "They can do it, but I never will." It never occurred to me that they had a few years' head start.

When it came to careers, I think I was partly influenced by each parent and partly by a random event. Like my father, a part of me respects logic and order and accuracy. Like my mother, a part of me admires creativity and style. Many nights after dinner, my father would retire to his study to prepare for class. I didn't want to work as hard as he and I certainly didn't wish to emulate his vast reputation: Exit the law. My mother's professional life, by contrast, seemed more enviable. She wrote at her leisure and wasn't tied to office hours. I wasn't going to emulate her, either (although I did finally publish a poem in *Esquire* about the unusual by-lines in *The New York Times*). What could I do? My natural ability held no clue. My math-science aptitude was always spectacular, and tests suggested I could be a splendid accountant or architect or engineer. Alas, none of those careers interested me: too dry and technical, I thought. Indeed, I was so intimidated by science that I almost flunked it every time I took it.

Sometime during my junior year at Milton Academy, an editor, perhaps *the* editor, of *The Wall Street Journal* spoke before the upper school. He described journalism as an endlessly fascinating experience. "One day you could cover a trial," he said, "the next day a fire." I was galvanized: This was the career for me. I will now quote *Growing Up*, Russell Baker's autobiography: "At this time I decided that the only thing I was fit for was to be a writer, and this notion rested solely on my suspicion that I would never be fit for real work, and that writing didn't require any."

Thus inspired, I wrote perhaps three stories for *The Orange and Blue*. The old self-starter.

I took up journalism for real in college. But not without problems. I was trying out, or "heeling," for the *Yale Daily News* against slews of former high-school editors. They had considerable talent and experience; I had neither. It took me two eight-week trials to make it. Then there was the constant conflict about what kind of journalism I should pursue. I knew news writing was "important" and "relevant" (father's orientation), but sportswriting was freer and livelier (mother's orientation). I wrote virtually nothing but sports and was associate sports editor my last year on the paper. Nonetheless, the conflict stayed with me through graduate school and beyond. My eventual career choice, like much I've done, emanated from happenstance. At one point I thought I would be an editorial writer in Decatur, Illinois, but I didn't get the expected offer. I did get an offer to cover sports, after a short news-side training period, in Minneapolis.

On the whole, I would rather have been in Minneapolis, and writing sports. I have nothing but happy associations with the Twin Cities, and sportswriting excites me as news-writing never did: The poet in me won out over the pragmatist.

Nonetheless, I wish I'd spent more time on the news side before going into sports. Too many sportswriters have covered sports and nothing else. The stories are right in front of them—on the field, in the clubhouse—and they don't learn how to dig, use public documents, interview tough subjects and all the other odds and ends that go into being a professional journalist. The sports side has some of the best writers and worst journalists in the business. I've had some news-writing experience at every paper I've worked on, and I've written freelance nonsports stories for publications like *The Times*, *The Village Voice* and the *News*. But I wish I'd spent a year or more under some crusty assistant city editor. Or even worked the lobster shift on the police beat. That's still the best kind of training there is.

Back from Boston. I couldn't decide whether to take a cab **17** home, nap and go to the office later; or take the JFK subway express directly to the Time-Life Building. Leaving the terminal, I saw a bunch of cabbies loudly arguing. That made up my mind: the train. Sometimes I can't stand the culture shock of returning to New York. The reason many visitors hate the city, I think, is that they're confronted by the worst of it: cab drivers driven crazy by carbon monoxide. From now on I vow to take fewer cabs and more trains.

18   Worked at home. Shelby Lyman, who did the TV commentary for the Fischer-Spassky series, called me with more information about the chess knight. My son Benjamin came over and we read *The Amazing Aventure of Dan the Pawn*, ate chicken, watched some TV. That's an unusually busy schedule for Benjamin, whose idea of a good evening is an engrossing book that he'll read from cover-to-cover. Matthew is more like me. He needs constant diversion—sports, movies, TV, games.

19   Dinner with Audrey and an opthalmologist friend of ours, Dean Stetz, at Lea Watson's. Lea, who works for the magazine's promotions department and is writing a tennis novel, jots down her goals for each month and then insists on meeting them. I realized for the nth time that I should be more organized myself. Generally, I find that the more I have to do, the more easily I can get things done; the less I have to do, the more time I waste. I also realized tonight that I don't concentrate very well. Lea said that her study of tennis players emphasized to her the importance of concentration.

22   I went over to the *News* to check up on my golf story. If I don't see a story before it's in print, there's always going to be some change that's annoying or inaccurate. In this case, there will be such a change even though I've seen the story. The piece is in the hands of a young copy editor. My lead was about shopping for a pair of golf pants and rejecting the ones that were offered to me because they weren't tacky enough. "On a golf course," I had written, "you're free to be bold, free to be brassy, free to be tacky, free to be you and me." The editor took out "free to be you and me," calling it a cliché. Well, to me, the line is funny, whatever it is. I couldn't convince her to leave it in, but I got my way in a couple of other areas.

I felt a lot of pain in my back while playing squash with Matthew. There was a story in the *News* about Tim Leary, a Met pitcher who got help for his back from a Manhattan neurologist named Daniel Alkaitis. Only one thing to do: I called Alkaitis and got an appointment for next Tuesday. **23**

Every year I seem to lose another athletic skill. In high school I was kicked in the finger two years in a row while playing soccer goalie. After the second cast was removed, I found I'd lost my aggressiveness and couldn't dive for loose balls. I was through forever as a goalie. When I came to the magazine, I was foolhardy enough to play touch football barefooted. I jumped for a pass, came down wrong and fractured an ankle. Then I badly sprained my other ankle playing basketball. As a result, my ankles became so weak that I had to give up both sports. Sometime later I threw out my right arm. So when I played softball, I had to be a pitcher and throw underhand or a first baseman and not throw at all. Of late I've been avoiding even softball because every time I sprint I seem to pull a muscle.

I think I'm so aware of aging and injuries because I cover people who are young and athletic. My injuries have widened the gulf between us. I suppose if I have a supressed desire, it's to be a great athlete. Why not? We crave the things we can't possibly have. What I must now avoid is the tend-

february

ency to excuse bad play by major leaguers on the theory that they had to be spectacular athletes just to get there. And I should remind myself that athletes—and a lot of other people—wish they could write.

25 Audrey and I had lunch with Neil Ginsberg, a Scarsdale High School teacher who has taken a leave of absence to put out a newsletter called *Inside Baseball.* Neil wants to do a regular report on each of the 26 teams. I told him I thought he'd be better off putting out one newsletter for all 26 teams. He's fighting an uphill battle, since he can only afford to pay his writers $35 per 600 words.

Too bad, because his newsletter would serve a purpose. It truly is about inside baseball—when to bunt, whether or not to take a pitch on a 2–0 count. Too little is written about the playing of the game. I guess that's what interests me most about baseball—the minutiae. Who's winning and losing is O.K., and a surprising number of players are fascinating as people, but all this is transitory. The game will outlive the people who play it and operate it and write about it.

28 I have two conflicting views of spring training, which begins officially tomorrow—the due date for all players who aren't already in camp. The first is the traditional one—that the baseball spring is a time of rebirth and renewal. Every team is improved, every rookie is a phenom. In the outfield, players, their caps purposely askew, throw balls between their legs. Other players—and coaches and managers—lean over the railing and strike up conversations with fans. The scene should be frozen forever.

But I also think about players who may be coming to spring training for the last time. Age and injury have dimmed their skills. For them, it's a time of desperation, not celebration: They might have to become sportswriters.

march

I spent an hour with Daniel Alkaitis, the neurologist. It was **1**
some experience. He asked me at length about my history—
personal as well as medical. He was discovering how much
stress has to do with my back problem. Pain can be caused by
stress, he said, and stress on top of pain creates more pain.
His suspicions seemed justified when he administered a
series of tests that disclosed no physical problems. Among
other things, he hooked me up to a machine, jabbed me with
needles, and administered electric shocks. "I'll confess anything," I said.

Though there was no evidence of pinched nerves, Alkaitis
gave me some exercises to do and advised me to put a hot
towel on my neck at night and type with a cervical collar on. I
might see him again in a month.

So there may be more to my physical problems than hypochondria. What kind of stress am I under? The stress involved in trying to perform consistently at a high level before
critical editors. The stress involved in merely trying to get
into the magazine (my National League story is virtually
guaranteed to run because the editors want it in the Baseball
Issue; a news story on a given week may be fighting for space
with stories about other sports or other baseball stories). Finally, the stress involved in satisfying a number of con-
stituencies in my private life. At times I feel I'm juggling the
different needs of my friends, and of my kids, and the balls
are going to fly out of my hands any second. And at times I

feel I'm not even putting another ball in the air—the one representing my own needs.

2   I spent the day at Bryn Mawr College outside of Philadelphia. I was researching a regional on "wellness," Byrn Mawr's answer to physical education. Wellness involves not only exercise, but nutrition and stress management. Everything from diet to emotional well-being is taken under consideration.

My schedule at the school was entirely planned for me. I was introduced to P.E. instructors; the wellness, health and nutritional directors; a couple of students; and the president of the school. Overwhelmed at first, I turned on my tape recorder and sat in a daze. By lunchtime I was more involved in the conversation—giving as well as receiving. The day's highlight was my session with the nutrition computer. I typed in two days' worth of meals—a seemingly healthy day featuring wheat bread, tuna salad and chicken; and a pig-out diet of Danish, hamburger, roast beef and chocolate cake. To my surprise, I found that both diets provided a satisfactory calorie count. However, both also provided too much protein and too little Vitamins A and D. The recommendation in each case was more fruits and vegetables. I believe, I believe. When I got home, I had a dinner of swordfish, lima beans, noodles and grapefruit.

I won't know how the story turns out until I transcribe the tapes and go through the wellness literature that the school's public-information director gave me. But I can see one problem: I spoke with only two students, the ones handpicked by the school. They were frank and revealing, but I should have sought out more.

It's easy to let management figures or their sporting equivalent (coaches, instructors, athletic directors) supply most of the information. The problem's not so much that they're guarded or publicity-conscious—the Bryn Mawr people couldn't have been more helpful—but that they're not the ones most directly affected by a given sports program. If there's a lesson for me in this experience, it's an old one— initiate, don't wait.

The night ended on a happy note when I received a call from the admissions director at Poly Prep: Matthew's in.

Audrey and I hopped* on a plane and caught a flight to **3** Tampa–St. Pete. This is going to be a 3½-week trip, and I packed accordingly: six pair underwear; six pair socks; three pair long pants and one pair shorts; three T-shirts; six sports shirts (long and short); two sweaters (one turtleneck, one long); jogging outfit; two pair sneakers; bathing suit; tennis and paddle-tennis racquets; golf clubs; brief case; Portabubble; raincoat. And I get paid to do this!

Say what you will about airline food, at least it's balanced: chicken, rice, assorted veggies, roll, bread, pecan pie. True to my Bryn Mawr diet, I forced myself to eat the veggies and eschewed the fatty butter and salt. I also had a screwdriver instead of my usual bourbon and ginger ale (fruit juice instead of cola). I can see the diet is already making me obnoxious.**

We're staying at the Don CeSar, a wedding cake of a hotel **4** made of pink, stuccoed Belgian concrete and topped by towers and cupolas. I had work to do, but first I couldn't resist a run on the beach, a swim in the heated pool. In the celebrated words of the umpire Bill Klem, you can't beat the hours.

By midday we were taking a 70-minute drive through traffic to Dunedin, the winter home of the Toronto Blue Jays.

---

*Audrey's version: "Audrey slithered on and Jim cranked and cramped on."

**Audrey: "True!"

march

"When I'm Dunedin," ex-pirate Willie Stargell once told me, "I'll get a glass of Clearwater and fetch Sara a Sota."

Spring training games don't start for a few days, so the Jays were practicing at their complex of fields and batting cages. Someone thought up spring training in part to dry up players who drank too much during the off-seasons, and there's some question whether it has any other relevance. Sure, players need a warm-up period, but for a month? And in Florida, Arizona and California? No matter. Nothing in the baseball year is half as pleasant as spring training, and it will be around as long as baseball is.

Spring is best before the games start. The players work out from about 10 in the morning until 1 in the afternoon. They shower quickly, grab a cup of vegetable soup and a couple of carrots and head out to the golf course or fishing hole. At night you'll see them betting hundreds of dollars at the horse and dog tracks and jai alai fronton (should the Commissioner be looking into this?).

There seem to be no losers by day (those struggling older players I referred to earlier lead lives of very quiet desperation here). Indeed, the players are so relaxed they willingly speak with fans and press. I followed my usual scouting-report routine: get the media guide in the P.R. office; go over the probable lineup and rotation with the P.R. man and manager and speak with new and/or pivotal players.

It's been a long time since I've conducted more than a day's worth of interviews, and I found myself going over some ground rules. The main thing is to converse with players rather than interview them. Conversations are relaxed, interviews tense; conversations can be revealing, interviews guarded. I'll thoroughly background myself before I speak with someone, but I won't depend exclusively on prepared questions. If one answer suggests another question, I'll ask it, even if it's not particularly germane to my story.

I try to avoid questions that can be answered by "yes" or "no." Those aren't very helpful answers most of the time. It may sound like a dumb question, but "How did you feel when . . ." or "How were you affected by that?" can produce long and revealing answers. Anything to elicit a meaningful response. The thing I like about those questions is that they're short. The subjects should be doing the speaking, not the interviewer. I don't recall hearing the guys on "60 Minutes" or Bill Moyers or Ted Koppel or even Johnny Carson asking long questions very often (Dick Cavett sometimes talks too much). And these guys, even Johnny Carson, are pros worth emulating.

The most important question I can ask is "Why?" and I'll keep asking it until I'm satisfied with the answer. Other good questions are "How do you know?" and "Can you give me an example?" The more concrete the better. What I try to get my subject to do is paint a word picture; that's easier to grasp than an abstraction. It literally illustrates the story.

What happens when a subject doesn't want to talk or won't say much that's quotable? I try to break him out of his usual pattern. Tony Cotton of our staff got the Red Sox' Jim Rice, a notoriously poor interview, to speak by blurting out "Why do you have a chip on your shoulder?" I find I can't interview these people as I would helpful subjects; the only alternative is to break them out of their hostile moods with something they haven't anticipated. Two of the things I'll say are, "Hey, look, I'm not trying to assassinate you—I just want a responsible answer," and "I think you deserve to have your side of the story told."

It's possible to bend over backwards without being ingratiating. I'll put myself in my subject's shoes, try to understand his frame of mind, and speak with him accordingly.

Everyone needs encouragement. When my friend Ira Berkow, a sportswriter and columnist for *The New York Times* and one of the best interviewers I know, met Willie Mays, it was on the occasion of a milestone homer Mays had just hit. Ira asked him how much longer he thought he could play, and Mays exploded. "Here I've just hit a big homer," he said,

march

"and you want to know how long I'll last! You could at least have congratulated me." A lesson well learned. "Even Willie Mays wanted people to acknowledge his achievements," Ira says.

By way of relaxing a subject, I'll start by picking a comfortable place to talk. I'll do anything to avoid speaking with a player in the clubhouse. It's his turf, and he may resent my being there. The dugout is better than the clubhouse, a restaurant is better than that, and the guy's home is the best place of all. I generally prefer a kitchen to a living room. A kitchen is by nature a casual place, where we can sit at the table, drink coffee and relax; a living room is usually a stiff and formal place, and the conversation may reflect that. However, other members of the family may troop through the kitchen. Above all, we must have privacy.

It may be necessary to speak with a subject for a long time before taking out the notebook or tape recorder. Humor is critical. If I can produce a laugh, I'll reduce the deadly seriousness that characterizes so many interviews. Any human touch is helpful. Everyone's story contains some sadness, poignancy and humor. I ask myself what's missing when I conduct an interview. The more life I can draw out of an interview, the more the subject comes alive. And the more he appreciates me as a human being instead of an impersonal question-asker.

Perhaps the most important way to gain a subject's respect is simply not to interrupt. When someone's telling a good story, keep quiet, no matter how many questions come to mind. You can always ask them later.

Of course, it's also necessary to get tough at times. When a subject is lying, I've got to challenge him. I can't be all-accepting. But I do try to be tactful: "Some people disagree with that. They say. . . ." If I ask a tough question in a relatively nonthreatening way, I'm suggesting that I don't necessarily disagree with my subject; I'm being a friendly interviewer, in fact, by giving him a chance to rebut. If I have a real zinger that could alienate him, I save that for last. In any case, it's a fact of journalism that some con men will come clean to people who challenge their honesty.

A final word of advice I give myself is, "Keep 'em talking." An old assistant city editor told me that my first night at *The Minneapolis Star*. "If you keep somebody talking long enough," he said, "you're bound to get a story." Quite simply, the longer someone speaks, the more likely he is to say something new.

The corollary to "Keep 'em talking" is "Keep 'em around." Some of the best interviews aren't interviews at all; they're observations. Gay Talese hangs around his subjects as long as six years. They eventually forget he's there, and he watches them react to events that shape their lives. I don't have that kind of time, but I do try to spend hours with them, especially away from the ballpark, to discover their private side.

I'm a nut for tape recorders because I take laborious and frequently unreadable notes. Further, I find my subjects quickly forget the tape and begin speaking freely. But the main reason I use tape is that I'll catch every word that's spoken, barring external noise or machine breakdown. With any other method there's no such certainty.

The problem comes in the transcription. It's boring and time-consuming. Also, tapes do break down. The advantage of note-taking is that I can begin typing the story right away: no transcription. The problem with notes is that an interview won't proceed naturally. I just can't write as fast as my subject speaks. It would have helped if I'd learned shorthand, as many British journalists do. Without it, I only take notes when I need a quick quote or two.

In some situations I take mental notes on what someone is saying because I'm in a situation where I'm unable or unwilling to write them down (driving a car, standing on a subway platform, hearing the interviewee say something he might not want to record) or because doing so would have upset the flow of conversation. The first chance I get, I'll put those mental notes down on paper. If I have any doubts about my accuracy, I must either discard the notes or ask the subject to repeat what he said.

Today I got at least one decent quote. I was speaking with catcher Buck Martinez about balding Dave Geisel, the only lefthanded pitcher in camp. "I like a guy who's losing his hair," I said.

"Well," said Martinez, "Dave's definitely the best balding lefthander in camp."

I don't think I'd be happy living anywhere but in a big city like New York. I hate cars, and around here it's drive, drive, drive. Audrey and I had dinner with some friends at a restaurant somewhere in the vicinity of three converging highways. Getting the wrong directions from the restaurant, I drove all over the map. Frazzled, we arrived forty minutes late. As far as I'm concerned, the greatest luxury in my life is that I don't have to own a car.

5 Larry called to say that I've been assigned a feature on Ron Kittle, a rookie outfielder for the White Sox. I was alarmed. All that space for a guy who has yet to complete a big-league season?

When Audrey and I arrived at the White Sox camp in Sarasota, Manager Tony LaRussa suggested that I do the piece on both Kittle and Greg Walker, a rookie first baseman who's considered just as good a prospect. Kittle and Walker are old friends, minor-league roommates and exact opposites in personality, so I readily agreed to do both of them. When I call Larry back, I'll argue eloquently for a two-player story.

Kittle is a much easier player to interview. He's an outgoing, good-humored, cocky bachelor. Walker's a shy, quiet, church-going family man, but I sense an interesting personality.

I spoke in general terms with the two players and LaRussa,

getting enough for maybe 200 of the 400–500 lines assigned. The rest will come from game details, observations and quotes from them and others around the Chicago camp.

We stuck around to watch a few innings of an exhibition game with Manatee Junior College. It was fun not so much because of the game, which Chicago won easily, as the company. We were sitting with White Sox P.R. man Chuck Shriver and Jerome Holtzman of the *Chicago Tribune*. One of the best P.R. men in baseball, Shriver had given me background on Kittle and told him to expect me. Holtzman is one of the most knowledgeable baseball writers in the country. He once wrote a book, *No Cheering in the Press Box*, in which he interviewed old-time baseball writers. Some of these guys were little more than press agents for the teams they covered, but Holtzman told me they had a lot going for them. "The writing was much more personal than it is today," he said. "I read an account of a boxing match that began, 'I arrived at the fight in good time.' They got incredible amounts of space and wrote journals rather than articles."

The old-time writers had immense power. There was no competition from TV and little from radio or magazines. The newspaper writers were, for all intents and purposes, the only game in town. Now they cover games that are either televised or reported on the evening news, so they have to do more than report the highlights. That's a tough job for journalists working under space restrictions and deadlines. *SI*, however, is helped rather than hindered by TV. A reader will see a game on television and want to know more about it. We have the time, space and resources to give it to him.

Today was my 39th birthday. No big deal. As a scholar I hit **6** my peak in the eighth grade. As an athlete I peaked around 23. I've been over the hill for 16 years. All that's left is me and my Portabubble.

march

Steve Wulf is also down here for the magazine. Audrey, Wulfie and I planned to attend the United States Football League opener in Tampa Stadium. We arrived in windy, searing weather, found we'd have to wait in line an hour, and left. "I'd forgotten what football crowds were like," Wulfie said as we watched legions of potbellied, beer-quaffing loudmouths enter the stadium. "At least most baseball crowds are more polite."

We reassembled at a golf driving range and hit a bucket apiece. Lots more fun than watching football. Then Wulfie headed back to St. Pete Beach while Audrey and I had lunch at the Colombian Restaurant in Ibor City. The place had tiles from Sevilla, American tiles depicting Don Quixote's travels, and good black bean soup. Afterwards, I dropped Audrey off at her plane, returned to the Don CeSar and dined alone on a hot fudge sundae. I also spoke with Larry, and he agreed on the two-pronged story. Thus did I pass into my 40th year.

7 I arrived at the ballpark in good time. It was the White Sox' spring opener, and Kittle drove in the game-winning run. I'm very lucky in that regard; my subjects invariably perform well.

I think I've assembled enough details on Kittle and Walker to write the 400–500 lines. I've called their parents, Walker's amateur coach, and Billy Pierce, the old White Sox pitcher who got Kittle a tryout with Chicago. Details, bury 'em in details.

When I'm on assignment I think less about writing than reporting. Good writing usually flows from good reporting. Once I've come upon some interesting facts, a turn of phrase invariably suggests itself. By contrast, good reporting never flows from good writing. Young reporters often go on a story thinking about knocking 'em dead with the writing. As a result, they skimp on the reporting. Suddenly, they're short on material—and ways to describe it. No amount of style can save an under-reported story. If the information is good, you can keep rewriting until the story reads well.

I know people who have gone on stories with the leads already written in their heads. They're locked into one way of doing the job. So when they've uncovered information that conflicted with their preconceptions, they've discarded it. They might as well have stayed at home. The interviews and events have to dictate the writing.

Once I'm done with the reporting and interviewing, I can put away my notebook and reflect for awhile before writing. Magazine articles aren't just factual—they're interpretive. To make a long story work, I need concepts as well as facts.

So—I reflected. As I thought about Kittle, I decided that he's as self-confident and optimistic a character as Henry Wiggen of the Mark Harris trilogy. I decided that Walker stands at the plate like a ballet dancer in the tendu position. These analogies came from my head, not from my notebook.

Wulfie and I drove down to Sarasota to see the White Sox–KC game and take Kittle and Walker to dinner. Reading my notes last night, I discovered that I haven't been getting very good quotes from them. It's not their fault: Speaking in the clubhouse just isn't conducive to good conversation. But over dinner at Walt's Fish House, they began telling humorous stories about their days in the minors. Driving back to the Don, Wulfie and I went over the evening's events and wrote down the best quotes. I'm not worried about the players' reaction—they knew we were taking mental notes. And I'm not worried about accuracy—every fact I use will be checked with them. All I know is that the story should work now: I've got the details and the color and the observations.

I have a theory—no, a revealed truth—about ballplayers. The longer they're in the game, the harder they are to deal with. Kittle and Walker are fresh and ingenuous—a delight. But no one was bothering them at the restaurant. Will they change when they're besieged by media and autograph hounds?

Another thing I've discovered is that athletes remember me later if we've been out to dinner. One dugout interview pretty much follows another and the interviewers blur in the mind, but a dinner with a writer is a little out of the ordinary for most players. With Kittle and Walker I think I've established bona fide contacts.

9   Today I wrote the Kittle-Walker story. I worked from 11:30 to 1 and 1:30 to 3, golfed and dined with Wulfie, then wrote from 8:30 to 10 and 10:30 to 11:30. This time I numbered the pages of my notebook and wrote a fairly detailed outline. I don't always write out of my head. With an overnight deadline, I decided I didn't want to waste time flipping through the notebook.

I'm very excited about the subject matter. Kittle and Walker may well be the best rookie twosome to come into the league since the Red Sox' Fred Lynn and Jim Rice made spectacular debuts in 1975. A righthanded-hitting leftfielder, Kittle hit homer after homer out of the Edmonton ballpark last summer and is expected to hit tape-measure shots this year, some of them possibly clearing cavernous Comiskey Park. Walker, a lefthanded-hitting first baseman, already has one of the best pure swings in the game—shifting his weight at just the right instant, letting go of the bat with his left hand after connecting, following through like a tennis player on a topspin backhand.

Above all, what Kittle and Walker demonstrate is how difficult it is to judge baseball talent. Scouts can be sure that a top college football or basketball prospect is worth drafting: He's already been playing in the very high minors. But there's simply no sure-fire preparation for baseball's major leagues. The skills are so refined it's almost impossible to predict how a rookie does until he plays in big-league game situations.

Who makes it? Frequently, late developers. Kittle and Walker, in fact, are reclamation projects from other organizations. Kittle was cut by the Dodgers, and Walker was drafted out of the Phillie system. The Dodgers gave up on Kittle when he failed to hit better than .250 for three consecutive seasons after suffering a neck injury. He went to work as a steelworker, and Pierce discovered him in an amateur league. Given a tryout at Comiskey Park, Kittle hit something like 7 of 12 pitches into the stands (the facts have been lost to legend). Walker's progress was delayed by a separated shoulder he'd suffered in football. A low draft choice of the Phillies, he had three seasons of mediocre stats in Class A. Nonetheless, playing in the 1978 Instructional League, he attracted the attention of Chicago's crack scout Jerry Krause. ' "You don't look for averages in the Instructional League," Krause told me. "You look for swings. Walker has a short swing for a big man. Guys with short strokes leave less room for error. A short, quick basketball shot is better than a long, sweeping one; a quick puncher hits hardest."

Kittle and Walker are a beautiful pair, and they get along famously. "Forget about the phony male-bonding of those beer commercials," I wrote, "this is a vintage friendship right out of Americana. Move over, Huck and Tom. Take a hike, Butch and Sundance. Make way, John Belushi and Dan Akroyd."

Some things I tell myself while writing:

Write as if you were speaking. The closer I come to that ideal, the more natural I sound. I try to use more verbs and fewer adjectives (Compare "A man was beaten, stabbed, gutted, shot and tortured" to "On a dark street, under a broken light, in the northeast part of town, a man was killed"; the first sentence reads much better, unless you happen to be the victim). I also use contractions whenever possible.

Don't get hung-up on the lead. That just delays the writing. I can always tack it on later if I'm initially stuck.

Vary the sentence structure. I try not to write several subject-verb-object sentences in a row, unless I'm doing it for emphasis.

Use anecdotes. Standard J-school teaching. Better to use the specific than the general.

Be obvious. We journalists are so close to the subjects we cover that we often forget to tell the readers basic information we think they already know. DeCinces once told me, "I don't know the men in my neighborhood. I work nights, they work days." Fascinating. Obvious. Unreported.

I drove two hours to Orlando and got all I needed on the Twins and Astros. A brilliant coup. I usually need a day on each club; now I'll probably get an unexpected day off later this week. Not so brilliant was a line in the Kittle-Walker story stating that each player could conceivably wind up in another team's uniform at the start of the season (Kittle could be traded for infield help, Walker could be sent back to the minors for more experience). Actually, that's a remote possibility, but Larry understandably picked up on it, wondering if a Kittle-Walker story was worth doing in the first place. Pete Carry, the interim M.E., wasn't as concerned. He told Larry that as long as the story was interesting, it should run. The writing must be holding up.

I returned from Orlando exhausted. I called Wulfie and he asked if I'd like to have dinner with him and Mark Heisel of *The Los Angeles Times.* At first I accepted. Then I thought, "This is ridiculous; I'm too tired to do anything but sleep." I called back to decline. For once I had resisted the fear of being alone, the need to be a "nice guy" and a "team man." I remember reading how Jeb Stuart Magruder of Watergate fame broke the law for much the same reason: going along to get along. That's company I don't need. Declining a dinner invitation is a world apart from refusing to break the law, but I still felt noble. It's O.K. to be gregarious, but as Billy Joel says, you always sleep in your own space. Tonight I knew where I belonged—in my hotel room.

Larry has decided that each scouting report should have a **11** sharp angle—a player, a problem, anything but the usual laundry list. Covering the Tigers, I latched onto Dave Rozema, who could be the key to the bullpen. He's also an interesting story. Rozema used to pull foolish stunts like sitting on a bottle of lip moistener and winding up with 11 stitches. Of late he's undergone a startling transformation after suffering a needless knee injury and undergoing a six-hour operation. It was the old coming-of-age-in-hard-times story, and Rozema gave me some good copy.

After leaving the Tigers' camp in Lakeland, I met Larry Kleinfeld and Sandra Thompson and had a Cuban-style dinner at the Alvarez restaurant in Ibor City. The Alvarez deserves a place in history—at least my history. I had chicken, fried bananas, soup, bread, flan and sangria for $5.43. There are still bargains in this world.

Later we saw professional jai alai. I loved it. Unlike some other betting sports, the principals are people. And what athletes they are! Whipping those hard balls off walls at speeds in excess of 150 mph and catching them in baskets attached to their arms, they're doing something I can't even imagine trying. What fluidity, what grace.

And what competition. At the Tampa fronton play is continuous and interesting. There are seven two-man teams, with two teams playing at a time. Team One plays Team Two, the winner plays Team Three, and so on. Each game counts as a point. The first team to reach seven points wins. We bet Quinellas, picking the first two finishers in either order.

march

Larry, Sandy, and I, betting as a team, won four of ten Quinellas and took home a profit of $20 apiece. No wonder I like jai alai.

13   The Reds' camp in Tampa personifies the Cincinnati organization: efficient, distant, sterile. It sits on a strip of land between two major streets. There are no palm trees, no atmosphere, nothing. If the practice fields and Al Lopez Stadium weren't there, the area would probably be one large parking lot.

The Reds worked out on the fields and arrived at the stadium a few minutes before their game with Pittsburgh. Wulfie's fiancee Jane (Bambi) Bachman, the magazine's chief of research, had asked me to find out whether Brad (The Animal) Lesley, a fearsome relief pitcher, would make the club. If so, a picture of the pitcher, as well as shots of other rookies, would accompany my Kittle-Walker story.

I first asked the Reds' P.R. man, Jim Ferguson. He said he wasn't sure. As the players trickled in, I got more and more positive responses. Finally, I cornered pitching coach Bill Fischer and told him my problem. "Go ahead and run the picture," Fischer said. "He'll make the club." (To everyone's surprise, Lesley flopped late in spring training and was demoted.)

Last year Johnny Bench had shown me a system for chipping with a wedge. The next day I used it on an "executive" course of par-3's and short par-4's and shot a one-under par 60, my best round ever. Today I reminded him of his good words, and we had a pleasant conversation. In the process he mentioned that he had concentrated too much on converting from catcher to third base last year, and his hitting had slipped. I'll be able to use that remark in the scouting report.

I also spoke with pitcher Rich Gale, whom I'd profiled in 1978. At the time he was a successful rookie at KC, where he had a good working fastball and a nifty slider. He was also a good subject: a rare New Englander in the majors, a squash player, and an intelligent, perceptive man (here I go again gravitating to the articulate athlete). Following his rookie year, he had an up-and-down record with the Royals and was traded, first to the Giants, now to the Reds. He pitched reasonably well today, allowing a run and four hits in three innings, and he has an excellent chance to catch on as fourth or fifth starter.

Because I'm in and out of cities and rarely follow teams for an extended period of time, I could probably count on my hands and feet the players who recognize me and remember my name. I hadn't seen Gale in two or three years, but he called out my name as soon as he saw me. As I reflect on that, I'm amazed. Here's a guy who has plenty on his mind. His career may turn on whether that slider drops or flattens out. I wonder what demons have pursued him the last four or five years. Why should he remember me? But he does.

The Kittle-Walker story closed tonight. I got a bunch of calls from my checker, Bailey Breene, and she had no major changes. Unfortunately, one of the assistant managing editors, Ken Rudeen, didn't like my lead. I had started with some anecdotes the players told Wulfie and me in the restaurant. Ken felt I should have started with hard news—rarely has one team had two such strong rookies, etc. Larry and I did our best to rewrite the opening to fit Ken's wishes.

I had the impression that Pete Carry hadn't objected to my lead: It had featured more writing and less reporting, after all. But any A.M.E., if he feels strongly enough, can effect major changes in a story or even kill it. My feeling about this piece was that Ken's idea was fine for a news story but not a feature. Technically, this story is in the front-of-the-book news area; but being more profile than results, it seemed to demand a featurish approach. Will people sit through 400–500 lines of what start out looking like hard news? The kind of straightforward, organized craftsman and painstaking word editor every magazine needs, Ken evidently thinks so. My preference was to soften up the readers with personality, humor, anecdote. With or without the changes the story will fly, but I'm not as pleased as I was a day or two ago. Every writer at the magazine has complained about overediting; today it's my turn.

14   It's been ten years since I bowled regularly, and the joy returned when Wulfie, Rick Hummel of the *St. Louis Post-Dispatch* and I spent a couple of hours at the Ten Pin Lanes in St. Petersburg. On the lane next to us was a family; the father, potbellied and balding, put a fine hook on his ball. Two lanes over were a guy and his date. On our other side an elderly couple was having a splendid time. Two young couples shared a lane; one of the women looked about six months pregnant. How quintessentially democratic, I thought, the good burghers out for a night on the town. "It's the most egalitarian sport I know," Wulfie said. "Anyone can outbowl a pro like Carmen Salvino in a single game. Imagine winning a game—or even a point—from Jimmy Connors."

The ritual was returning: the four-step approach, the lane arrow to aim at, the feel of a 14-pound ball. The three of us staged a strike competition, and I won it in overtime. At the beginning of the evening, I was nervous and preoccupied over other matters. At the end I was exercised and exorcised. Let's go bowling!

15   I was running on the beach when I came across Thomas Boswell of *The Washington Post*. We talked for half an hour. Later we saw "48 HRS.," both of us for the second time, and agreed it was time well spent.

Boz is one of the best baseball writers—no, sportswriters—around, and he had his usual store of insights and opinions.

• Commissioner Kuhn, supposedly a lame duck, will remain in office. The owners responsible for his "firing" will reconsider, based on the new $1 billion TV contract he helped negotiate. "I don't ever again want to hear about a team's financial hardships," Boz said.

• The Orioles will win the AL East.

• The Dodgers won't get anywhere near as much out of rookies Greg Brock and Mike Marshall as they would have from departed veterans Ron Cey and Steve Garvey.

Boz is invariably a few steps ahead of the pack. For a feature on Brock and Marshall, both recent standouts in the Pacific Coast League, he went through the stats of every present big-leaguer who played in the PCL. What Boz discovered was that many a major-league nonentity had bonzo stats in the PCL, a notorious hitters' league. And what of the players who went on to become big-league stars? Even Garvey and Cey took a while to establish themselves after coming out of the PCL. Conclusion: For all their billing, Brock and Marshall won't be instant sensations. So the Dodgers could be in trouble.

I've often wondered how Boz covers baseball as well as he does. Certainly his superior intelligence is a factor. He doesn't merely see facts—he sees associations. He writes well and is well read. But the clincher, I think, is that he loves baseball. He asks questions not because he's paid to, but because he's sincerely interested in the answers.

Boz is nothing if not cosmic. Once he was interviewing Mike Flanagan, an Oriole pitcher. "Mike," Boz said, "do you realize that when you hold the ball on the mound, you control the universe. The world stands still. You're the initiator. Nothing can proceed without you."

"Tom," said Flanagan, "there's a little piece of food under your lip."

march

16   For the last two days I've been writing my scouting reports. I've only got 80 lines for each, and I had to make them awfully spare and factual—good journalism, average writing. I didn't even have room for the line about the balding left-hander.

After finishing my sixth and final report, I played golf with Boz at nearby Isla del Sol, a short but narrow course with water on every hole.

Boz is a better golfer than I am. He often breaks 80, which I've never done on a full-length regulation course. But his game isn't exactly in midseason form. How did he react to his poor play? Intelligently, I thought. Instead of plodding after each badly hit ball and glumly marking sevens and eights on his scorecard, he took many practice shots and didn't keep score. And instead of holding in his anger, as I usually do, he swore a lot and threw some clubs. He got out his frustration and felt great afterwards.

17   Matthew arrived last night (Benjamin is coming in tomorrow) and insisted on taking a midnight swim in the Don CeSar pool. O.K., but this morning he was again pushing me into the water. No sooner had I swum a few laps when I felt a pain in my left arm. Three swims, one run and 18 holes of golf in 24 hours is too much.

I filed the scouting reports, and Matthew and I had supper with Boz and John Schulian of the *Chicago Sun-Times*. Schulian's an interesting character. An opinionated, controversial, and gutsy columnist, he once referred to Yankee manager Billy Martin as a mouse studying to be a rat. "What," asks John, "is he going to do to me?"

19   Matthew and I drove down to Sarasota for the White Sox–Red Sox game (Benjamin stayed at the pool reading a book).

Kittle and Walker hadn't seen the story, but LaRussa had and loved it (of course, he also suggested it). Feeling comfortable with the club, I decided that we could sit on the field near the White Sox dugout. It was quite a thrill, especially for Matthew, who got to take close-up pictures and chat about photography with first base coach Dave Nelson.

I could hear the players calling to each other. They all seemed to have nicknames: Kitty for Kittle, Vinny or Mormon (!) for Vance Law, Pudge for Carlton Fisk. Even Tony LaRussa has been given a nickname by his underlings: T-bone.

Funny how things can change in a week. Kittle now has left field sewed up. When I asked Walter how things were going, he held his hand parallel to the ground and moved his thumb up and down: so-so. It looks as though he won't start but won't get sent down either: LaRussa likes him coming off the bench.

After we left the park, we spent some time at a go-cart track. Another major thrill for Matthew: his first driving experience. I'd never drive a go-cart, but I wasn't thrilled. I act as if I've experienced everything, because nothing seems new. Actually, I've experienced very little.

I've got the next week to hang around and sniff out stories. **20** Some time ago I got Larry's permission to do Nolan Ryan when he sets the all-time strikeout record (he's 14 short). The Astros were playing the Cardinals today, and Ryan threw for the first time in a game situation. His line: 5 IP, 2 R, 3 BB, 4 K. Not bad. Afterwards, I visited Ryan in the clubhouse. He was seated with one ice pack on his right shoulder and his right elbow in a tub of ice. Standard procedure: Pitching is an unnatural act that produces swelling and requires therapy.

I've never found the right adjective to describe Ryan. "Modest" and "self-effacing" are pretty tired expressions, but they come close. "Phlegmatic" isn't bad. Basically, Ryan doesn't see himself as any big deal. To him, pitching is something he does when he isn't working around his farm in Alvin, Texas. He seems surprised that people make a fuss over him. When he pitched for the Mets, kids hung around his home in Queens waiting for autographs. That offended him. He had it better when he pitched for the Angels and lived in relative obscurity. Then he moved back home to Texas. Just a pleasant, hard-working guy who makes about $1 million a year.

21 I took the boys to Al Lang Stadium in St. Petersburg, and the first thing I discovered was that John Stearns, the Mets' catcher, is out at least until June with elbow trouble. I knew he'd been hurting, but the news was worse than I'd expected. "He had one of those things where the tendon is pulled away from the bone," New York general manager Frank Cashen told me. "We had him in a treatment program and were very confident, but he got too excited, threw too hard and overextended himself."

I suggested that one of baseball's major problems is players returning too soon from injuries. It has happened thousands of times. "Well, not so often any more," said Cashen, "now that they've got long-term contracts." He frowned. Some baseball men feel that well-compensated players are too quick to remove themselves from the lineup.

There's another view, though. Managers are always bragging about players who run through walls. Well, you can't run through walls and come out unscathed. The problem with long-term contracts isn't that players malinger; it's that they try too hard in order to justify their salaries, and sometimes wind up having bad years. The next season they tend to relax. Do they put themselves on the disabled list at the first opportunity? I doubt it. Some players are getting second opinions and taking better care of themselves; to old-fashioned officials, that may seem like malingering. But some doctors who aren't on team payrolls maintain that players persist in returning from injuries too soon. "A lot of times all they need is rest," says Daniel Akaitis, the neurologist who treated me and the Mets' Tim Leary, "but they're trained to work through pain."

The atmosphere at a spring training game is quite unlike that at a regular-season game. No one worries about the final score because the starters are replaced after a few innings. They run their laps in stockinged feet, padding along the grass behind the outfielders. Then they shower, change and leave the park. The movement of people in the stands is every bit as fluid. Fans drift in, drift out, show up for the sixth inning. At Al Lang Stadium there's a celebrated hot-dog vendor named Tommy Walton. When he makes his grand entrance, people applaud, and surprised players turn around to see what's happening. "World's worst hot dogs!" Walton cries out. Later he breaks into a raucous tenor and sings *Take Me Out to the Ball Game* and *He's Got the Whole World in His Hands.*

We watched today's game with Roger Angell, the fiction editor and baseball columnist for *The New Yorker.* Roger's a sensitive and charming fellow, but he couldn't restrain himself when he saw one of his least favorite players, first baseman Dave Kingman of the Mets. Roger stuck out his tongue, blew on it and gave Kingman the raspberry: "btfstpk!"

"Roger!" said his wife Carol.

"Btfstpk!" Carol was blushing and laughing now. Their 12-year-old son John Henry had one of those "Oh, Dad!" looks on his face.

"Btfstpk!" Angell blared again. Met fans turned around and looked nervously at him. Whereupon Kingman hit a long homer.

"Keep it up," one of the Mets fans said. "It helps."

"Btfstpk!"

march

22   Wulfie, the kids and I have become a foursome: two big
kids and two little ones. We play pinballs, bowl, go to ballgames and movies. An English major at Hamilton College,
Wulfie came to the magazine by a roundabout route. Upon
graduation, he got into his car. "I drove to every single daily
newspaper in New England," he says. He eventually took a
job writing sports for the *Evening Sun* in Norwich, New York.
Later he drove south, stopping at every major daily on the
way, and landed a job with the *Fort Lauderdale News*. "I was
hired as a desk man and horseracing writer," he said. "I had
been to one race, and that qualified me."

From the beginning Wulfie was one of the rare sportswriters who could use literary references. But that's not what
distinguished him from the other ink-stained wretches.
Wulfie seems to do his best work in his sleep. In Fort Lauderdale, he was asked to watch the Super Bowl on television and
write the game story. He fell asleep during the second half,
woke up with a few minutes to go and wrote an article that
placed first in a statewide competition.

A few years later, freelancing somnolently in Boston, he got
a call from Merv Hyman and was hired as a researcher. Before
long Wulfie wrote some excellent stories and was run up the
masthead. On Saturday night deadlines he'll go to sleep with
the lead in his head, get a wakeup call at 5 A.M. and write
steadily until the 10 A.M. deadline. I can't imagine how he
does it. I also can't imagine how Wulfie does interviews: He
mumbles something awful. I can only assume that once athletes pick up what he's saying, they crack up, relax and talk
freely. Either that or fall asleep.

We were eating dinner recently at Ted Peters Famous
Smoked Fish, a St. Pete restaurant, when I mentioned that it's
possible to take smoked fish back to New York on the plane.
Of course, I added, you also have to put up with the smell.
"In that case," said Wulfie, "you can't sit in the No Smoking
Fish section."

A good part of the day was spent at a clinic. I don't mean a **23** baseball clinic. Matthew had swimmer's ear, and we went to a medical clinic for medication. The doctor gave him prescription ear drops, but Matthew was in pain for much of the night. I went downstairs, and the guy at the desk gave me an envelope full of generic aspirin. They worked splendidly. Next morning a guest on the Donahue show was talking about prescription drugs. "Extra strength," he said, means more of the same drug sold at a higher price.

A complication arose over my Minnesota scouting report. I've pretty well panned the Twins, but the consensus at the office is that they'll climb to fifth in a seven-team race. Larry told me that my report had to be more positive, so we spent an hour rewording it. We inserted that the Twins had the league's third-best defense, won 44 of their last 92 games and proved they could be almost respectable if reliever Ron Davis is effective. I'm skeptical. The Twins always seem to close well, after they're far out of contention.

This was my chutzpah day. The kids and I arrived at Payne **24** Park in Sarasota sometime after the game started. I drove around and finally parked in a lot reserved for a bar. "I'm sorry, sir, but you can't park here," a kid said. "It's reserved for the restaurant."

"I've been driving around for half an hour," I said. "How about if we buy a few Cokes inside?"

"That's all right," the kid said, "y'all go ahead."

Flushed with success, I talked our way into the park and onto the field. Once inside, I introduced Matthew to Russ Kennedy, a photographer for the Associated Press. Russ gave Matthew professional advice and allowed him to use some equipment.

As we were leaving the field, Greg Walker came up and thanked me for the article. That's a rare gesture. Usually ballplayers don't read the article, don't say anything or don't thank me. I was utterly thrilled.

Walker said he still wasn't certain of making the team. "The way you swing the bat, I'm sure they'd call you up by June," I said.

"I hope so," he said, sounding unconvinced. Obviously, it's a day-by-day thing. I can't imagine my next story determining whether or not I remain with the magazine.

25 At midday I stopped at a mall to get a haircut. The barber shop was a dingy place. Tacky photos were mounted on a pegboard. Two barbers—an elderly man and an old woman—were cutting hair and watching "Broken Arrow" on a small black-and-white TV. The man gave me a hair-and-beard cut for $6—a bargain until you consider that the price was right for the trim. After paying the $6 and a $1 tip, I asked for a receipt. He fumbled around for paper and pen, then suddenly turned on me. Thrusting the money back into my hand, he gave me a shove and shouted, "Keep out of here! I'm sick of receipts!" I dropped the money on the cash register and fled.

The boys' old buddies Elizabeth and Sophie Knight arrived with their mother Joan and her friend Bill. The seven of us got lost on the way to a St. Pete restaurant. We stopped at a bar for directions. When a female bartender had trouble directing us, a male patron, drunk and loud-mouthed, bumped into me and whined, "What do you expect from a stupid broad?"

Florida presents a strange face to visitors. Two groups I've rarely seen are bona fide southerners—black and white. Two groups I always see are the very old and very young. Both depress me. I see old men in restaurants, sitting glumly in loud pants and white loafers while their wives dominate conversation. A vision of me in the future? And I see young people on the beach, flipping Frisbees through their legs, jumping on surf boards and generally doing things I can't. A vision of my lost youth? I stop being jealous when I talk to these kids and discover that they have no intellectual curiosity whatsoever. Wulfie says Floridians' brains get addled by the sun.

I'm ready to go home.

On this, our last full day, we had the only perfect afternoon **26** of our stay—sunny and hot. I took to the beach for the first time—and gaped. There's something more going on than skimpy bikinis. Women are wearing bottoms that barely cover their, well, bottoms. On the front of one bikini bottom was a picture of an ice-cream cone. I'm a card-carrying ACLU member, but I'm revolted that sex is being marketed and advertised like so much merchandise. I never thought I'd have anything in common with Jerry Falwell, but I'm frightened by the thought that movie houses showing Charlie Chaplin films are being replaced by porno houses. The come-ons I've been seeing on sit-coms and TV ads are coarse— nothing less, nothing more. What we're seeing isn't openness, it's mindlessness. Or am I just getting old?

The kids and I have been running from one activity to another, and we've missed a lot in the process—the chance to walk on the beach, soak up some rays, reflect, read, slow down. Some March we'll learn.

The boys and I abandoned Florida's driving rainstorm only **27** to encounter the same thing in New York. On the plane back I thought about spring training. What stuck with me longest is a conversation I had with Roger Angell. He's doing a story on catching. From what he told me, I gathered that he asks his subjects the most obvious questions—how do you take your stance behind the plate; what do you say to a pitcher to help his confidence; how much pain is there. Part of my problem with being something of a baseball "insider" is that I tend to think I know it all. So I don't ask basic questions, and instead fall back on ritualistic ones ("What pitch did he hit?"). By contrast Roger remains, in the best sense of the word, eternally naive. He knows his readers aren't insiders and he covers the game from a fan's perspective. He continues to maintain a sense of wonder about baseball.

28　I always find it a thrill to read for the first time the final edited copy of a story. This morning I read nine such stories: the six scouting reports; my National League feature; the chess knights regional and my golf story, which ran in yesterday's *News*.

Despite a typo or two and some edits I didn't like, the golf story turned out all right. I got some compliments at the office, including one from Assistant Managing Editor Mark Mulvoy, who has written some golf books. And the good people at Dyker Beach will be thrilled; that was one of my main reasons for writing the story. I must keep telling myself that.

I wish they hadn't cut my favorite line from the chess story ("Chess legend: The knight is the favorite piece of the Russians because it can move in eight different directions, none of them straightforward"). What are the editors thinking when they do something like that? To accommodate the inevitable life-sized pictures—accent the *illustrated* in *Sports Illustrated*—Larry had to make substantial cuts in my NL piece. Gone was my lead about the seventh game of the Series. Larry felt that the research will carry the story. It won't be pretty, but it will be persuasive. I must keep telling myself that.

Substance over style. I must keep tellilng myself that.

april

Audrey and I went to a Passover seder. Not being religious, **1**
our hosts David FeBland and Lynda Mandlawitz decided to
forego the service for a gala dinner. It was a quintessential
New York party: excellent food, unforgettable company.
There was a guy named Manny teaching people to mambo; a
young black businessman from Michigan and a woman
lawyer from Omaha, both relocating here; a businessman-
turned-journalist; a woman into holistic everything; artists
and teachers.

There's an unfortunate part of me that wants everyone to
be the same—conforming, reassuring, nonthreatening. At
times like this I remind myself that democracy at heart is
nothing more than our ability to tolerate—no, celebrate—
people who are different from ourselves.

With the start of the season just two days away, I don't **2**
know how I'll be spending the first week. Nolan Ryan has
been put on the disabled list with a urinary-tract infection, so
it will be some time before he breaks the strikeout record.

I'm a little bothered by the fact that I don't have any other
ideas for stories. A certain lassitude has set in. By now I
should have written the Bryn Mawr story; I haven't even
transcribed the tapes. I'm a real case of mañana. Plainly, I
need assignments and deadlines. Plainly, I'm still not enough
of a self-starter.

april

3   It was the kind of Mad Monday that will undoubtedly characterize the baseball season. I arrived at the office and learned that I would be doing a column on Bruce Bochte, a fine player who retired from the Seattle Mariners at the peak of his form. Interesting guy, interesting story idea. Trouble is, his agent says he's not speaking to the press. With time running out before the travel department closed, Larry told me to do the column on Buddy Bell, the Texas third baseman. Many teams were after Bell at the winter meetings, but the Rangers didn't deal him. Why not? How does Bell feel about remaining with an apparent noncontender? What makes him so desirable? A story with possibilities.

The only time I ever spoke with Bell, several years back, I asked him an obnoxious question after a bad loss. Understandably, he snapped at me. He probably won't remember the incident. What the hell, he'll either speak with me or he won't. Baseball's back!

4   There is no starker contrast in baseball than that between spring training and Opening Day. Informality is replaced by formality, humor with seriousness, warmth with cold, speculation with reality. Suddenly, the red-hot rookie who wowed 'em in Florida is gaping at the sight of the mammoth stadium he must play in now that play is for real. Suddenly, the players must back up the boasts the manager has been making about them all March. That's why everyone has butterflies in his stomach—manager, coaches, veterans, rookies.

Opening Day used to merit the capital letters. The game was played in the afternoon. Businesses would close and schools would let out early. The President threw out the first ball for the Senators' opener in Washington and elsewhere mayors and other dignitaries were on hand. In a very real sense, the business of America stood still for the national pastime.

No longer. There's no team in Washington and the President hasn't thrown out the first ball for the better part of a decade. And now, in a lot of cities, they're playing Opening Day as Opening Night!

Here's the thinking: More people will come out at night, so play the opener under the lights. Baseball has joined the world of commerce and industry. Damn you, Cincinnati Reds, for starting night baseball in the majors in 1935! And what of the ballgame itself? The hoopla used to hype the game; in the past decade or so, the game has become lost in promotions. Fans ogle celebrities; parachutists land at second base; scoreboards explode, mascots mascot.

Why? Because baseball is competing for fans with other sports—and even more important, with television. This is the age of the seven-second attention span, and baseball, a slow game, is attempting to be continuously entertaining.

I'm skeptical. Baseball is as much a game of reflection as reflexes. It's quite literally a pastime, created for people who enjoy lying in the sun with their shirts off and cups of beer in their hands. And that's the way it should sell itself—as an alternative to pop culture, not part of it.

Flying in from Newark, the only major New York–area airport where planes seem to leave on time, I arrived at Arlington Stadium a couple of hours before gametime. I spoke at length with nearly everyone I needed to see except Bell, who has the flu. He said he'd be up to an interview tomorrow.

I don't particularly like pressboxes, especially glass-enclosed ones that are insulated from what's happening on the field. But it was cold and windy in the stands, so I traded immediacy for comfort.

Altogether too many pressboxes are enclosed, and the beat writers sit in them game after game, bored and detached. Cynical comments and one-liners ricochet around the room like ping-pong balls in a bottle. When Billy Sample, the Texas leftfielder, made a fine sliding catch, a writer said, "Stay on your feet, you hot dog."

Writers keep the same crazy hours as players from March through October. Even when they're home they're away in a sense, because most of the games are at night. With teams traveling by jet and routinely crossing time zones, the baseball beat has become so exhausting that many papers use two or more writers.

A major problem for beat men is keeping a distance between themselves and the players. The writers have to deal with the players every day. If they're too critical, they can lose a contact for a whole season; if they're not critical enough, they can become "house men," or shills for the team. It's a difficult balance to maintain day after day, and the best writers do a highly professional, even heroic job of it.

I have a much easier time with the players than the beat writers do. Most of the time I'm assigned to cover athletes on teams that are winning. If I have to write a negative story, I can be as nasty as I want, knowing I probably won't see the same team for weeks or even months. I doubt I could be a consistently tough or critical beat writer; I wouldn't even want to try.

6 I spoke with Bell. He's the son of Gus Bell, a former outfielder for the Pirates, Mets, Braves and Reds who hit 206 homers in 15 big-league seasons. The Bells are the only father-son combination that has played in All-Star Games.

Competing for losing teams in Cleveland (1972–78) and Texas (1979–), Buddy Bell isn't as well known as third basemen like George Brett, Mike Schmidt and Graig Nettles, but his peers consider him just as good. "He's the guy I'd build a franchise around," says Chicago White Sox pitcher Jim Kern in a statement echoed by Detroit manager Sparky Anderson.

"He's got an interesting combination of Graig Nettles and Aurelio Rodriguez: Nettles' reactions and range and Rodriguez' arm."

"I'm probably one of the least scientific players around," says Bell, a nice, simple guy who has won four consecutive Gold Gloves and averaged .304 the last four seasons. "If you think too much, you make the game too complicated. You hit the ball, catch the ball, and that's about it. When I go to clinics, the other instructors don't think I'm very bright."

He does not lack for competitiveness. Few players do. Speak with a guy whose team is out of contention at the All-Star break and he'll tell you, in so many words, that he's just marking time. Bell was hopeful about being traded between seasons, but deal after deal fell through—possibly because the Rangers decided to build from within, possibly because owner Eddie Chiles was unwilling to risk making yet another bad trade. How does Bell live with a team that doesn't figure to contend in the near future? He fidgeted with the question and a cigarette. "Realism and optimism aren't the same thing," he said, "but you have to be optimistic." Nonetheless, he spent the next few minutes alternating between utopian thinking and crueler realities. "When you lose 98 ballgames," he said, referring to the previous season, "it's tough to say you'll win 98 games. But I like to think of us as a contender. They've fired some good people around here, but then they turned around and hired a guy like [manager Doug] Rader, who's just as capable." He paused, groping. "We'll be O.K. We'll be O.K. If the club shows patience with what we've got, we could have a gold mine."

He wasn't convincing. I feel for him.

I've been staying at the visiting team's hotel. That's useful in several respects: I can take the team bus to and from the stadium, grab players for interviews when they're away from the park, have drinks with someone after the game. Tonight I sat in the lounge with Ken (Hawk) Harrelson, the slugger-turned-White Sox broadcaster. Baseball is a game of many empty moments—during the game, on the plane, in the hotel—and it takes good talk to fill them up. The Hawk is one great talker, and he said something striking about defense: "Good pitching isn't worth a damn without good defense, and the White Sox have a problem with their defense. That's why I picked them to finish third." And that's why LaRussa benched Walker, who cost the Sox the opener yesterday with his poor play at first. Defense is something people take for granted, but I wonder how many clubs have won titles without good men in the field.

Herm Weiskopf of our staff is here pursuing items for Inside Pitch, a new weekly column replacing Baseball's Week. According to a Pub Memo, the front-of-the-book publisher's letter, Inside Pitch will "provide a behind-the-batting-cage look at the game, something closer, more intricate, more knowing." I mentioned my feelings about defense to Herm, and he fully agreed. We both hope to get some defensive tidbits in Inside Pitch.

Another thought about writers. When they begin calling their team "we," they're in danger of becoming house men. "Have we gotten back-to-back hits this year?" a Chicago writer asked as the Sox lost their third game in three starts to the Rangers.

Chicago president Eddie Einhorn watched the game from the pressbox and brooded. "Now we have to go to Detroit and face Morris, Wilcox and Petry," he said, referring to the Tigers' fine rotation.

I've viewed computers as some kind of panacea, but tonight I learned a sobering lesson. Steve Daley of the *Chicago Tribune* was composing on his Teleram—the same model I use—when the thing went crazy. "Some of the letters haven't been working properly," he said later. "I was reduced to using codes—'4' when I wanted 'a', for instance—but tonight ten more letters went out. I had to borrow a typewriter. It was an old model, and the photocopier wouldn't work with it, so I had to dictate under deadline. It was a disaster." He paused and scowled into his drink. "I hate to write badly," he said.

I spent most of the day typing. Earlier in the week, Larry told me I'd get 200 lines. That was useful information because the story has some complicated elements that would take a long time to explain. I had to gloss over them. Just as well—they'd have cluttered up the story. Kern had given me numerous examples of Bell's intelligence, combativeness and courage. Instead of citing each one, I wrote, "According to Kern, Bell has a catcher's combativeness, a manager's mind and a masochist's pain threshold."

I managed to take a few hours off to play nine holes. Typically, I was paired with a nice partner; I got his number and I'll have someone to play with the next time I'm in town.

Later I had dinner with one of my college roommates, Jim Stripling. A Fort Worth lawyer, he has a nice wife who is expecting their first child, a spectacularly attractive stepdaughter and, best of all, a love for games. Indeed, after dinner he took me to a Scrabble club.

As we entered the room, Stripling introduced me to the group, and people gathered round to tout Scrabble and ask me questions. I got an eerie feeling—and a possible insight about sports. Just as athletes are so insecure because they have so much to lose—fame, money, respect—I asked myself how I'd feel if people began ignoring me. Sure, the questions get repetitive and I shouldn't need the raves to feel good about myself, but a part of me does. How would I feel if I had to sell myself on my personal virtues, not my prestigious employer? Probably a lot more insecure. I think a lot of people remain with the company far too long because of its reputation. As a result, they can feel better about themselves without bettering themselves.

april

8   Thoughts on the plane ride home:

After one game, I saw the White Sox' superbly conditioned Tom Paciorek eating a banana. Soon as I got home, I looked up my Bryn Mawr nutrition test and saw I wasn't consuming enough potassium. Right to the old Korean market.

Arlington Stadium is a strange place to play baseball. It sits in the suburbs next to the Six Flags Over Texas amusement park. No doubt neither Dallas nor Fort Worth would allow the park to be situated in the other city. Too bad. My idea of an ideal ballpark is one located downtown, where people can stroll over at lunchtime or after work.

An expanded minor-league park, Arlington Stadium looks disjointed in appearance. Far down the rightfield line is the Ranger clubhouse. It's a Texas-sized room with brown easy chairs and a plush blue carpet. A man don't hardly know where to spit. But Arlington Stadium has two important advantages over most new parks: real grass and little foul space. The ball takes honest bounces, not moon hops. And the place is "intimate," meaning that the stands are close to the field. "Even when the crowd is small," Bell told me, "you feel like there are a lot of people in the stands."

10   Audrey and I were checking out the Brooklyn Bridge Centennial exhibit at the Brooklyn Museum when I realized that 1983 is also the 25th anniversary of the Dodgers' departure from Brooklyn. It's easy to connect the two events: the bridge as the flawed promise of technology, the Dodgers' betrayal as the loss of innocence. A natural Viewpoint:

> May 24 is the Brooklyn Bridge Centennial. Lost in the ongoing celebration is a local milestone of commensurate significance: the 25th anniversary of the Brooklyn Dodgers' departure for Los Angeles. The two events should be inextricably linked in our memories.

The bridge was Manifest Destiny personified. Chief Engineer John A. Roebling felt that his creation—the greatest technological achievement of its time—signaled the conquering of the frontier. If men could link Manhattan and Brooklyn, everything Out There, from the elements to the Indians, would fall before our westward sweep. The bridge inspired engineer and artist alike, as the current exhibit at the Brooklyn Museum attests. Poet Hart Crane described the bridge as "harp and altar." Novelist Thomas Wolfe asked, "What bridge? Great God, the only bridge of power, life and joy, the bridge that was a span, a cry an ecstasy—that was America. . . ."

The great bridge also signaled the birth of a borough. Linked to the city, there burst forth a wondrous community of neighborhoods and parks and churches and, pedestrians beware, electric trolleys. Hence, the name Dodgers to describe the baseball team that became Brooklyn's most unifying force.

To our chagrin, we eventually learned that technology didn't hold the solution to all our problems. The machine could conquer the moon, but it respected neither the environment nor the soul. And when the Dodgers left Brooklyn, we lost our innocence forever. Love and loyalty, we were shattered to hear, were only so much mush to people in power. Almost inevitably, it seems in retrospect, the events that followed—expansion, divisional play, nighttime Series, artificial turf, the designated hitter—honored financial expedience rather than good baseball sense.

The building of the bridge was the birth of an illusion. The exodus of the Dodgers was the death of a dream.

As I was leaving the office at lunchtime, Staff Writer Bruce **11** Newman stopped me in the lobby. "I guess you've heard about yourself in the George Will column," he said. I hadn't, but I ran right out and bought *The Washington Post*. Let's pick up from the column:

Mathematics now has proven what clear-thinking moralists always hoped would be true: The American League's designated hitter rule, America's worst mistake since electing President Buchanan,

april

is a deserved affliction to its perpetrators. *Sports Illustrated's* Jim Kaplan, a prophet who will not be without honor in his country while I draw breath, notes that for the first time the National League has won four consecutive World Series with four different teams. Also, the National League has won 19 of the last 20 All-Star games. Some MIT mathematicians told Kaplan that the odds against such a result between equals is 23,800 to one, so Kaplan concludes the leagues are not equals.

Writing with a judgmental tone not heard since the Old Testament prophets were cataloguing the shortcomings of the Israelites, Kaplan says to the American League: Your failures are the wages of sin, and the DH is sin. True, Kaplan cites other factors, such as better farm systems, and fewer small parks that encourage mindless, swing-for-the-fences baseball. But the DH has also made managers dumber: "Because pitchers don't bat in the American League, managers have tended to leave them in the games when they are losing. As a result, there has been less thinking, less strategy, less managing." With the DH, teams lust incontinently for a big inning, so there is less aggressive scrambling for runs. Sloth. Sin.

I have warned President Reagan: He will be judged by whether he rids the nation of the DH.

12 Off to Kansas City for a column on Bob Stanley, the Red Sox reliever. This is my first venture of the season to the Midwest, where I went to graduate school and had my first job. But any trip to the heartland is a pause that refreshes.

It's said that if you live in the East, people ask you where you went to school; in the Midwest, what corporation you work for; in the South, who your family is; and in the West, what car you drive. The Midwestern stereotype seems least offensive to me. I love the place: It's truly can-do country— full of hope, free of cynicism. Ah, the achievement-oriented Middle West: Johnson, Johnson, he's our man; if he can't do it, Swanson can!

Before the 1982 season I did a project for the magazine using the Elias Sports Bureau, a statistical service based in

New York. Our task: Create a new standard to judge relief pitching. Relievers are evaluated almost exclusively by saves—a category that credits only those "stoppers" who finish games for winning teams. What of long relief, middle relief, spot relief and relief in losing causes? The Elias Bureau's Steve Hirdt and I created seven different categories in addition to saves. Among them were innings pitched; success at preventing runners from scoring; success with first batters faced, and "holds," which are given to pitchers who don't save or win but do keep things in check. The baseball establishment adopted none of these criteria, but somehow, somewhere, someone was enlightened.

No one was ever suited better to a new system of evaluation than Bob Stanley in 1982. He wasn't a save leader, but he was the main reason the Sox finished third, only six games out. Stanley set an American League record with 168 innings in relief; held the lead or tie 27 of 38 times he came in; prevented 34 of 48 runners left on base by the previous pitcher from scoring; held opponents to a .255 batting average, and succeeded in 12 of 14 save opportunities. In all, he contributed to 31 of Boston's 89 wins.

I spoke briefly with Stanley, who didn't pitch tonight, and we set up a lunch date for tomorrow.

A good workman, Stanley had a good workman's lunch— **13** chicken gumbo soup, cheeseburger, baked beans, two Cokes. It was his first meal of the day, and he wouldn't eat again until after the game. Later I saw Stanley running laps and doing calisthenics; he strikes me as the kind of player who is always prepared for work. Most ballplayers are like that. People think that because of the money, players must be underworked and overpaid. I think they work harder than ever precisely because of the money: They don't want to jeopardize their earning power. (Money more than any other reason, I think, is why so many players are still active at age 40.) As Stanley told me, "I've got a wife and three children to support, and I like to live comfortably."

Last season Stanley pitched for the most part in long relief. If a pitcher was knocked out early in the game, he got the call. Long relief is generally one of baseball's least glamorous jobs, but Stanley gave it some panache. He frequently bailed out Sox starters, who survived the fifth inning only 51 of 162 times. He would pitch long stretches and keep the other team from piling up runs, and the Red Sox used that valuable time to get back in the game. He was especially useful at Boston's "bandbox of a ballpark," Fenway Park, where a game is truly never over until it's over. "I ain't going for no Rolaids," he says, referring to the annual relief award that invariably goes to short relievers. "I'm not complaining. I just go as hard as I can for as long as I can. The Red Sox need a good bullpen to win."

Tonight's game was delayed for 45 minutes, and I spent the interval in the Boston clubhouse. To kill time, the Sox played miniature golf with bats, balls and paper cups. One of the best things about baseball, Buddy Bell told me a few days ago, is that, as a player, you never have to grow up. When they tired of golf, the Sox began imitating each other at the plate. Second baseman Jerry Remy, impersonator par excellence, brought down the house with his portrayal of first baseman Dave Stapleton hanging his head after hitting a popup.

I think ballplayers razz each other for two reasons: They've got a lot of time with nothing better to do, and they play under too much tension to take everything seriously. "You have to have a very thick skin to be a ballplayer," Sox pitcher Bruce Hurst told me. While looking for a house in Boston, Hurst and his wife have been living with the Celtics' Danny Ainge, who once played baseball for the Toronto Blue Jays. "Danny and I were talking about baseball and basketball," says Hurst, who played hoops at Dixie College in Utah. "We agreed that it's tougher to take a ribbing in baseball. When you're playing with 24 other guys instead of 11, there's a greater chance someone will get under your skin."

14 Last night and this morning I sent three stories to the office—the Bob Stanley column and the Brooklyn Bridge Anniversary and Bryn Mawr regionals.

Checking out at 10:45 A.M. today, I felt terrific. My work was done and there was ample time to get to the airport for a noon flight. In the cab I stole a look at my plane ticket. Omigosh, it leaves at 11! But not even a missed plane was going to ruin my day. A 12:30 flight to St. Louis, a 2:15 connection to New York, and I was home in plenty of time.

On the way, I thought about a ballplayer's life. Last night's game ended at midnight, and the Red Sox immediately flew home. I suppose the players straggled into bed at 6 A.M. The club saved a night's lodging, but what does this schedule do to a guy's system? Taking late-night flights and crossing time zones has to be tougher than traveling by train, as teams routinely did before baseball moved west in 1958.

I met a Princeton grad named Bob Tufts, who has caught on with the Royals as their last pitcher. Tufts used to play for the San Francisco Giants. His wife finished law school and prepared to take the California bar with the knowledge that she might have to practice elsewhere. "I hope you don't wind up somewhere like Kansas City," she told him.

15 I've just read my Buddy Bell story in this week's magazine, and I'm very disappointed with the editing. A given story will go through many hands—the checker, the copy editor, the proofreader, the lawyer, the editor in charge of the sport and two or three managing editors. Somewhere, someone took the edge off my story.

Let's start with a minor if nettlesome point. I wrote the

following sentence about Bell: "A fair-haired boy in every respect, he hits, fields, hustles, coaches for the Boys' Club and would help old ladies across the street if there were any pedestrians in Arlington, Texas." The editors stuck a dash between "street" and "if." That, to me, makes the joke too obvious. What I wanted to do was subtly slip in the clause with no punctuation at all. That's what makes a joke funny—understatement.

Later, discussing trade rumors concerning Bell, I wrote that a lot of clubs were after him: "the Orioles, the Dodgers, the White Sox, the Blue Jays, the Yankees, the Cardinals, the Reds, the Bad News Bears." This time the funny part—"the Bad News Bears"—was printed in the subtle fashion I'd written it. Why now and not then?

But what really irks me is the penultimate paragraph. In the April 6 entry of this journal I fleshed out Bell's agony and conflict over remaining with what appears to be a lousy team. The editors have shortened those good quotes and observations to this:

"Finishing in the second division every year can put gray hair on the most carefree player, though. 'Realism and optimism aren't the same thing,' he says, 'but you have to be optimistic. I think we'll be O.K. If the club shows patience with what we've got, we could have a gold mine.' "

Where's the pathos? Where's the emotion? What's left is bland and homogenized. Once again, I'm suffering from our editors' worst failing: overediting.

18   Monday madness: First, I was given a complicated scenario that could result in one of three stories. Go to Montreal for a three-game series between the Cardinals and Expos, writing about which team does better; but be prepared to go from Montreal to Atlanta and do the Braves instead if they stay hot. So I would be writing about the Cards, Expos or Braves.

Larry felt that one of those stories could wind up in the news area. The alternative—covering Nolan Ryan's quest for the strikeout record—would have resulted in a column if he did it this week or nothing if he failed. Larry said I'd be better off doing a sure news story.

However, the editors later decided that Ryan could be a big news story, so off I went to Houston. Larry gave me some editorial food for thought: Here's a record that has stood for 55 years, and people are just now catching up. But three different players—Ryan, Gaylord Perry and Steve Carlton—should pass recordholder Walter Johnson this year. Why did the record stand for so long, and why are so many modern pitchers going to pass it this year? Is the strikeout record a pitcher's equivalent of the home run or hit record? Larry suggested that I call Bob Feller, one of the greatest strikeout pitchers of all time, and send wires to correspondents for quotes from other greats.

All of which is known as "getting the big picture." Sometimes an editor can see the forest when a writer is looking at the trees.

19 I called Bob Feller and he turned out to be a querulous feller, more interested in bemoaning the years he lost to World War II than crediting Ryan.

20 I came to Houston two days before Ryan was due to pitch. Unfortunately, a dozen other writers had the same idea. The result was a mass interview. But Ryan was unusually expansive. He's not as interested in breaking the record as he is in calling attention to the positive side of his career. Critics have long maintained that he's too inconsistent and wild, noting that he's only 19 games over .500. Ryan wants to remind people that he's been durable and at times spectacular. And he has a point. The records of the teams he's played for have been worse than his own, and he's had winning records in nine of the last eleven years. "I definitely beat myself sometimes with walks," admits Ryan, who is running up an all-time record. But again, his critics are on the defensive: He has cut down on walks since learning to get ahead of hitters and use his curve as an out-pitch to supplement his feared hummer.

It's true that he tries to overpower hitters rather than finesse them. But who can blame him? He throws almost as hard—97 mph or so—at 36 as he did a decade earlier, when he was clocked at 100 mph, and he gets stronger in the latter stages of a game. No wonder he's blown only a dozen leads in the last three innings of the games he's pitched.

Why are so many pitchers threatening the strikeout mark? "Batters don't worry about striking out anymore," Feller told me. "Joey Sewell played in 155 games one year and had three strikeouts." By contrast, Mike Schmidt has never struck out fewer than 100 times in any full season, and the top 20 strikeout victims all started their careers after 1950. Today's starting pitchers can throw as hard as they want for as long as they want; in the pre-relief era, starters had to pace themselves. Expansion put more patsy hitters in lineups. Finally, today's pitchers are better conditioned, better coached and better motivated by big money. So they stick around longer and rack up more K's.

I had an interesting conversation with Tim Sullivan, a young writer for the *Cincinnati Enquirer.* Sullivan will leave the baseball beat after his third season. "I'm writing too many stories on injuries and agents," he said, "and not enough on the things that interest me. I'm finding that my whole being is contracted. It hit me one night last year when I was sitting in a Philadelphia bar. Tom Seaver came in, and he started asking what I'd been reading. I realized how easy it is to become insulated on the beat."

So do I. It's been two months since I finished a book. I rip open the papers, glance at my favorite columnists (Anthony

Lewis, Jimmy Breslin), check out the comics and head right for the baseball boxes. I didn't know about the terrorist bombing of the American embassy in Beirut for 24 hours—or was it 48? Scary.

Well, I guess there is such a thing as a bad golf game. I was **21** paired with three interesting-looking players—a wavy-haired matinee idol type, a good-old-boy Southern lawyer and his black colleague. I wanted to speak with them—hell, half of golf is conversation—but they kept speeding ahead in their electric carts. Very rarely do I become totally flustered on a golf course, but it happened this time. I four-putted two consecutive greens.

The baseball was much better. One of my favorite situations arose in the 10th inning of the Reds-Astros game. The Reds were leading 3–2, but the Astros had the bases loaded, nobody out. Where should the outfielders play? I strongly believe they should move a good five steps closer to the infield. Why? Because most inside-the-park hits are in front of the outfielders, and if they didn't move in a base hit would score two runs and cost them the game. But baseball managers invariably play the fielders back on the theory that "someone might hit one over our heads and beat us." What they're really saying is, "Someone might hit one over our heads, and I might be second-guessed." Cincy manager Russ Nixon kept his troops back. The Astros' Phil Garner hit the ball over the centerfielder's head anyway, and the Astros won 4–3.

Meanwhile, people are talking about Ryan. Houston general manager Al Rosen says Nolan has the same class as "Affirmed at the post." Some of the Houston players were talking about how Ryan's record fifth no-hitter had them all white-knuckled. They're excited about the possibility that he'll get the record tomorrow.

Yet the event isn't being heralded locally. "I bet we only get

20,000 tomorrow," says Dave Smith, a pitcher who played college ball with Armen Keteyian of our staff and is proving to be a good source. "The fans here aren't very knowledgeable about baseball. They only come out when you're winning." The Astros have been losing.

Smith unwittingly put his finger on one of the game's lingering problems. Baseball has expanded and probably will continue to expand in cities that have large, often indoor stadiums and are situated in attractive television markets. Most expansion cities also have poor baseball traditions and fans who are more likely to be taken with mascots and exploding scoreboards than good pickoff plays. In such fashion does baseball become richer—and poorer.

22 Ryan failed to get the seven strikeouts he needed to tie Walter Johnson. It would have been a beaut of a story: breaking the record at home against the Phillies; perhaps doing it by striking out Pete Rose, future hit king; revitalizing the Astros, who had lost their first nine games. Nonetheless, a part of me wasn't rooting for the record. Sad to say, my major concern was putting off today what I won't have to do until next week.

Actually, I felt terribly conflicted during the game. My head said, "Do it, Nolan, and give me a great story." My gut said, "Don't do it. I don't want to sit in front of the screen all day tomorrow." I kept fighting myself (Ryan struck out three in six innings and took the loss). By game's end I felt sick. No wonder.

23 On the plane home I ran into Jack Levin, a former neighbor of mine in Brooklyn who has started his own law firm. "There's a spirit of competition pervading the profession," he told me. "That competition will reduce costs, not just by cutting rates, but by streamlining laws and litigation procedures. This is a terrific time to be an entrepreneur in the legal profession."

Well, what about journalism? More often than not we report the news rather than make it. But we do affect people. We inform and enlighten, offend and bother. We traffic in ideas, which are always changing. And when attitudes change, so do actions.

And sportswriters? As I reflect, I'm more and more impressed by the importance of sport. People spend more time reading the sports page than almost any section of the paper. When men get together, there's always one easy subject of conversation: sports. Increasingly so for women. We have more leisure time today than ever before, and that means watching sports on TV if not participating in them. So when we affect people's attitudes toward sport, we affect the way they view their lives. This is a terrific time to be in the sportswriting profession, too.

My interest in ballplayers usually relates to how recently I **25** wrote about them. Kittle was benched yesterday after going 0-for-15 while striking out seven times. That after four homers and 19 runs batted in—figures placing him among the league leaders. "Kittle is able to laugh at his output so far," *USA Today* notes, "saying things like, 'My weaknesses fluctuate' and 'It's an experiment with me each time I go to the plate.' "

I'm a little surprised that Kittle has slumped so soon. Usually a young slugger terrorizes the league his first time around. Then the pitchers adjust, find ways to get him out and force him to change his style.

"I've seen a lot of everything," Kittle said in the newspaper article. "They are still feeling me out, too. Being a power hitter, they're pitching me inside a lot, and with it being so cold, that makes that strategy even more effective." Hitters dislike the cold because their hands hurt when they hit inside pitches.

"But I'm not swinging at bad pitches or making a fool of myself up there. I'm just missing some good pitches."

In the words of the article, "In Kittle's absence Walker was the designated hitter and went 3-for-4."

26 I'm off to Montreal, where Ryan pitches tomorrow. He needs four strikeouts to tie the record, five to break it. If the game is postponed, he'll pitch Friday in Philadelphia. And if he doesn't get the record this week, he undoubtedly will next week in New York.

This time I want him to break the record. We're talking four pages in the magazine and a possible cover. Besides, it'll be a madhouse if he has to break the record in New York.

After the most cursory of customs inspections—"Citizenship? What business are you in? Why are you here?"—I was outside looking for a cab. *Sacré bleu*—all taxis at the Montreal airport are limos! A besuited driver, soft music, the works. My room at the Hyatt Regency has all sorts of angles and curves, not the usual square shape. There's muted light in the room, dressing-room lights in the bathroom. I turned on the TV and got "Hockey Night in Canada." The Edmonton-Chicago game was hockey at its best—not fighting, just breathtaking skating and stick-handling.

I could have a good time here. Too bad I'll have to leave after tomorrow's game.

27 It was a perfect setting for a record: a dominant pitcher against an outmatched hitter. On the mound was Ryan, one strikeout away from the alltime record. At bat was Brad Mills, a substitute infielder playing his first full big-league season.

Expo manager Bill Virdon had summoned the lefthanded-hitting Mills to bat for righthanded second baseman Doug Flynn against Ryan, a righthanded pitcher. The "book" play. Mills had singled off Ryan in their only previous encounter, last season, but he was struggling now and Flynn had never struck out against Ryan. Virdon will be second-guessed.

Ryan walked around behind the mound, telling himself not to rush his delivery. He braced on the rubber, raised his hands above his head, tucked his left knee under his chin and threw with his simple and fluid motion—pushing off with his left foot, shifting his weight and releasing from an 11 o'clock motion. In came a fastball over the outside corner for a called strike. Now a curve, low and inside, but Mills couldn't check his swing. Strike two. Ryan wasted a fastball outside. One-and-two. Tugging at his cap, Ryan walked on and off the mound and shivered like a dog shaking off water as he looked in for the sign. A big, sidewinding curve over the outside corner. Called strike three!

In the crazy quilt of activity that followed, no two characters seemed to mesh. Mills stood forlornly. "I was looking for a fastball, he threw a curve and I got vapor-locked," he said later. Umpire Bob Engel was animated. He turned and threw a hard right—a memorable thumb for a record-breaking strikeout. As the 19,309 fans at Olympic Stadium rose to cheer, Ryan hesitantly raised his hat. Meanwhile, stoic as monuments, giant likenesses of Ryan and Johnson appeared on the electronic scoreboard in center field.

Like Johnson, Ryan is a modest and clean-living man from rural America who has pitched uncomplainingly for generally mediocre teams. He was born in 1947, the year after his predecessor died. Like Johnson, Ryan relies primarily on his heat. Johnson was the celebrated Big Train. Ryan—Nollie and Tex to his teammates—throws the Ryan Express. Oh, there are differences. Johnson threw almost nothing but a sidearmed fastball, which all but blinded the hitters of his day. Ryan goes over the top and throws a nifty curve about 30 percent of the time. But Johnson and Ryan will forever be linked as recordholders and the most overpowering pitchers of their time.

Baseball men will debate the importance of the record. Some quotes from my correspondents' files: "Three thousand strikeouts is the equivalent of 3,000 hits," says Gaylord Perry, who is just 34 short. "Strikeouts are important if you need them to win a game, but I don't know if they're a measure of how good a pitcher is," says Hall of Famer Bob Gibson, one of seven members of the 3,000 Strikeout Club. "Wins and losses are the important thing," says Atlanta pitcher Phil Niekro. But Cincinnati's Frank Pastore counters: "With wins, you're dependent on your team. You get the strikeouts yourself."

In 1974 I saw Hank Aaron break the career home run record and Lou Brock set a single-season stolen-base mark. The next season I happened to be at a Milwaukee game when Aaron, with little fanfare, set a career mark for runs batted in. After Ryan's feat, hoping to witness ambience as well as action, I accompanied the Astros to Philadelphia. It was well worth the trouble. I got some additional information from a writer, a coach and Ryan himself, and heard the co-pilot announce that Ryan had set a "hit" record.

Before going to sleep in some Marriott-by-the-freeway, I wrote down the following outline:

- The moment (flesh it out).
- Ryan vs. Johnson.
- Importance of strikeout record.
- Why it came at a good time for Ryan and Astros.
- Why the celebration was brief.
- Perry, Carlton will also break record.
- Why modern pitchers are so dominant.
- Ryan-Carlton rivalry.

The writing went so well that I took time off to play golf **28**
and have dinner with a friend. Unfortunately, the hay fever
season opened today, and I was miserable.

But back to baseball. I know I've done a better story on
Ryan than anyone. I've done more thinking, had better advice, spent more time and received more space—all of which
gives me more perspective. I've followed Ryan for two weeks
to three cities in two countries. This is the magazine at its
best, and I hope to get the opportunity more often.

I drove back from Philly and stopped at Poly Prep. The **29**
great all-sports athlete Gina DaVito is rumored to be going to
Princeton. I walked out to the softball diamond, where she
was warming up with the girls varsity. They were throwing a
ball around like major-leaguers. So much for the myth that
girls are constitutionally unable to throw like boys. I told her
that Yale would be happy to house her if she visited the
campus another time. She said she understood, but the way
she spoke suggested she wasn't interested.

I took my boys to the Braves-Mets game at Shea Stadium.
We had field-level box seats—and couldn't see. One of the
many wonders of Shea is that the seats face the middle of the
field, not the pitcher's mound. As a result, we were craning
our heads at a 45-degree angle while trying to look over spectators and vendors. I couldn't blame the boys when their
attention wandered.

One of the biggest problems with today's salaries is the
ugliness big money has created between fans and players.
Tonight there was the usual quota of drunks yelling about
overpaid bums. "Foster gets $2 million a year—for what?"
one fan lamented. On the next pitch George Foster homered.
"Kingman gets paid $700,000, and what does he do?" On the
next pitch Dave Kingman hit one of the longest homers I've
ever seen. The Mets won a good game 6–5.

I figure the evening cost me $40—$24 for seats and $16 for parking, concessions and programs. Tickets in basketball, hockey and football, geared for corporate expense accounts rather than Joe Citizen's budget, cost considerably more. "Baseball has always been a working man's game," Detroit manager Sparky Anderson once told me, "because of the fan identification. You can come out and yell at these guys all you want. Football? Not the same. When they're out of uniform, you don't even know what the players look like."

30   I played paddle tennis with my kids at Riis Park in Queens. Next to golf, paddle is my favorite participant sport. Not to be confused with platform tennis, paddle is a simpler, smaller form of tennis—with a low, taut net; a miniature court; a deadened tennis ball, and a small wooden paddle. I call it tennis without tears.

Paddle is played in New York City, St. Augustine, Florida, Southern California and a few other pockets of culture. I took up the game six years ago, and I've played in the national doubles four times. Not because I'm so good, but because there are so few players. No matter: Anyone can play anyone else because paddle is a game of equalizers. The serving team has a huge advantage because it generally controls the net, so sets tend to be close. The dead ball and the required under-hand serve minimize a power game. So it's possible for a weak team to play respectably in the nationals. We all have our Mittyesque dreams of competing with champions. In paddle tennis, dream becomes reality.

may

A major discovery last week: There are more good guy   **1**
ballplayers who love the game and hate to lose than I
thought. While waiting for Ryan to set the record, I sat in the
pressbox at Montreal's Olympic Stadium with Hal Bock of the
Associated Press and Henry Hecht of the *New York Post*.* The
three of us tried to compose an all-star team made up of
jerks—and couldn't fill the positions.

Back in New York, Audrey and I spent a couple of hours at
the Brooklyn Botanic Garden. The Cherry Blossom Festival
was in full bloom, and the Japanese were out in force. So
were several other groups of little-noted New Yorkers: Ras-
tafarians, Colombians, interracial couples. I had a feeling of
total harmony among the city's frequently feuding ethnic
groups. That's what parks and gardens are all about: recrea-
tion for the people. During our two hours there I saw no
more than half a dozen cigarettes, one radio and one Walk-
man. On the way out I noticed that I didn't have the sugar
craving that comes every few hours. I wonder: If people got
together like this more often, wouldn't the world be a
more. . . .

Naaah.

*Hecht joined *Sports Illustrated* in 1984.

may

2 I'm going to Toronto this week to write a column on Randy Moffitt. He's Billie Jean King's kid brother, but that's not the most interesting part of his story. A reliever for the Toronto Blue Jays, he's back from baseball's scrap heap. He was waived by the Giants a few years ago and almost died of a rare stomach disorder. Now he's not only restored to a major-league roster, but healthy and starring.

Before leaving, I spoke with Peter Carry, the first interim managing editor, about my Bryn Mawr story. He says I still have to prove two things: that the school's wellness program is unique, and that it's relevant to other places. Otherwise, why write about it? Back to the drawing board.

3 I spent most of the day in Brooklyn. First, I shot a 95 at Dyker Beach. Almost every drive was true, and almost every chip was dubbed. There followed a one-hour session with the pro, Tom Strafaci. He gave me these chipping instructions: Keep the grip firm and tight, squeezing hardest near the tips of the fingers; accelerate on the downswing; pinch the knees and keep the ball midway between the feet; keep the left knee still while moving the right knee toward it, and keep the head down even during the follow-through. Got that? "Just keep in mind the grip," Tom said.

Later I played chess with Gil Feldman, a classics teacher at Poly Prep, and acquitted myself well before losing. Afterwards we had dinner in Bay Ridge and attended a "college night" at John Dewey High School. College nights are occasions where high school students can question college admissions people—or their stand-ins like us. I answered so many questions—mostly, "Is there a minimum SAT score for admission to Yale?" (answer: no)—that I got a sore throat.

In many respects Toronto has every city in the U.S. beat. The streets are clean, there's very little crime, and the neighborhoods improve the closer you get to downtown. I'm tempted to take the kids to Toronto this summer. I was more than tempted to take a look around the city after my lunch with Randy Moffitt. Then I thought about why I was here. If I really care about baseball, I'll be out at the park early, absorbing atmosphere and ambience. The Moffitt story especially requires this approach. The key to the piece won't be the facts about him, but his thoughts and feelings and personality.

Moffitt was a joy at lunch: interesting, intelligent, amusing. Among other things, he talked at length about horseracing. "I go to the track in the morning and usually leave before the races," says Moffitt, who has worked as an assistant trainer and has a groom's license. "I love the backstretch. It's a completely different world: the smells, the linaments. It's a little community with its own church and dental office and kitchen. Everybody knows everybody else, and there's all kinds of whispering about how 'That guy's training the horse wrong' and 'If I had that horse I'd train it differently.' You're so busy on the backstretch that you forget everything else."

Unfortunately, I never got to see Moffitt pitch. Consider the situation: last of the ninth, two outs, runners on first and second, Blue Jays leading 6–1. The pitcher is lefthanded Dave Geisel, the batter lefthanded-hitting George Brett. If Brett gets a hit, I'm thinking, the Royals will bring in the righthanded Moffitt to face righthanded Hal McRae. Brett singles sharply to right. I rise halfway out of my seat, beaming. But what's this? The KC third base coach is waving in the runner, John Wathan—with his team five runs behind! Rightfielder Jesse Barfield throws a strike to the plate, Wathan's out and the game's over. I had to get a description of Moffitt's motion from the pitching coach. I'm not always lucky.

may

9   I called Moffitt's doctor and got a big surprise. First, he said that all stories written about Randy's physical condition have been inaccurate. Then, he said he wouldn't speak to me without written permission from Moffitt. I'm getting another insight about why we do a better job than the newspapers. Lacking time to get permission, reporters working on deadlines got Moffitt's version—a layman's account of a complicated medical problem. These writers didn't have time to write to the doctor.

But maybe I'm being a little too lenient. I was able to get the facts without written permission after all. I pushed the doctor, and he said he would speak to me if Randy called him and gave permission. Randy was only too happy to comply, and I had the interview. Why didn't the Toronto reporters think of that? Why was the best local story about Moffitt one dealing with him and his sister Billie Jean King—an old angle? And why didn't anyone but me call Moffitt's wife—an excellent source? The real problem, as I've said before, is that most sports reporters are used to having the stories present themselves on the field. They aren't ingenious and resourceful because they haven't worked on the news side.

12   Back in New York, I took a cab downtown with an Armenian driver from Turkey. He asked me if all newspapers were Democratic or Republican. "In Turkey," he said, "if there's a president from one party, the papers who supported the other party are shut down." Boy, do we take a lot for granted.

I finally got the printer fixed. Took the damn thing to the Smith-Corona shop, and a guy made a few quick, simple adjustments and printed out the February entries. I felt great.

Not such a great feeling: My toaster caught on fire and the apartment filled with smoke. I managed to douse the flames with water—after pulling out the plug, of course. A thought: Suppose I'd been in the laundry room when the toaster caught on fire? Or worse, suppose a fire starts when I'm asleep? I pulled out a lot of plugs at the very thought. Boy, do we take a lot for granted.

Of all the ongoing scandals in baseball, the worst by far is **15** the beanball. Its perpetrators have several excuses for committing the crime. "It's part of the game," they say. Or, "I got to have the inside of the plate." Or, "I was just trying to move him back."

It used to be "part of the game" to call all Jewish players Moe. It used to be "part of the game" to have no black players. It used to be "part of the game" for players to wear no protective headgear or catcher's equipment. Baseball discarded these idiocies, but not the beanball.

If pitchers want to move batters back, they could throw at the waist or the shoes. Boston pitcher Carl Mays said he was trying to move Cleveland's Ray Chapman back one afternoon in 1920; he accidentally killed him with a beanball. (Baseball finally adopted batting helmets—forty years later.) The real reason to throw at the head is to instill fear. Understandably, this practice often succeeds in its objective. What isn't understandable is why baseball tolerates it. Umpires have the right to warn both benches before games that the first time they even suspect a beanball they'll eject the pitcher. You'd be amazed at how accurate pitchers would get.

Art Shamsky, a broadcaster and ex-Met, wrote a thoughtful column on the subject in today's *Times.* I was listening to the Yankee broadcast when Phil Rizzuto alluded favorably to the column. But Rizzuto's partner, Bill White, made light of the subject. "Why not eliminate the pitcher?" he scoffed. "Have everyone hit off tees."

Seething, I wrote White a letter complaining that he had reduced the debate to an absurdity. "There will always be pitchers, Bill," I said, "and they will always know exactly when they are throwing at hitters. Not for nothing is an 0–2 brushback or a beanball on the pitch after a homer called a 'purpose pitch.' I have another name for it: assault and battery." I went on for a few more sentences and concluded, "The sport you're broadcasting should bear no resemblance to hockey or prizefighting."

Wulfie read the letter and said, "Kaplan's thrown a beanball of his own." (But sometime later I mentioned the episode to a nonplayer in a major-league organization. He said that he had once hit, helmetless, against White in a casual batting practice. "Don't you think he threw the first pitch about six inches behind my head? He thought it was very funny, and, of course, not wishing to be humiliated by the onlooking players, I laughed, too. But I've never forgotten it. Strict baseball mentality.")

16   A day of wonder, it began at the Greek's. For $4 I had French toast made with challah bread; milk and orange juice. A "Greek's"—I'm referring to a counter-style restaurant run by Greeks rather than a Greek-food restaurant per se—is one of the highest forms of American democracy. The food is decent and cheap. And that's not all. At a Greek's you can hang out forever over your coffee. You find old folks and people who aren't exactly well-heeled. Better by far than a welfare hotel or a "shelter." The Greek's.

The day ended with another tribute to American democracy. Audrey and I saw a live performance of "A Prairie Home Companion," the National Public Radio weekly show, at Town Hall. It was all so . . . evocative. Garrison Keillor's monologue was about the first day of spring at Lake Wobegon, his fictitious town in Minnesota. He talked about mandatory choir practice and the stern teacher who made him solo while the girls tittered. There's something in that kind of anecdote to stir all of us—even if we never saw the inside of a church.

Afterwards Audrey, staff writer Alex Wolff and I were dining at The Century Cafe, which is across the street from Town Hall, when Keillor and his party came in for a late supper. With him were Roy Blount, Jr., the celebrated humorist who used to write for *Sports Illustrated,* and his wife, Joan Ackermann-Blount, one of our freelance "contract" writers. Joan saw us and invited us over. We spoke with Keillor, who smoothly handled introductions while smoking Pall Malls and downing a cocktail. A country slicker.

Earlier in the day I was reading a *Saturday Review* article about Keillor. In it Garrison referred to a letter he'd written to an old teacher in which he complained that ethics were disappearing, swallowed up by science and technology.

And, I would add, by hype and advertising. In sport these days, every event seems to be known by some corporate name. There's the Camel Scoreboard that's published in some newspapers, and various products are known as the official camera (soft drink, blue jeans) of the U.S. Olympic team. You can't go to the ballpark without seeing products and promotions hawked on the electronic scoreboard or hearing them mentioned on the P.A. system. The very standards of excellence are known by corporate names. It's not enough to have a contest for top relief pitchers; it has to be called the Rolaids competition. Is anything sacrosanct? If Budweiser bought the rights to the World Series, it would probably become known as the Budweiser World Series. Or maybe the Busch League Playoffs.

Earlier in this journal I was complaining that baseball's Opening Day had become just another business venture. Hey, look, I don't want to sound naive. Baseball was always a business venture; advertising and sponsorship date almost from the beginning. As far back as I can remember, ballplayers were endorsing bats, and Gillette was sponsoring the World Series. But, somehow, business always seemed to be in the background. Gillette *sponsored* the Series; the Series wasn't a blatant excuse for selling blue blades. The viewer appreciated the sponsor instead of resenting it. Indeed, when I came of age, I would no sooner have shaved with another brand of blade than moved to another country.

It's impossible to feel that way any more. The commercials have become longer and more frequent, the sponsorship bolder and louder. In part, this phenomenon is owing to the prominence of television money among baseball owners. But there's something larger involved, too: the vast power of corporations. What they want they get—anywhere, anytime. Taste? Sentimentality? Don't be silly.

17 Larry assigned me to go to St. Louis tomorrow for a column on Houston shortstop Dickie Thon. I quickly made arrangements. Then Audrey and I saw a screening of "Champions of Sport," a Home Box Office TV production written by my friend Ira Berkow of *The New York Times.* Some of the old footage was excellent, and Ira got athletes past and present to make new and interesting observations. I'd like to see the production again to go over Ira's questions.

18 I arrived in St. Louis just in time for the Cardinal-Astro game. Thon is a promising shortstop, but an erratic one. In the seventh inning the Astros were up a run, with St. Louis runners on first and second and no outs, when Willie McGee hit a grounder up the middle. Cardinal shortstop Ozzie Smith would either have converted it into a force out or a double play. Maybe Thon had too much on his mind—catching the ball, stepping on second, throwing to first—but he appeared to look up. The grounder skipped off his glove and rolled into right field, a clearcut error that was scored, incredibly, as a double. The Cardinals went on to score eight runs and eventually won 9–5.

So the story won't be a puff job by a long shot. Good. So

much in baseball is gray and ambiguous. Unfortunately, I often have to write positive, almost gushy pieces because I'm usually assigned to a hot player or team.

After the game I flew to Pittsburgh. I would have been on the Astro charter but Donald Davidson, the Astros' feisty little traveling secretary, put a double-whammy on me. He said that only local writers were allowed on charters and besides, there wasn't any room. The Astro beat guys found this incredible. "How many seats do you need—a dozen?" one asked.

It was raining in Pittsburgh, and I spent the entire day in **19** the hotel. First, I had breakfast with Thon, taping the conversation as usual. He was cheery and pleasant—completely recovered from yesterday's flub. Like many outstanding ballplayers, he's had excellent training—in his case, from his father and grandfather, who were athletes in Puerto Rico. "I first saw Dickie Thon in 1977 A-ball, when I was with the Padre organization and he was in the Angel system," Ozzie Smith told me. "I could tell he'd be a fine addition to any club. The first thing I look for in a shortstop is soft hands. The next thing is quick feet. Then you go to the arm. He has all these qualities."

I spent the afternoon transcribing the tape and trying to reach Thon's wife (success) and father and grandfather (failure). Then I had a swim in the hotel pool and a productive dinner with Kenny Hand of the *Houston Post.*

One of the subjects Kenny and I discussed was official scoring. Next to beanballs, scoring may be the worst ongoing problem in baseball. Because one of his major decisions is awarding either hits or errors, an official scorer can determine who throws a no-hit game and who wins a batting title. His decisions affect not only baseball's all-important statistics but to some extent its salary structure and player movement.

That's because stats have become so important in salary arbitrations and are used in the formula to determine which teams losing free agents require significant compensation.

So who does the official scoring? Predominantly newspaper reporters who cover teams. And what's wrong with that? For one thing, these writers are being paid for scoring by baseball—the very industry they cover. If that's not a conflict of interest, I don't know what is. Second, they can't possibly be expected to concentrate fully on scoring because many of them are writing during the game. Third, they're under constant pressure to go easy (i.e., award more hits and fewer errors, except during potential no-hitters). A writer who scores an error on a tough chance can expect to take heat when he goes into the clubhouse. As a result, many scorers are too lenient, especially on the home team. "It's reached a point where guys are saying, 'Well, we expect to get calls at home and get jobbed on the road,'" one player told me. "It shouldn't be that way. It should be based on what's a hit and what's an error."

In recent years the better newspapers have been acknowledging the conflict and refusing to allow their reporters to score. Unfortunately, beat men have been replaced as scorers by retired baseball writers who miss a lot or are hardened in their ways, or by suburban scorers who don't travel with the team. Scoring has never been worse.

The solution seems obvious: Hire a fifth umpire for each crew. The umps would be rotated as they are now, with each one scoring every fifth game. To date, though, the leagues have refused to increase their umpiring payrolls by 25 percent. I'm not holding my breath.

20   While the Astros lost again, I sat in the stands with my old college classmate, John Dickson, and his wife Carol. Funny how people change. When Dickson and I spent two spring breaks in Bermuda, neither of us was exactly a fulltime student. Now Dickson's a solid citizen, teaching high school and coaching basketball in a town outside of Pittsburgh. He still has his sense of humor, I'm happy to report. Carol is so busy carpooling their three sons and doing volunteer work that she hardly has time to play golf. I quickly set about rearranging her priorities. We had a terrific time, and I'm delighted that I've hung onto my two-year-old copy of *Fifteen Years Out*, a compendium of addresses and phone numbers for the Class of 1966. Travel is a pleasure when you can see old friends.

Larry felt I was a little too critical in my Thon story and **23** asked for a rewrite. "You can't belittle him when you're discovering him," he said. I can see his point. Because I saw Thon make some mistakes last week, I probably went overboard. It would have been better to "discover" him and give him some tempered praise.

No matter. I'll see Thon a couple of times this week when I do the Cardinal infield. St. Louis will be in Cincy and Houston, and I'll be writing the feature-length story I've long wanted to do on defense, the least appreciated feature of winning baseball. In short, the ultimate story on the ultimate subject by—oh, go for it—the ultimate writer.

I'm going to be following the Cardinals all week, and that **24** means taking the team charter from Cincinnati to Houston Wednesday night (unlike Donald Davidson, the St. Louis traveling secretary, C. J. Cherre, is most obliging).

I can already see that the story is going to be successful. I came armed with questions suggested by Larry Keith, the activist baseball editor. How does one infielder know where another infielder is? How do they give signals? How do they win games with their gloves? What makes a Gold Glove infielder? How good is the Cardinal infield—the best ever? How do they play hitters? What are the strongest and weakest points of every fielder? What about cutoffs and other strategy? Are there useful examples from games this week?

25   For the last two games, I've sat at Cincinnati's Riverfront Stadium with Charles Newman, a novelist *(White Jazz)* who's writing a story on the Cardinals' pitchers for *Vanity Fair*. Occasionally it takes a person with totally fresh perspective—someone from outside of baseball—to reveal some truths about the game.

"There must be a lot of frustrated managers," he said. "The job's not that difficult, but they're being asked to work with players somebody else got for them. Whitey Herzog controls player transactions in St. Louis. Power flows upward from him rather than downward to him.

"In most organizations the pitchers throw pretty much the same way. Here they don't even throw the same pitch the same way. The older pitchers throw the slider like a curve and the younger ones throw it like a fastball. Other clubs may use a speed gun or chart their pitchers or videotape them. The Cardinals do all three. When they play the tapes, the pitching coach, Hub Kittle, never shows the pitchers what they're doing wrong. He shows them pictures of when they're going well to remind them of the right way to do things."

Newman stood around casually smoking a pipe while speaking with players, and he took no notes. With his novelist's sense of dialogue, he was able to converse—not interview—and later write down the highlights verbatim.

The reason ballplayers are spoiled isn't so much because they're well paid as because they're pampered. There's been a story in the Cincy papers about the Reds' Cesar Cedeño refusing to board a flight because he wasn't given a seat in the first class section. Another burning issue is shoes. The Reds are the only team that requires black shoes, and the players have filed a grievance. The issue isn't shoe color as much as advertising revenue. The team actually offered the players a deal with the Pony company in which each Red would get $600 in cash and $500 in merchandise. The players turned it down. "Some guys on other teams get $30,000–$40,000," Frank Pastore, the Cincinnati player rep, told me. "Some guys on our team pay for their own shoes." (The issue was resolved some weeks later, with an agreement for free black shoes with red stripes, and higher payments to the players.)

Cardinal players have everything taken care of—laundry, travel, even golf reservations at private courses on days off. The club picks up hotel bills, and players take care of meals (the postgame spread is free) and other incidentals out of their $43.50 per diem. We took an Ozark charter tonight from Cincinnati to Houston, and it was first class all the way. The team bus carried us from the ballpark directly to the spot on the airport ramp where our plane was waiting. There was so much room on board that everyone who wanted an empty seat next to him had one. Food? We started off with a cold appetizer featuring shrimp, lobster, artichoke and lox. Then it was on to a main course of either lobster, chicken or chateaubriand. There was a spinach salad, and the flight attendants offered assorted cakes and pastries for dessert. I had a rum ball and topped it off with amaretto in a chocolate cup. Burp!

During the flight I thought some more about the Cardinal system. "The Cedeño incident never would have happened with the Cardinals," Rick Hummel of the *St. Louis Post-Dispatch*, one of the game's most talented and sensitive beat men, told me. "Whitey would have challenged him to a fight." Hummel added that he knows of no dissent on the team. On the contrary, the players seem to pick up on Whitey's methods. Pitcher Joaquin Andujar was grousing about something or other on the bus to the plane. During the flight rightfielder George Hendrick ragged him mercilessly. After landing, we piled onto a waiting bus. By now Andujar was smiling. The order of seating was roughly the same as it had been on the plane—coaches and manager up front, followed by writers, then players. Arriving at Houston's Shamrock Hilton Hotel, the players took their preassigned room keys and headed upstairs. Their luggage would be brought up to them. By now Andujar was smiling and joking. He had nothing to complain about. Neither did his teammates.

26   It was one of those quintessentially happy baseball scenes. Rookie Dave Von Ohlen had been summoned to pitch in the third inning, with the Cardinals leading the Astros 4–2. He went 5⅔ innings, allowed just one run and got his first big-league win.

Afterwards, Von Ohlen—mustachioed, ingenuous—told bunches of microphones and notebooks that he was happy, thrilled and excited. His gruff but proud pitching coach, Hub Kittle, stood watching the scene. "He isn't afraid to throw strikes," Kittle said. "That's how you win in this game." Indeed, Von Ohlen admitted that the only time he was in trouble was when he started "nitpicking—going for the corners instead of throwing the ball over the plate." Pitching is basically very simple.

Von Ohlen was so hospitable to the press that as the 11:10 P.M. bus time approached, he was still in his underwear. "To hell with Von Ohlen," Herzog laughed as he left the clubhouse. "We can't use him tomorrow anyway."

27   Here's how the lives of baseball writers and baseball coaches differ dramatically. I played golf at Memorial Park, a public course, while Cardinal broadcaster Mike Shannon and coaches Chuck Hiller and Red Schoendienst played at River

Oaks, a fancy country club. I played nine holes in 2½ hours, waiting on almost every shot; they played 18 in maybe three hours on a virtually empty course. I was paired with some grotesque characters who kept making snide remarks about the interracial couple ahead of us; the Cardinals played with their buddies. On the other hand, they had to meet an 8 A.M. tee-off in order to get to the ballpark on time, and I got to sleep late.

I'm becoming utterly entranced by this story. I swear it: The most memorable moments in baseball are great fielding plays, frozen in time and space. Wambsganss. Gionfriddo. Amoros. Mays. Nettles. Brooks Robinson. Any serious baseball fan can fill in the blanks. Those are people who've made memorable fielding plays in World Series; there are countless subtle moments in routine games, too, and I've been noticing them. With a runner on first, someone cracks a line-drive single to center, and shortstop Ozzie Smith pretends to catch it. The runner who had been on first stops at second instead of going to third because Ozzie has caused him to break stride. In a sacrifice situation first baseman Keith Hernandez takes a couple of steps toward home as if he were anticipating the pitch, then wheels and heads back to first for a pickoff throw. He and the pitcher have decided on the pickoff by some subtle signal; after Keith's second step toward home the pitcher throws toward the bag. "We're not really trying to pick the guy off," says Hernandez, "just keep him honest." So many subtle moments.

"Where else but in a fucking kids' game can you start out at **28** night and end up in the morning," Schoendienst called out at 12:10 A.M. "God a'mighty, ain't it wonderful!"

We'd just seen an extraordinary 18-inning game that the Cardinals had won 3–1. In the last of the 17th the Astros had a man on third with one out when Alan Ashby had hit a ball deep in the hole. Everyone had assumed the game was over. Either the ball would go through, scoring a run, or Ozzie Smith would field it too late to throw home. But Smith had dived, grabbed the ball, leaped to his feet in one motion. Then he'd checked the runner back to third and thrown out Ashby by two steps. He'd also thrown out the next runner. The Cardinals had rallied to win the game in the 18th.

"Best shortstop in the history of the game!" croaked Hub Kittle, who has been in baseball 48 years. The rest of us walked around the clubhouse with great big smiles on our faces. "I'd *pay* to watch Ozzie Smith," I kept saying.

Then something struck me: Scenes like this don't occur very often these days. I don't want to romanticize the lot of old-time ballplayers, who had lousy salaries, poor medical care and virtually no rights, but they may have enjoyed the game more than today's major leaguers. Baseball was their reason for living, and they loved playing. Today's players think constantly about money: How much they make, how much others make, how little time they have to strike it rich. No one wants to turn the clock back, but I wish there were more pure, joyous scenes like the one in the Cardinal clubhouse. We're forever talking moneyball, not baseball.

I got a lucky editorial break tonight. All afternoon I'd been writing the story, anticipating a deadline tomorrow morning. During the game Larry called and said the pictures in Cincinnati were poor and the story would be delayed a week. Why was this a break? Because under the original deadline, I'd have had time merely to make an insert on Ozzie's spectacular play tonight. Now I can rewrite the story and lead with it.

29   On the plane back from Houston I was sitting next to a woman and her 10-month-old son. The kid was carrying on something awful; I could hear him through the sound of the

Stray Cats on my headset. So I did the only thing possible under the circumstances: I whipped off the earphones and placed them on the kid's head.

The little boy immediately lit up. His mother was delighted. The flight attendants cooed and people pointed and laughed from across the aisle. It was a good move.

Good moves aren't as earth-shattering as existential moments, but they're every bit as much fun. Last October I arrived in St. Louis for the playoffs with a letter in hand from a local stockbroker, who was chiding me for having picked the Cardinals to do poorly. I called the guy up. "Hello, Mr. Slocum, this is Jim Kaplan from *Sports Illustrated*."

Long silence.

"I got your letter," I continued, "and you were absolutely right—I completely misjudged the Cardinals. Listen, I've got a couple of extra tickets for tonight's game—are you interested?"

A good move. The same week I made an even better move. On the way to the park I shared a cab with a Canadian doctor who was in town for a Masters and Johnson conference. We had an interesting conversation, one thing led to another, and he eventually snuck me in for a session of the conference. No telling what a good move will open up.

june

I've got two stories scheduled for the issue closing this week—the Cardinal feature and the Moffitt column. Since both pieces are completed except for updating and checking, I've got a rare week in the city.

The Angels are in town, so I called up DeCinces and asked him if he'd like to have lunch. He couldn't meet me, but he did offer an alternative—sitting with his wife, Kristi, at the ballpark.

The visiting wives' seats are along the third-base line at Yankee Stadium, and we sat just a couple of rows from the field. This vantage point presented an interesting change from the pressbox. From my seat alongside Kristi, I could see the infielders' expressions and watch them talking to the umpires and reacting to hard-hit grounders—the closer you get the tougher they look. But unless you're directly behind home plate, as you are in the pressbox, it's difficult to follow the action. Several times batters made contact and I had to watch the fielders to pick up the path of the ball.

Listening to Kristi, I could also sense the tradeoffs in the life of a player's wife. The DeCinceses have two children, Timmy, 9, and Amy, 3, and Kristi hopes that Doug, who's 32, retires soon enough to spend more time with the kids. "But not too soon," she says sensibly. "He hasn't done everything he'd like to do in baseball, and he has to get it out of his system." Nevertheless, the time apart isn't easy for either of

june

them, and Doug's constantly sore back has both of them worried. "I pray for him a lot," Kristi says.

There's a stereotype of a ballplayer's wife—cute, dumb, living for her husband. Like most of the wives I've met, Kristi doesn't fit the image. She's attractive and smart and interested in things like art, writing, interior decorating and special education. When she spoke of a trip the DeCinceses had taken to Japan, it was obvious they hadn't spent their time hanging around the Hilton.

As the Yankees won, I was distressed by Reggie Jackson's heads-down play. In the first inning he hit a hard single directly at the leftfielder, foolishly tried to stretch it into a double, and was easily thrown out. Later a weak hitter was up and Reggie didn't move in from his usual rightfield position until someone frantically waved. Another time Reggie got a terrible jump and was thrown out trying to steal third. Afterwards, I saw Reggie in the clubhouse. He's usually open and friendly with me, but this time he walked by, scarcely recognizing me. We all have our ups and downs, but Reggie's seem to be higher and lower than most.

Later, the DeCinceses, Audrey and I had dinner at The Century Cafe. Our conversation, as is often the case with the DeCinceses, was as much personal as it was professional. Doug said he doesn't get on umpires much anymore. "I know that they're doing what they want to do, that no one's forcing them to, but it's still a thankless job," he said. "They never get noticed until they blow one." Asked why managers are constantly arguing with umpires, he said, "It's partly to show the players they're behind them, but it's also to take the heat off the players. The manager wants to get between the player and the umpire before the player starts screaming and gets thrown out."

One of the most perceptive and intuitive players in the game, Doug's always dropping gems like that on me. He has experienced a great deal in baseball—good health, debilitating injury, playing for contending teams and this year, it appears, playing for a loser. He also has had some unusual experiences. He broke in as the designated replacement for Brooks Robinson, Baltimore's Hall of Fame third baseman. The pressure—and the abuse he took from fans—was so intense that Doug briefly underwent therapy, an experience he cheerfully and openly discussed with me when we met in 1979. (It's a sign of how much baseball has matured that Doug was never ridiculed by opponents for seeing a shrink; on the contrary, another player asked him where he could go for help.) Doug has greater perspective still because he was the American League's player representative for some years and has fully prepared himself for baseball's afterlife, having worked in his father's construction business. On top of all this, Doug is exceptionally frank. All in all, a player worth talking to—as well as a good friend.

At one point in the dinner the conversation got around to "Dream Girls." I mentioned that I'd seen the cast in the Democratic telethon. Indeed, not only had I watched the telethon, but I'd pledged the requested $12 a month until the 1984 elections. As Woody Allen once said, I was raised to be a Jew and a Democrat, and I never learned which one was my religion.

Kristi recoiled in mock horror. "Don't tell me you're Democrats?" she exclaimed.

If it's possible to profile a prototypical ballplayer, he's a white, conservative American; a practicing Christian; a native of a small town or suburb in the South or the Sunbelt; an outdoorsman who likes fishing, hunting and/or golf, and a family man who doesn't want his kids to see movies that have sex or swear words. I think Ronald Reagan would have handily carried a vote of the players association.

The conversation resumed without rancor. The DeCinceses are so openminded and generous of spirit that they'll break bread with people who cancel their votes.

june

5   The Moffitt story got delayed, but the Cardinal story ran. Larry said it was the best piece I've done all year, and Peter Carry wrote me a nice note. I'm on a roll, hitting homers on every story. They're coming up to the plate looking like watermelons.

6   Why am I on a roll? It's worth examining. The main thing is, I'm not trying to divine what someone else wants. I'm initiating the stories myself, developing them as I see fit, writing in a style that suits me. The key word is initiating. Everything's coming from me. I'm looser, livelier. In short, I'm finally keeping a New Year's resolution.

    Another complicated parley coming up. Tomorrow Steve Carlton and Nolan Ryan will fight it out for the strikeout leadership. Carlton, who is one behind Ryan, will face the Cardinals in Philadelphia at 7:35 P.M. An hour later Ryan will be pitching in Houston. I'm going to Philadelphia and reporter Cathy Wolf will be in Houston. If everything goes perfectly, Carlton will break Ryan's record, Ryan will break back, and the record will change hands throughout the night. I suggested to Larry that the story could be done in a series of short items like the kind that run on AP machines:

    "Bulletin: Philadelphia, Pa.—Steve Carlton established a new strikeout record tonight. . . ."

    "Bulletin: Please hold previous dispatch. Nolan Ryan has just. . . ."

    "Bulletin: First dispatch was correct. Here's update. . . ."

    If the Carlton-Ryan story doesn't come off, I'll go to Omaha for the College World Series.

7   To my chagrin, the story didn't work. Carlton struck out six batters, and as I listened to the Houston game by picking up the Astro radio station over the phone, Ryan only struck out three and didn't break back. Carlton lost 2–1, and Ryan left after five innings with the score tied 2–2.

The most interesting part of the evening was a conversation I had with Hal Bodley of *USA Today*. His paper has a large sports section that includes some good charts and a daily feature. Bodley, the baseball editor and a writer and columnist, gave me a good idea of his job. He takes about three plane trips a week. One day he'll be in Pittsburgh, the next Montreal, the third home in Philadelphia. Each month the office gives him an expense check averaging about $2,500, and he has no trouble covering it.

He also has to contend with editing by committee (we commiserated). The *USA Today* braintrust in Washington, D.C., is always calling him with ideas, and stories are frequently cut for space. Bodley's game story tonight said that Carlton set the strikeout record but would have preferred to win the game. No, no, said the office—concentrate on the record. So Bodley filed again—and complained. His original story ran.

All the while, this relaxed, down-to-earth guy is writing Pete Rose's autobiography and a weekly Phillies file for *The Sporting News*.

My days don't get much more exhausting than this one. I **8** left Philadelphia at 10:15 A.M.; drove to New York; had lunch with the kids; packed; flew from New York to Minneapolis; changed planes; flew to Omaha; checked in at the Holiday Inn; spoke with tournament officials, and went to bed around 3 A.M.

On the way, I picked up this week's magazine. The Cardinal feature ran at almost exactly the length I'd written and wasn't heavily edited, though I lost some metaphors for no good reason. The story should be both enlightening and readable. However, there may be a few letters about the words "Mex" and "Taco," which are nicknames given first

june

baseman Keith Hernandez by his teammates. As I've said, ballplayers can be tactless, and these strange nicknames—Hernandez is of Spanish, not Mexican descent, and he hardly speaks Spanish—will offend some readers. Nonetheless, I used the words to be consistent—I was reporting other infielders' nicknames as well. Just watch our readers behead the messenger who brought the bad news.

9   Covering the College World Series is very, very different from covering the majors. The entire city of Omaha seems to be behind the event. The Optimists Club has been bustling about, taking players from the eight teams out to dinner. A folksy P.A. announcer asks fans to shake hands with their neighbors. After games, players shake hands with everyone on the opposing team. All in all, I find this a positive and comforting introduction to the next generation of major-leaguers.

Nonetheless, I'm disoriented and confused trying to write a story. There are too many teams, too many unfamiliar faces, too many games. I'm scratching about desperately for a theme. I simplified things a bit by arriving after four of the eight teams had been eliminated, and I've attached myself to Alabama, a Cinderella team with a .500-plus hitter. Alas, the Crimson Tide lost tonight to Texas. Alabama is still alive because the tournament is double-elimination, but Texas, the only unbeaten team, offers no convenient angles.

One thing I noticed immediately is that the journalists here are less competitive than on a major-league beat. Before one game Texas was taking batting practice. No writers were on the field. I asked an official if B.P. was closed, and he said no. So I had the Texas team to myself.

While I was watching the players hit, Cliff Brown of ESPN came over and asked if he could interview me before the third inning. "Sure," I said, "but I don't know anything about college baseball."

"That's all right," he said, "I'll prep you." We decided on two questions—about the ball jumping off the aluminum bats ("I'm glad they don't have them in the majors, or someone would be killed," I said) and the Series atmosphere ("It's hokey, but I love it"). My 20 seconds on the air went fine.

The ESPN encounter proved to be a bonanza for me. The pressbox is air-conditioned and enclosed, as remote from the action as many a big-league pressbox. I spent most of the games in the ESPN box down the third base line, where I could concentrate on the game, watch replays on the monitor and get insights from the chatty and informative Brown. Now if he'd just give me an angle.

Taking the elevator in the Holiday Inn, I was approached **10** by a spokesman for an aluminum bat company. He took issue with my claim that the ball jumps off aluminum bats faster than wooden bats, and said he had surveys to prove his case. I guess it's sheer coincidence that run production took a quantum leap after aluminum bats were introduced at the College World Series.

After today's game only Alabama and Texas are left in the tournament. Texas can end it all tomorrow (Saturday) with a win; Alabama must win tomorrow and Sunday.

After getting my notes in order tonight, I walked across the hall for a drink at the tournament lounge and got into a discussion with Steve Fleming, a graduate assistant at Alabama. Fleming signed with the Pirates out of high school, broke an ankle and never advanced past Class A. Fortunately, his contract stipulated that the Pirates pay for his college education. Intelligent and motivated, Fleming made the most of his opportunity.

His case is atypical. Far more common is the kid who signs out of high school, marries his girlfriend, plays awhile in the minors and gets waived. What's to become of him? Having lost his amateur status, he can't play in college. By now he's probably got a kid or two to support. Untrained for anything but baseball, he's lucky to get any kind of job.

And the kid who isn't married isn't much better off. He's away from home for the first time, living with strangers and getting little supervision for the 16 or so hours a day when he isn't playing ball. It's a recipe for trouble.

Fleming's solution: Eliminate the lower minors and send most prospects to colleges and junior colleges. "Unless a kid's getting six figures and the club won't release him until he gets to Triple-A (the highest minor-league classification), he's crazy to go to the minors," says Fleming. And, oh, what advantages the colleges have over the low minors—security, education, socialization, counseling. Yet when Fleming speaks with high-school phenoms, they often assume he's just shilling for Alabama, and they pass up college for the quick bonus. I suspect the grimmest cases are those of poor kids, who get bad advice and are suckered by the bonus fix.

11   I had my usual good luck. Texas went through the tournament undefeated and won it tonight; I won't face the dreaded Sunday night closing. Also, the Longhorn who gave me the best angle drove in the winning run.

All in all, not a bad week. I had a nice golf game with Don Kausler and Chris Welch, two reporters from Alabama, and a steak lunch with Jack Etkin out of Kansas City. I also did some good things with the copy. I was flexible enough to change directions late at night, and smart enough to sleep on the story and read it over in the morning before sending it.

12   I've been on a roll so high I had to come down. The College World Series story isn't running. Why? Because the pictures weren't good. The photographer was shooting last Friday at twilight, on a poorly lighted minor-league field, and the results were atrocious. Six days on the road went for naught.

Remember, this is sports *illustrated*. Many a story has been lost because of poor pictures, and under Gil Rogin photography has assumed an importance virtually commensurate with text. So even a mere column such as this—a column that may carry just one picture—can die. The photographer did get a usable shot of Alabama's Dave Magadan—the .500 plus hitter I told him to shoot—but the policy is to run shots of winners. The big story? No story.

When I heard the news, I felt impotent and outraged. All that work for nothing! And because of a lousy picture! Some papers fell out of my in-box, and I kicked them around the office. I calmed down a little when I heard that the story replacing mine was my own Randy Moffitt column, which probably would have died this week.

But I'm going to bed with a lot of weariness and anger to sleep off. I've spent a week on the road. For nothing. And this isn't the first time we've been to the College World Series without a story. On another occasion the final wasn't played until Monday, which would have involved an expensive late closing that just isn't done for columns. The excuse this time can't be very comforting for the tournament organizers. When are they going to run out of patience with us? And what happens to writers who get story after story killed for some reason other than the writing? *My* patience is being tried a little, too.

Now there's a new reason my story was killed. Turns out **13** we did shoot the guy I led with, Texas first baseman Jose Tolentino. A photographer tracked him down after he returned to Austin, Texas, and the photo department booked a flight to get the picture to New York. But at some point last night Ken Rudeen, the new acting managing editor, read the story and killed it. "I felt it bogged down," he told me today. "There was too much play-by-play."

I'm a little confused. The only time I wrote in detail about a game was to describe a spectacular confrontation between Texas pitcher Calvin Schiraldi and Dave Magadan that resembled the Bob Welch–Reggie Jackson drama of the real World Series. I think Ken was telling me nicely that he just didn't like the story.

Different managing editors have different priorities. Carry wanted superior writing, and I tried to give it to him. Rudeen seems to value clarity and order over flair. I should keep that in mind.

I thanked him for his explanation and started to leave his office. "Oh, by the way," he said. "I thought your Cardinal story was excellent."

Apparently a lot of people did. The readers have yet to complain about the Hernandez nicknames. "That was an excellent story," Rogin said when I saw him in an elevator. "I never realized baseball was so complicated."

Next week's story doesn't exactly sound simple. Here are some notes from my conversation with Larry: Column on Phillies' hitting woes, specifically Rose, Morgan, Perez. Team in turmoil. Traded Krukow and Ruthven, Christensen out for year. Owner Giles told a writer two weeks ago that manager Corrales would be fired, but he wasn't. Troubled manager. Rookie Hayes playing poorly. Team could turn it around this week, of course. Team batting: last in NL, next to last overall. How is defense? Concentrate on hitting, but bring in other factors. Pictures? Rose, Corrales.

Another, more long-range story I may be doing is the controversy over installing lights at Wrigley Field. I'll presumably get to this in a few weeks. More notes: What is name of organization opposed to lights? How well Cubs are doing probably won't affect story. Backdrop: Cubs going to night baseball in a year or two if mgmt. gets way. Get Royko column on letter to concessionaires. Advantages of night ball: Team won't wear out in heat of summer days. Disadvantages: Effect on neighborhood (noise, poor parking). Find out what studies have been done. If none, whom should we talk to for advice?

I've just finished reading *Growing Up* by Russell Baker. Like many readers, I was enthralled by Baker's stories about his family and boyhood. But I came away from the book with something far more personal. Baker is truly an educated man. He not only reads great books, he remembers them. I feel a sense of loss. Being goal-oriented rather than process-oriented, I studied to get good grades and, ultimately, a good job. It was learning without joy. And I'm sure I'm not alone. As the *Saturday Review* puts it, American kids are being well trained and poorly educated.

Another thing. I don't know Baker, but I suspect he's the kind of guy who does well when he's alone. I don't. I seek out golf games and friends to fill the void. Nothing wrong with that per se, but what happens when I'm unavoidably alone? In a plane or hotel room I grow lonely—waiting for something to happen.

14 The Cardinals and Phillies played an excellent game in St. Louis, but the highlight of my day was a postgame drink I had with Joe Morgan, the Phillies' second basemen. Morgan is one of the brightest people in the game.

He told me he's living in a Philadelphia apartment while his wife and two daughters remain on the West Coast. He misses them, but he doesn't want to disrupt their lives. "My wife runs a women's clothing store," Morgan said. "She's known as Gloria Morgan, not Mrs. Joe Morgan. I think that's great. I hope it rubs off on the girls."

Morgan once wanted to manage. No more, he said. "There are too many guys who don't know the fundamentals. They think all they have to do is show up at three or four o'clock. I could never manage because I see so many things that bother me. Suppose there's a runner on first. The first baseman has to keep him close, and that creates a huge gap on the right side of the infield. So you'd think they'd do everything possible to keep the batter from hitting over there. But they don't. They're pitching inside to lefthanded batters!"

Morgan was right. Because of expansion, more and more players are being brought up who aren't sufficiently schooled in fundamentals and strategy. And long-term contracts don't reward the guy who can move up the runner. "I'm not opposed to big salaries, but I wish they'd tie them to team play," Morgan said.

15 An hour before the trading deadline, the Cardinals broke up my miracle infield. They traded first baseman Keith Hernandez to the Mets for two pitchers.

At times like this I hate baseball. All I could do was think of the pain and frustration Hernandez must feel. I tried to put myself in his place, imagining how I'd feel if I were sent to a Time Inc. bureau in, say, Atlanta. I pictured myself adjusting to a new city with new office mates, wondering when I'd see my kids and girlfriend again. I think ballplayers begin to turn sour when they realize, in the words of the late Red Smith, that they're "so many cattle to be bought and sold."

16 The story on the Phils isn't working. First, they were winning without hitting. Then they were neither hitting nor winning. Now they're hitting and playing .500 ball. What does it all mean? I called Larry and suggested that I write the column on Pete Rose. The most prolific hitter of our time, he's suddenly riding the bench and leaving doubt whether he can break Ty Cobb's hit record. He's still some 275 short, a formidable distance for a slumping 42-year-old. Larry agreed to the change. "Just make sure your story is definitive," he said.

Rose pinch-hit, as usual, and grounded out to second, as **17** usual. Afterwards, he told me, "Maybe it's easier pinch-hitting. You only have to get up for one at-bat." A few minutes later he learned he'd be starting tomorrow. "I don't want to worry about getting a couple of hits," he said. "That would be putting too much pressure on myself." But soon afterwards he came back and added, "If I keep getting a couple of hits a game, they won't be able to take me out of the lineup."

Poor guy. The countdown to Ty Cobb's record has already begun, and Pete can't get it out of his mind. Of course, no one will let him forget it, including me.

Here's the problem. Rose has too little power now to hit homers and too little speed to beat out infield hits. The pitchers are inducing groundouts to second by throwing him inside fastballs he can't get around on. He's coming off his worst season (.264) in 18 years, he went 0-for-20 recently, and he may be released at season's end, as I learned (exclusively?) today from Philadelphia owner Bill Giles. All of which is causing Rose to talk bravely in public while privately asking friends if they think he'll break the record. I'm glad I demanded to write this piece: It's a story and a half.

I had dinner and drinks with some Philadelphia writers. It was a dizzying evening of talk, sometimes hilarious, sometimes tiresome, mostly about women and baseball. I'm amazed at how much some writers talk like ballplayers. Women aren't women but broads, to be leered and whistled at. Writers also use the same nicknames as players. Richie Hebner of the Pirates came over from a nearby table. "Hi, Hacker," everyone said.

I guess the pattern's inevitable. If you travel with a group of people, you adopt their mannerisms. The problem is that you're also likely to become overly protective of them. A certain amount of compromise is necessary—you have to maintain your sources—but how far can you go? The most

june

critical beat men seem to come from cities with competitive newspapers. (Perhaps the best example is Boston, where Red Sox coverage has historically been hypercritical.) In one-paper or single-ownership cities, the writers can be unabashed house men. In Philadelphia, where the *News* and *Inquirer* are jointly owned, however, the coverage is tough, professional and critical. This may be owing to the city's previous history of competitive journalism, or to the increasingly prominent suburban papers, which do compete in various ways with the metropolitan dailies. It also helps that Peter Pascarelli of the *Inquirer* and Bill Conlin of the *News* (who also writes *The Sporting News'* National League column) are as hard-nosed as the players they cover.

18   Here's the first few paragraphs of my Pete Rose story as I sent it in:

"The good news is that Pete Rose gave a virtuoso batting performance last week. The bad news is that he did it playing pepper.

"Rose took his swings in Busch Stadium several hours before a game with the Cardinals. Throwing to him were Hank King, his personal batting practice pitcher and confidant; reliever Tug McGraw and rightfielder Von Hayes. 'Pete bats like a musician fine-tuning his piano,' said King. 'Ping, ping, ping, bong. Whoops: Sandpaper that bat. Ping, ping, ping.' Rose swung casually, effortlessly. No matter how bad the throw, he hit smartly to each fielder in turn.

"An onlooker noticed something peculiar. The Phillies were about to face a righthanded pitcher, John Stuper, but the switchhitting Rose was batting righthanded. 'It's a funny thing,' said Rose, 'but I never could hit lefthanded in pepper.'

"It's a funny thing, but people are beginning to ask how well Pete Rose can hit, period. After going 0-for-20 and slumping to .238 on June 7, he was benched for the first time in his professional career. He kept playing as a late-inning pinch-hitter and defensive replacement—indeed, he tied his personal streak of 678 consecutive games last weekend—but his run of nonstarts reached nine before he started again Saturday night and tked. At week's end he was batting .tk and on the bench again (.ch. tk).

"When you're 42 years old and 277 behind Ty Cobb's career hit record of 4,191, every missed at-bat has to hurt. Rose has batted under .300 two of the last three years and last season dipped to .271, his lowest average since 1964. In the wake of his benching, he had some hard questions to answer: Has he lost some ability? How does he feel about being benched? Is he worried about Cobb's record? Rose for the defense: . . . ."

"Tk" is a printer's term meaning "to kum," and "ch. tk" means "check to kum." They're devices to indicate that I don't have the information or that it won't be available until after I file; the researcher will have to look it up. Anyway, here's the opening of my story after Larry edited it:

The good news is that Pete Rose gave a virtuoso batting performance last week. The bad news is that he did it playing pepper.

Rose took his swings in Busch Stadium several hours before a game with the Cardinals. He swung casually, effortlessly. No matter how bad the throw, he hit smartly to each of the three fielders in turn. But when the game began Rose was on the bench.

For the first time since people began to think of Rose as Ty Cobb's heir apparent for career base hits, there is serious doubt about his chances. Even Rose, in a rare unguarded moment, admitted as much last week. "It's obvious I can't catch Cobb if I'm not playing regularly," said Rose, who trailed Cobb by 277 hits, 4,191 to 3,914 at the end of last week.

That's a formidable distance when you are 42 years old, coming off your worst season in 18 years, batting .2tk, playing irregularly and the owner of your team is talking about releasing you.

After going 0-for-20 and slumping to .238 on June 7, he was benched for the first time in his 21-year career. He kept playing as a late-inning pinch-hitter and defensive replacement—indeed, he tied

june

his personal streak of 678 consecutive games last weekend—but his run of nonstarts reached nine before he started again Saturday night. The prospect of that start caused Rose to say, "My job is to play my tail off, get two hits a night so they won't want to take me out." Rose did what tk. At week's end he was batting .000, with tk hits in only tk at-bats.

Nevertheless, Rose is not about to admit to anything so obvious as the ravages of age. With characteristic upbeat bravado he has an answer for every question.

The other editors undoubtedly had some further changes, but Larry has already made his mark. What he's done is give the story focus. Sure, my anecdote about Rose playing pepper was amusing enough—I do regret losing King's quote— but Larry felt we should get to the point faster. Why are we writing about Rose? The paragraph starting with "For the first time" alerts the reader much earlier in the story than I did. Larry further sharpens the focus by bringing in quotes and other information that I had used later in my file or mentioned to him conversationally.

Obviously, I should go over my stories and how they're edited as carefully as I'm going over this one. It's the only way to learn. Unfortunately, I rarely do take this much time.

20   I called my agent, Dominick Abel, and told him about my (correction: my son Matthew's) idea for a book on defense. "Fine," Dominick said. "Why don't you write up a proposal?" He was as casual as if he'd been saying, "Why don't we meet for lunch?"

The idea is for a ten-chapter book—one on defense in general, each of the others on fielding one of the nine positions. The title will be *Playing the Field*. I'll work on the proposal this week, but I won't finish it until after I've spoken with as many players as I can at the All-Star Game in Chicago July 6. That way I can give the publishers my best shot.

june

There's no moon-spoon-June pollyanna about this book. It will be simple and modest, but useful. I think it can work.

21

I find I'm now rooting against Rose in order to justify the contentions in my story. I might as well be spitting on the flag. Of course, I still hope he breaks the record, but only after a struggle.

27

I passed my last week before vacation in the city. As is my wont, I failed to break 90 at Dyker Beach, shooting a clutch 42–49–91 (I once shot a 40–50–90). I also saw a couple of movies and a couple of plays and played paddle tennis. And did some office work and minimal research on the book proposal.

An article by Bill Madden in the *Daily News* traced the White Sox "revival" to Tony LaRussa's decision to use Greg Walker as the everyday first baseman. Benched for six weeks after making those errors Opening Day, Walker has come back strongly and pushed his average over .300. The batting coach, Charlie Lau, says, "He's just a natural hitter who I think will be one of the best in the league for years to come." Meanwhile Ron Kittle, who is among the league leaders with 17 homers and 51 runs batted in, is a cinch to make the All-Star team. I knew it. I just knew it.

Some other updates. In the NL: Dickie Thon (.302, 8 HR, 38 RBI), Nolan Ryan (5–1, 2.04 ERA, 54 K's in 57⅓ IP), Pete Rose (.248, 55 hits in 66 games), Steve Carlton (8–8, 3.01 ERA, 117 K's in 131⅔ IP). In the AL: Bob Stanley (5–3, 2.12, 16 saves), Buddy Bell (.281, 8 HR, 36 RBI), Randy Moffitt (3–0, 6 saves, 1.65 ERA).

Conclusions: Thon is an emerging star. Ryan is an enduring star who, true to his word, may not have the staying power to match Carlton's K's. On the other hand, Carlton may not have Ryan's staying power as winner. Rose, as reported, is in deep trouble. Bell's having a workmanlike season but won't make All-Star team. Happily, DeCinces will replace him. Moffitt's stats aren't as glitzy as Stanley's; Big Foot is bigger gun, will play in midsummer classic.

28 I'm in Toronto for a week's vacation with the kids. We flew to Buffalo on the People's Express cheapie and drove the rest of the way, stopping at Niagara Falls. While we were there, we took the Maid of the Mist boat under the falls, getting a happy soaking in the black ponchos passengers are given. It was no big thrill, just something you have to do once in a lifetime to say you did.

In Ontario it's mandatory to wear seat belts. Last week I had been driving somewhere in New York when I heard on the radio that the Supreme Court had told the Reagan administration to get serious about installing automatic seat belts or air bags. I counted the number of drivers wearing seat belts and figured it was somewhere between 10 and 20 percent. A nation of suicidal nuts. Today the boys and I calculated the number of Canadians obeying their mandatory buckle-up law. About 75 percent.

29 I was reminded early today that I'm getting old. After an hour of swimming, ping-pong and video games, I felt soreness in my neck and legs and had spasms in my upper arms. In the past, I was able to rationalize my disabilities. When my ankles became too weak for basketball, I convinced myself I wasn't interested in the game any more. But now I'm getting headaches from playing golf in the heat. What's left?

On to happier tidings. We visited the Ontario Science Center. It's a hands-on museum where visitors can push buttons and turn dials as well as just gape. In brief, education cum gimmicks. Then we had a Chinese dinner with our friends Fran Greenbaum and Peter Harper and their son Matthew, followed by our first game of Trivial Pursuit, a board game in which players answer trivia questions in six categories. In brief, gimmicks cum education. Brainstorm: Has the magazine ever done a story on the game? First order of business tomorrow: Call Time Inc. index and find out.

We haven't done Trivial Pursuit! **30**

We returned to the science center and later worked our way around the local park's Vitas Parcours, a European running course punctuated by exercise stations. Doing the step test on a high log, I pulled a hamstring.

The kids love Toronto. If I have any complaint, it's that everyone's a little too upbeat. I could use a little more alienation. No wonder people say writers are a little off.

july

We spent the day at Exhibition Place, visiting the ballpark **1** and amusement center.

The amusement area is no big deal. Exhibition Stadium is thought-provoking. The Blue Jays joined the league in 1977, and for the first five years the sale of beer at the park was prohibited. It was legalized last year. Today the fans behaved well and cheered gallantly, even as the Jays lost 11–2 to Seattle—and on Canada Day, yet. There was no smell of marijuana, no sign of drunkenness or profanity. Despite today's loss, the Jays are contending seriously for the first time in their history. No wonder everyone was so cheery.

But Canadians have more than earned their beer. I'm not sure the same applies in U.S. parks. Crowd control is improving in the States, but crowds—or individuals in them—can still be unforgivably unruly. I think Canadians view an afternoon at the park as an opportunity to strut their best behavior, while we see it as a chance to release our worst. Unless we adopt Canadian manners, someday there will be a riot or murder. Then we may be reduced to passing through metal shields and going without booze.

Unfortunately, Exhibition Stadium is not as pleasant as its patrons. The place was originally built for football, and most of the seats face the middle of the field instead of the mound. When are the Lords of Baseball going to realize that they'll never profit—at least, not esthetically—from multipurpose stadiums? The playing surface is artificial. No need to comment on that. And Torontonians are constantly bombarded by announcements, gimmicks, promos, music and one of the worst mascots in the majors.

Incredibly, the fans put up with it all. This gives me pause. Why don't these decent, tasteful people object to commercialism? Maybe they don't understand what's being done to the game in the name of entertainment. Baseball is an esthetic experience as well as an intellectual challenge. To truly appreciate it is to sit quietly, between pitches, and allow the game to affect your senses. You watch the alignment of the fielders, the silent communication between catcher and pitcher and coach and batter. You listen to the conversations around you and the cries of the vendors. You smell the hot dogs, you taste the beer, you bask in the sun. "I don't need drugs," a man once told me, "when I've got art and music and dance." I don't need hype at the ballpark when I've got baseball. But even as owners rail against drugs, they're giving us entertainment fixes. We're constantly distracted—by the electronic scoreboard, the P.A. system, the mascot. Baseball's sights and sounds and smells have been replaced by videos and promos.

As I had these thoughts, I felt sick and depressed. It occurred to me: I can make these arguments until I'm blue in the face, but I'm not sure I'll enlighten today's fans—even Canadian ones.

I considered myself. Two major victories in my life were convincing the boys to play chess as often as backgammon and pinballs as often as video games. Chess is reflective, backgammon reflexive; pinballs are personal, video games inhuman. Yet backgammon and video games have become all the rage.

I considered myself further. I read a little. I write a lot. I insist on good grammar. I don't like to dance. I do like to wear ties. I don't use drugs (I don't "do" drugs either). In short,

I'm hopelessly old-fashioned. How much weight will the arguments of a traditionalist carry in a society that's changing every seven seconds? Like Arthur Miller's description of Willy Loman, my name is carved on a block of ice in the sun.

We drove two hours to Eugenia, Ontario, where Fran, Peter **2** and Matthew have a summer cottage. There followed a Day of Heaven: sailing, swimming, canoeing, boomeranging, relaxing. I picked a bouquet of flowers for the first time in memory. We had shishkabob and some of the best corn-on-the-cob and strawberries-in-cream I've ever tasted, followed by another rousing game of Trivial Pursuit. I'm not much of a trivia buff, but I'm starting to love the game. It's not only educational but engrossing. You're constantly involved, answering questions to yourself when it's not your turn.

Oh, did we sleep soundly.

We drove four hours from Eugenia to Buffalo and flew to **4** Newark. After dropping the boys off, I met some friends and headed for East River Drive. After a 45-minute walk through crowds, we saw a fireworks display. I don't like fireworks anymore. I find them at once scary and boring.

I feel pleasure and remorse—pleasure at attending the festivities surrounding the 50th Anniversary of the All-Star **5** Game, disappointment at having missed so many of these occasions in the past. The White Sox, who were hosts of the first game in 1933, have put on a golden anniversary celebration. At today's Old Timers Game, stars old and new mingled in the clubhouse.

"Is this your locker?" Willie Mays asked Andre Dawson.

"No, sir, it's yours," said Dawson.

july

Following the Old Timers Game, the White Sox threw a party at Navy Pier. The room was so large that Joe DiMaggio in his prime couldn't have thrown a ball across it. The mood was that of a Polish wedding: relaxed and boisterous. And the live entertainment was Chubby Checker, Dottie West, the Four Tops and the Oak Ridge Boys. Doug and Kristi DeCinces sat holding hands as the Four Tops sang. "We used to neck to this music," Kristi said.

The central figure at the party was Ron Kittle, who has become the most popular athlete in town. Kittle stood in the ballroom wearing snakeskin boots, slacks, an open shirt and a jacket. "I'm not wearing my glasses," he said. "I don't want to be recognized."

What a joke. Everyone was after Kittle's autograph—little kids, old men, and women of all descriptions—including the wives of other ballplayers. In Chicago, a city of few sports heroes and even fewer winning teams, Kittle is already a bigger hero than Mr. Cub, Hall of Famer Ernie Banks, ever was. Banks says so himself.

Kittle has a few things Banks lacked. He has been an instant success, hitting 18 homers, driving in 55 runs and almost singlehandedly preventing the White Sox from dropping out of the race early in the season. He hits mammoth taters, which fans love in spacious Comiskey Park—where homers of any variety are unexpected. He's a local product, having grown up in nearby Gary, Indiana. He was a steel-drivin' man before he was a ballplayer—you think Chicagoans don't like that? "And he's having so much fun," says former White Sox owner Bill Veeck. "How can you *not* like him?"

Kittle has hardly changed at all. Keeping his cool under intense scrutiny, he arrives early and leaves late at shopping center promos and interviews. "The hardest thing is to be able to say no," he says. "You have to be able to find out who your friends are."

"He has a Chicagoan's knack for being confident without sounding conceited," says *Tribune* columnist Steve Daley. After the Old Timers Game, Kittle grabbed a bat and ran around the American League clubhouse getting signatures. I took a look at the bat. The biggest and boldest signature scribbled on it was that of Ron Kittle.

I asked Kittle about Walker and he said that Greg was doing fine, although that day he had gone out on a boat in Lake Michigan and gotten seasick. Later I spoke with Walker. He has survived rookie jitters and grown comfortable with his status as a major-leaguer. He admits that the benching depressed him, but he adds, "I decided that even if I got sent down to the minors, I'd play my best and work my way back up."

Purists are always complaining about the All-Star Game. **6** They don't like the fact that in selecting the starters, the fans often pass over the most deserving players for the most popular. So what? The game is an exhibition, not a championship event. Fans like to see Ozzie Smith doing his cartwheels at shortstop and Reggie Jackson taking his mighty cuts, even if they're both hitting .212 at the time. And so do I. Anyway, starters can be replaced after three innings.

I couldn't help noticing how happy the players were to be here—happy to be designated as stars, happy to be rubbing elbows with stars. The celebration is primary, the competition secondary. That's what the purists don't seem to understand.

Of course, the competition was primary for me this year, since I had a vested interest in a National League victory. As I buried my head in my hands, the American League won 13–3.

The good news is that hardly anyone said anything to me about the result. The bad news is that I feel awful, in retrospect, about the way my NL story ran in the magazine. What jumped out was how "superior" the NL is to the AL. That wasn't really my point. I was arguing, you'll remember, that the differences between the leagues have helped the NL win all those Series and All-Star Games. Actually, what has been happening of late is that AL teams are playing the more adventuresome NL style of ball. My insights will be lost now that the AL won so handily. It will appear that I was wrong to call the NL superior.

Though the All-Star Game was played on Chicago's South Side, I wasn't unaware of that controversy brewing on the North Side, at Wrigley Field. While I was in town, I fleshed out some details for what may prove to be an interesting story.

The *Chicago Tribune* Company, which purchased the Cubs in 1981, wants to install lights in Wrigley Field. Why is this significant? Because Wrigley Field is the last unlighted park in the majors: An entire way of life is threatened.

"I know in my heart that the Cubs can't win playing daytime baseball," says Cub general manager Dallas Green. According to the pro-lights argument, Cub players take a terrible beating by constantly switching from day games at home to night games on the road. What's more, it's said, the steady diet of daytime games in the July and August heat wears out the team by September. Finally, the Cubs won't be able to pay today's inflated salaries until they draw better, and that won't happen until they install lights.

The pro-day argument is more personal. Neighborhood groups say the Wrigley Field area can't accommodate the traffic and noise that would come with night crowds. Evidently, it's one thing to tolerate tie-ups and crowd noise on the few afternoons when there are sellouts, another to suffer congestion every few nights in a pennant race. And a lot of people just flat like sitting outside on a hot afternoon drinking beer. A group called Citizens United for Baseball in Sunshine (CUBS) successfully lobbied for an amendment to the state's environmental protection law prohibiting Wrigley Field events after 10 P.M. in which the decibel level exceeds 45. However, the law only bans noise from stationary sources such as P.A. systems and organs. Presumably, the games themselves could continue after 10. CUBS is now pushing for an 8 P.M. limit, and the controversy is certain to continue.

I asked Ernie Banks for his observations. "Lights would help," he said, "because the players can get more rest. Playing today requires discipline and stamina. The schedule is so quick—bing, bing, bing, bing, bing—and the Cubs don't always have time to adjust before they go someplace else. They've been moving some starts from 1 P.M. to 3, and that's helped because it's more like a night game.

"But I really enjoyed day baseball. You had regular hours like anyone else, leaving home in the morning and coming back at night. You had a chance to be with young people when school was out. My kids used to be with me at the park, playing catch. Every day I seem to run into someone who says he was at Wrigley Field when he was 10 and 11. You had women and families coming out. People grew up watching you and there was a lot of love from the fans, who were very knowledgeable about baseball.

"It was a kind of a double situation, though. The better you'd play, the more people wanted you to do on the outside. The biggest thing was community activities. Many times I'd come home and a Little League would want me to come out. Since the activities started at 7 or 8 in the evening, I could do it. I'd get home at 10 and have to be up at 7. The pace was too great.

"But there's no better place in the world to play than Wrigley Field. You've been there, haven't you? It's beautiful."

july

7   I flew to Boston directly from Chicago. The Angels are
playing the Red Sox at Fenway Park, and I'm doing a column
on California's Fred Lynn, the Most Valuable Player in the All-
Star Game. I shared a cab from Boston's Logan Airport with
Angel teammates DeCinces and Rod Carew. Carew is considering retiring after the season, although I suspect he'll
stick around another year or two to get his 3,000th hit. A
sensitive man, he's driven to distraction by the demands of
autograph seekers. "They were calling me at seven, eight,
nine in the morning in Chicago," he said. Carew wearily
girded for the next assault. Assuming an extreme Boston accent, he called out, "Gimme da bawl, sign heeyah."

8   I had lunch with my father and DeCinces in Maison Robert,
a restaurant built into the old City Hall. DeCinces had trout, I
had swordfish and Dad had an omelette—all uniformly excellent.

As was the conversation. Dad asked DeCinces, a third
baseman, if he knew of any lefties at the position. He didn't
(actually, there have been ten lefthanders since 1900 who
played third for very brief periods). Dad wanted to know if a
hitter could look back and catch the catcher's signal to the
pitcher. Doug said it wouldn't be advisable because there
might not be enough time to see the signal and get set for the
pitch.

I could see that my father was impressed with DeCinces.
By association, perhaps Dad was a little more impressed with
me. In the academic community exercise is considered ac-
ceptable primarily because it keeps a man mentally alert.
Sports is not exactly pushed as a profession. Sportswriting?
My father would have preferred that I go into law or
medicine, though he never said so until I confronted him.
"Professions like medicine or law are more secure," he said.
"If a newspaper or magazine fell through, you wouldn't have

anything to fall back on." Mind you, this is an understandable view for a guy who grew up in the Depression. At least he wasn't putting down my profession. I once got into a political argument with one of my father's colleagues. "Oh, well," I heard him mutter to himself, "he's just a sportswriter."

My father seemed especially interested in an exchange Doug and I had. Doug is suffering from a rib separation and has aggravated the injury by trying to come back too soon. I pointed out to him that *The Baseball Encyclopedia* is filled with the names of men who ruined their careers by playing with injuries. "No question," Doug said. "You're under a lot of pressure—from your peers, from the writers asking you every day how you feel, from the fans and, most of all, from yourself. You want to keep your stats up, and you know your team needs you in the lineup. I'm having a good year, and any time I don't play, a lefthanded pitcher who faces us is going to benefit." (He bats righthanded.)

Nonetheless, I hope Doug doesn't play during the three-game series in Boston. The back injury has led to spasms, and he feels great pain every time he throws or stretches for a grounder. I breathed a deep sigh of relief when he wasn't used in the All-Star Game, except to pinch-hit. Today he went out to the park four hours before game time, took a heat massage, used an electronic muscle-stimulator to move fresh blood into the damaged area and lifted some weights. An hour or so later Arthur Pappas, the Red Sox physician, poked Doug's ribs. He immediately went into a back spasm. "No way you're playing today," said Pappas.

I overheard the California trainer say Doug was considering traction. A few minutes later I found Doug in the clubhouse. He was distraught. "I thought I could DH today, but I can't even run." he said. "The problem is, the rib condi-

9

tion keeps affecting my back. Maybe I should go into traction, take some drugs and do nothing for awhile. Or maybe I'll have to give up the month of July. But then I think of the numbers I need to have this year."

I tried to put myself in his position. He's making about $400,000 a year and will become a free agent at season's end, the Angels having refused to negotiate a contract extension with him this spring. On the open market he'll be worth $1 million a year, the going rate for premium third basemen. But now, with his medical condition, it could all go poof: the contract, the career, the future. At least, that's what has to be going through his mind. No wonder he's depressed.

10   Fred Lynn is a fascinating study. Though he was a Rookie of the Year (1975) and a Most Valuable Player in both a playoff series (1982) and for a whole season (1975); and though he's averaged .300, with 18.5 homers and 78.5 runs batted in from '75 through '82, many observers feel he's only scratched the surface of his talent. They say he's forever taking himself out of the lineup with questionable injuries, especially when his team is about to face lefthanded pitching. (He bats lefthanded.) "Fred is as good as he wants to be, day in and day out," says California shortstop Rick Burleson. "As far as ability goes, he's among the best in the game. I sometimes wonder if his motivation is there all the time."

In his defense, Lynn has suffered a considerable variety of real injuries and has wisely taken himself out when he couldn't run hard in center field. "You're a liability," he says, "if you play half-speed when you're hurt and can't contribute. Is it better to play two games and then miss two months, or miss two games and play two months?"

Well spoken. If there's a more legitimate criticism of Lynn, it's that he tires mentally sooner than some other players. "Some people are good for 162 games," says a veteran Lynn-watcher, "he's good for about 140."

The story went very well. So why am I a little worried? Because Lynn was so nice, and my writing was a little critical, albeit balanced. It isn't easy to be tough on so nice a guy. Athletes don't realize that they'll often get bad press when they don't speak with reporters, and better press when they do. It's human nature.

I've got two stories to write this week: a third, updated **13** version of the Dickie Thon piece and a column on Yankee pitcher Dave Righetti. I went to Shea Stadium looking for quotes from Tom Seaver, who yielded two homers to Thon last week. I got the quotes, and a potpourri of memorabilia to boot.

The Reds' incomparable catcher, Johnny Bench, is retiring after this season, and as he makes his final appearance in each National League City, he's receiving a fond farewell. Today at Shea Stadium he's getting a send-off from New York fans and players.

Mets pitcher Tom Seaver, a former teammate of Bench's in Cincinnati: "John was never intimidated by the tag play at the plate, no matter what the collision was going to be like. He and Jerry Grote were two of the best I've ever seen at blocking the plate, throwing runners out and giving the umpire a good view of the ball as it came over the plate."

Mets broadcaster Tim McCarver, a former catcher: "Bench was the best one-handed catcher ever. In fact, he popularized using one hand. Before about 1940, Birdie Tebbetts and others said to catch with two hands. That's a bunch of bananas. When you catch one-handed, you can snap the ball right back to your throwing hand, whereas the movement's too bulky with two hands. With one, it's an oval-like movement.

"The other thing John popularized was the hinged glove, as opposed to the old ones with the little pocket in the middle. If you caught everything in the pocket, it would sting your hand, so you'd try to catch in the webbing. If the ball sailed, you'd miss it. The new gloves are designed for catching the ball in the pocket without pain, because the new, hinged pocket is between the thumb and index finger. It's like a first baseman's glove. Now, if the ball sails, you catch it in the webbing."

Bench on himself: "My fondest memory? The idea that as a catcher you could have a good day four different ways. You could call a good game, block home plate, throw out runners and get some hits. The things I hated most were the foul tips. But when I was a world champion, all the aches and pains went away.

"I had the ability to change the game with the one-handed glove. I could stand away from a sliding runner and avoid a collision by making a sweeping tag. You just have to go "*¡Olé!*" like a guy making the tag at second. Catchers never had the time to do that when they had to use two hands with the round glove. You've got to keep the ball moving to make the sweep tag; don't just put the glove in front of the runner's foot. It's like catching an egg; you've got to give with it.

"Handling pitchers? There were different personalities. There was the guy you patted on the back, the guy you had to tell about different situations and the guy you just told, 'Let's go.' If a pitcher believes in you, he'll throw his best pitch. I may get away from calling the pitch when he's not throwing it well, and then come back to it later. You spot it."

14   Larry says I haven't got much about Thon's personality in the story. Never mind that he's an amiable but rather unquotable fellow, I obviously didn't get much out of him. Why didn't I push him more? Why didn't I ask more follow-up questions?

Fortunately, I didn't have time to mope. I went right out to Yankee Stadium to interview Dave Righetti. He gave me a good interview (I think) and his phone number, which his agent says he's loath to part with. I must have done something right.

The Baseball Writers' Association of America is the only **15** one I know of that's limited to writers from daily newspapers. At one point there was good reason to restrict the membership. Friends of the general manager and other freeloaders would mob the pressbox. Even today, reporters from local radio and TV stations can drive the daily guys crazy with their mikes and terrible questions. "Basically," says Jack Lang of the *News*, the association's powerful secretary-treasurer, "we want to keep out phonies."

From the beginning, though, the association has gone too far. Lang's old paper, the *Long Island Press*, originally was given less-than-full credentials because it was considered a suburban paper. The association later admitted suburban writers, but not representatives from a major national sports magazine.

The imbalance creates numerous problems for us. We don't get to vote for awards; we get lousy press seats at the All-Star Game, playoffs and Series and, worst of all, we don't get a BBWAA card, which allows us into the clubhouse (the league pass gets us into parks but not all clubhouses).*

In order to be admitted to Yankee Stadium, I had to call the public relations office for a daily pass. Because I arrived at 5 P.M., an hour before passes were available at the press gate, I had to talk my way into the ticket office. They gave me not one but three passes—one for admission to the park, one for the clubhouses and one for the press dining room. I went down to the clubhouse, but no good: My pass hadn't been signed by one Mr. Kelly. I went upstairs, found him and got

*In 1984 the league passes were accepted at all parks as working credentials.

july

his signature. "Sorry to put you through this," he said, "but last year someone got in who shouldn't have." Yeah, George Steinbrenner.

16   In addition to the interview with Righetti, I got quotes from several members of the Texas organization where he started out, and more still from his parents. I fleshed out some details: That at age 24 he could become a 20-game winner earlier than Steve Carlton or Sandy Koufax; that he has the largest contract ever given a player who wasn't in arbitration or on the verge of free agency ("His teammates call him Rags," I wrote. "They should call him Riches"); that his slider, curve and changeup set up his excellent fastball; that maturity is the real reason for his success. I had enough personal and professional details to write 400 lines instead of the usual 200. I thought I wrote a hell of a story.

Nonetheless, Larry told me he had "no sense of what the guy is like." Maybe my problem is that I've been writing so many columns I'm getting stale.

18   I'm eligible for four weeks' vacation, not including the week all editorial staffers get at Christmas. I took the first week in Toronto, and I'm going to take the second and third weeks at my parents' place on Martha's Vineyard. Earlier today, I took the subway to a Piedmont Airlines office, which last week sold me two tickets to Boston over the phone for $34 apiece. Today the saleswoman told me I was paying $55 for each. I went into a controlled rage, pointing out what they'd offered before. She went off to check with her supervisor, came back and let me have the tickets at the lower figure, even though other customers will pay $55 (the phone quote had been a mistake). Just like Doug and Wendy Whiner on "Saturday Night Live": People will invariably appease a grouch rather than deal with him.

Jim Kaplan and sons Matthew and Benjamin.

Kaplan and playwright Mark Levin *(right).—photo by Ted Stephney*

Ron Kittle, Chicago White Sox.—*UPI/Bettmann Archives*

Nolan Ryan struck out 12 New York Mets in this game.—*UPI/Bettmann Archives*

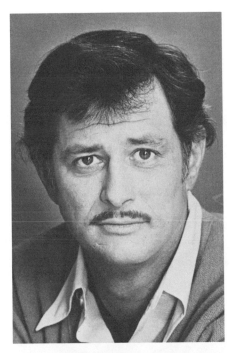

Frank Deford.

Larry Keith.—*photo by Ted Steph-ney*

Steve Wulf *(left)* interviewing Pat Gillick, vice-president for baseball operations, and manager Bobby Cox of the Toronto Blue Jays.

Pete Rose stretches to take a throw from Marty Bystrom of the Philadelphia Phillies as Eddie Milner of the Cincinnati Reds gets back safely to first base.—*UPI/Bettman Archives*

Al Holland, Joe Morgan and Pete Rose look on as the Phillies lose the third
game of the 1983 World Series to Baltimore.—*UPI/Bettmann Archives*

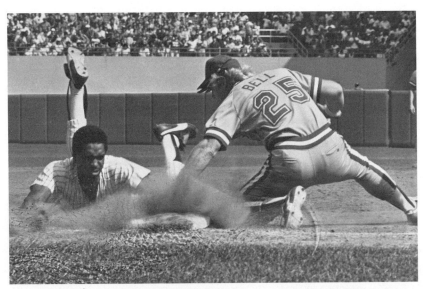

The Yankees' Dave Winfield slides into third under the tag of Buddy Bell,
Texas Rangers.—*UPI/Bettmann Archives*

Dickie Thon, Houston, throws to first as Dave Concepcion slides into second base.—*UPI/Bettmann Archives*

Johnny Bench, Cincinnati Reds.—*UPI/Bettmann Archives*

Bob Stanley, Boston Red Sox.—*UPI/Bettmann Archives*

1936 New York Yankees display at Baseball Hall of Fame, Cooperstown.—*Hall of Fame*

The celebrated pine-tar incident. An enraged George Brett, robbed of a home run against the Yankees, is held off the offending umpires.—*UPI/Bettmann Archives*

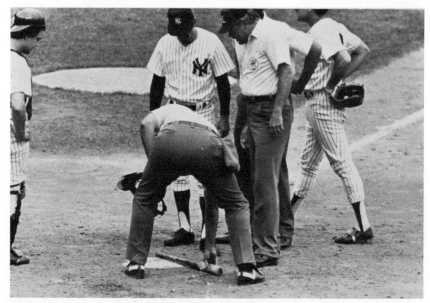

More pine-tar. Kansas City manager Dick Howser (*center*) looks on as the umpires measure the tarred area of Brett's bat against home plate.—*UPI/ Bettmann Archives*

The Philadelphia Phillies' Mike Schmidt.—*UPI/Bettmann Archives*

Fred Lynn of California Angels in action against Milwaukee.—*UPI/Bettmann Archives*

"Mister Cub," Ernie Banks.—*UPI/Bettmann Archives*

Jim Kaat as pitcher for St. Louis Cardinals.—*UPI/Bettmann Archives*

Another view of Jim Kaat.—*photo by Matthew Kaplan*

Doug DeCinces, California Angels, and wife Kristi.

I had 10,000 things to do: Get money; do laundry; hold the mail; pack; pay bills; leave my phone number with the writers' secretary. My last act was to finish my expense account, and I'm afraid I cheated myself. I didn't come close to recording every cab I took or drink I bought for someone. I've just finished reading Bob Greene's "Rules of the Road" in the current *Esquire,* and I have an addition: Write down every expense immediately after incurring it.

19

Matthew has been on the Vineyard several days. Benjamin and I caught the Piedmont flight to Boston; drove to Woods Hole; arrived two hours before our ferry was due to depart, and caught an earlier one. We arrived in time to take a swim, down a splendid swordfish dinner (my choice if I were a condemned man), and see "Harold and Maude." One night on the Vineyard and I feel as if I'd been on vacation a week. An island will do that to you.

21

My vacation is not without work. I've been transcribing the diary entries onto the old Portabubble. And I had a long conversation today with my agent, Dominick Abel. He has read my book proposal, and he isn't enthusiastic. After a general chapter on defense, I had outlined one chapter on each position. "It's too didactic and instructional," Dom said. "Excitement and entertainment are lacking. The way you've outlined it, people could skip a chapter if, say, they weren't interested in right field. Maybe you could organize it in terms of chronology, style of play or profile. You're organizing it like a story for *Sports Illustrated;* there isn't enough wonder, and you don't luxuriate in the history of the game. Remember, the people are more interesting than the positions."
I'm going to have to think about this.

july

26   I've been transcribing about 5,000 characters (1,000 words) a day. Because I forget almost everything that happens to me, keeping a diary preserves and in a sense immortalizes my life. Especially the good parts. And that runs counter to human experience. Go to it, Mark Antony: "The evil that men do lives after them; / The good is oft interred with their bones." So a diary should make our lives fuller and richer and happier.

27   My friend Julie Cass came over for a swim and a visit. The Southern correspondent for *The Philadelphia Inquirer*, Julie covers everything from floods to river baptisms. I could get in the swim of a job like that.

As we took a walk on the beach, we discussed how different we journalists are from "normal" people. "I'd love to take a course some time," she said, "but I never know when I'm going to be in town." That's the joy and curse of our profession—glamour without predictability. I wonder if the managing editors ever consider the stress writers suffer from their abnormal lives. In fact, I think I'll ask one of the bosses: "When you're about to be promoted to a management position, are you given any training at all in human relations?" I'm sure the answer is no. That's too bad, because I think the people are as important as the product.

We worked our way down to Vincent's Beach, where bathers have the option of using suits or going nude. Three things happen when you go to a nude beach: 1) You gawk; 2) You quickly become accustomed to seeing people au naturel, and 3) You wish most of them had kept their clothes on.

In the evening I took Benjamin and Mary Fagan, my mother's mother's helper, to a party at the home of Julie's hostess, Marie Jemison. There were a lot of old LBJ cronies, including Liz Carpenter, Lady Bird's former press secretary. They were all furious about the book Robert Caro did on LBJ.

Another thing I learned: Southern women love to talk about sex.

I'm covering the pine-tar incident from afar, but I didn't **28** have to be at Yankee Stadium three days ago to appreciate its significance. I have no doubt it will be the highlight of the baseball season. Why? Because it's something we can all get our hooks into. It's funny, serious; complicated, simple; trivial, important. It's baseball at its best, with new angles and controversies sure to open up almost daily. People will argue about it for months.

I'm particularly enjoying the episode from here since it affords me the opportunity to read unhurriedly two of my favorite *Times* writers, Murray Chass and Ira Berkow. Yankee beat man Chass begins to salivate and chortle as things grow complicated; no one does a better job, for instance, covering the game's business and labor sides. And Berkow consistently finds humor and irony where others miss it.

The facts of the case are known to everyone who hasn't spent the last three days in a disco. With two outs in the ninth and the Yankees leading the Royals 4–3, K.C.'s George Brett hit a two-run homer off Goose Gossage. Or did he?

Yankee manager Billy Martin had been waiting for just this opportunity. In an earlier game with the Royals, some of Billy's troops had discovered Brett using an illegal amount of pine tar on his bat. There had been no reason to mention that to the umpires until Brett caused some damage.

Now that Brett had put the Royals ahead 5–4 in the ninth, Martin pounced. Rushing to the mound, he informed home plate umpire Tim McClelland that the pine tar extended more than the legally prescribed 18 inches from the tip of the handle of the bat. Martin, McClelland and the other arbiters began sniffing about the plate like dogs around a tree. McClelland held the bat over the plate, which is 17 inches wide, and

july

discovered that Brett had "heavy" pine tar 19 or 20 inches from the handle and lighter stuff for another three or four inches. The umpires conferred. Suddenly, McClelland threw up his right fist, banishing Brett, his bat and his homer from the game. With the homer reduced to an out, the Yankees were declared winners by the original 4–3 score. Brett had lost a game by homering. Gossage had earned a save by serving up a gopher ball.

In a trice, Brett vaulted from the dugout to McClelland's throat. No race car on the Bonneville Salt Flats ever executed a quicker 0-to-60. Brett was forcibly restrained. (In a subplot, K.C. pitcher Gaylord Perry, who has been known to use some sticky stuff on the *ball*, spirited the bat into the clubhouse. The umpires recovered it.)

The umpires base their belated reversal on three clauses in the Official Baseball Rules:

1.10 (b), which states, "The bat handle, for not more than 18 inches from the end, may be covered or treated with any material (including pine tar) to improve the grip. Any such material, including pine tar, which extends past the 18 inch limitation, in the umpire's judgment, shall cause the bat to be removed from the game. No such material shall improve the reaction or distance factor of the bat";

6.06 (a), which states that a batter is out for "illegal action" when he hits an illegally batted ball; and

6.06 (d), which ejects a player and forfeits any advancement on the bases if he "uses or attempts to use a bat that, in the umpire's judgment, has been altered with or tampered with in such a way to improve the distance factor or cause an unusual reaction on the baseball."

Did George Brett use too much pine tar on his bat? For sure. Should the bat have been thrown out of the game? Absolutely. Should Brett's two-run homer have been disallowed? Query.

The issue seems to be whether Brett used excessive pine tar in an effort to affect the "distance factor."

Brett thinks not. "I don't wear batting gloves," he says. "I like the feel of raw skin on raw wood. But you also don't want to hold the bat where the pine tar is, so you put it up higher on the bat, get some on your hands when you need it, and then go back to the bottom of the bat. Where I hit that ball, it was on the meat part of the bat, about five inches from the end. There's no pine tar 29 inches from the handle. That ball wasn't even close enough to the pine tar to smell it."

Here's where things get curiouser and curiouser. The umpires upheld the Yankee protest even though crew chief Nick Brenigan agreed that pine tar shouldn't affect distance. Evidently, they still considered Brett's homer an "illegal act." Meanwhile Martin, ordinarily an archetypal villain figure, is basking in the delicious furor he has created. Chass describes him as being "as peaceful and snug as he could be about the whole incident." Says Billy, presumably puffing on his pipe, "It turned out to be a lovely Sunday afternoon."

Ah, but the issue won't die. The Royals have filed a protest, to be heard this week by American League President Lee MacPhail. What we have here is a big, continuing story being run, quite properly I think, on page one of *The Times* adjacent to lesser events from the Middle East and Central America.

Enter Ira Berkow. One of the things Ira does best is ask obvious questions that are rarely asked because they're so obvious. In asking them, however, Ira invariably gets interesting answers. He was at the AL offices Monday, shortly after the offending bat arrived for inspection. I quote now from his story:

Reporter: Were there any fingerprints on it?
[MacPhail's assistant Bob] Fishel: I didn't see any.
Reporter: Are there any now, after you held it?
Fishel: Not mine. I can tell you that. I held it by the ends.
Reporter: As if you were eating corn on the cob?
Fishel: Sort of, but without the margarine.
Reporter: Margarine?
Fishel: Butter's high in cholesterol.

Later, Berkow asked Yankee general manager Murray Cook why he was opposed to the Royals' appeal.

Cook: You can't have foreign substances going all the way up the bat. Say you want to bunt. The ball would stick and aid the batter.
Reporter: But his ball didn't stick, it flew.
Cook: [Shrug, smile] Strange, isn't it?

And still later, Ira called Hillerich & Bradsby, makers of Brett's Louisville Slugger. Brett's bat, said Rex Bradley, a vice president for the company, is a T-85 Marv Throneberry model.

Reporter: Marvelous Marv Throneberry? The Mets' legend, the guy who did things like hit a triple and miss both first and second?
Bradley: One and the same.

MacPhail is to issue his ruling on the case today. I can't wait.

29 In a decision worthy of Mr. Justice Holmes at his best, MacPhail upheld the protest, reversed the umpires' reversal, reinstated the homer and left the Royals leading 5–4 with two outs in the ninth.

MacPhail's decision is laudable both for his logic and tact. "It is the position of this office," he states, "that the umpires' interpretation, while technically defensible, is not in accord with the intent or spirit of the rules and that the rules do not provide that a hitter be called out for excessive pine tar." Cutting to the heart of the dispute, MacPhail points out that pine tar doesn't increase distance. In conclusion, he makes two particularly generous statements:

"Although Manager Martin and his staff should be commended for their alertness, it is the strong conviction of the League that games should be won and lost on the playing field—not through technicalities of the rules . . ." and "Although the umpires are being overruled, it is not in my opinion the fault of the umpires involved, but rather is the fault of the Official Playing Rules, which in some cases are unclear and unprecise."

(Actually, as my favorite magazine will point out next week, the umpires demonstrated incredible ignorance of "precedent, rules and interpretations." In 1975 K.C.'s John Mayberry used excessive pine tar while hitting two homers against California in an 8–7 victory, but MacPhail upheld the result when the Angels protested. "Pine tar," he wrote at the time, "is not to be considered in the same vein as a doctored or filled bat under rule 6.06 (d)." Furthermore, American League regulation 4.23 states, "The use of pine tar in itself shall not be considered doctoring the bat. The 18-inch rule will not be cause for ejection or suspension.")

MacPhail had consulted rule-makers, umpires and former umpires before making his latest decision. "They all said the rule was put in not to call a batter out or discipline a player but to clean up the bat and eliminate delays in the game. Before the rule was put in, batters were putting pine tar all the way up their bats, and every time the ball was hit it became soiled and had to be removed from the game. That created delays."

Alas, MacPhail's tact was reciprocated by neither the Yankees nor the umpires. "I thought the umpires were right and should have been applauded, not degraded," says Martin, ordinarily no friend of the men in blue. Rather than accept their well-earned defeat, the umpires are maintaining the rightness of their wrong decision. And George Steinbrenner, as usual, had the last word: "We use pine tar on fences in Florida, and it makes them harder."

To be continued, I'm sure.

Here's a fish story: **30**
My friend Jim Fesler and I went fishing on Lobsterville Beach. No fish, nary a bite. We whipped over to the Menem-

july

sha jetty, where everyone was pulling out blues. Even some beetle-turtle kid with a one-foot rod was getting hits. But not Fesler and Kaplan. We chucked out poppers and darters and swimmers. Nothing. Finally, I maneuvered to a casting position close to the water and thought I got a bite. Instead, I found I was tangled with a kid's line. "Get off it, he's got a hit!" someone yelled. As I moved along the wet rocks toward his line, my feet slipped out from under me. "Oh, God, I'm going to fall on my head," I thought. Fortunately, my back, and not my head hit the rocks. Unfortunately, as Fesler was guiding me back to the car, I felt dizzy and nauseated.

As I lie here, my legs, left arm, left buttock and neck are sore, but nobody believes the aging hypochondriac.

That's why it's a fish story.

august

I'm driving directly to Boston for the owners' meetings. **1**
They may dump the Commissioner. Here's the story the
editors want me to do: Bye-Bye Bowie; his reaction; who's the
new Commish or whose names are suggested; how baseball
reached this point.

I asked Bambi Bachman, the chief of research, if she could
free a reporter to work with me. "It'll give someone an opportunity to establish contacts," I said. It'll also give us a chance
to double-team a difficult assignment. There are going to be a
lot of people to speak with, and getting something new is
difficult because the newspapers cover these meetings very
well.

Supposedly Commissioner Kuhn was fired last November. **2**
He needed a three-quarters vote from each league to remain
in office, and he only got 7 of 12 votes in the National League.
So he's supposed to step down when his term expires August
12.

But of late there's been a revisionist movement to keep him
in office. Supposedly, 18 of the 26 owners are behind him,
including everyone on the powerful executive committee.
The committee may not even bring up a vote on the new
Commissioner and may simply reappoint Kuhn when his
term expires next week. How will the minority owners react?

"It'll be a bloodbath," says one. This is how the geniuses in charge of our national pastime routinely behave.

Another possibility is a compromise. Some of the pro-Kuhn owners are circulating a plan to retain him while reducing his powers. A fellow named Fred Kuhlman, fronting for St. Louis owner Gussie Busch, leads the dump-Kuhn movement. I'm told that if Kuhlman can be induced to switch his vote, the others will fall in line. The matter should come to a head tomorrow.

Tonight Jim Fesler, Ira Berkow and I had dinner on the wharf. Recently Ira wrote the men's column for the *New York Times Magazine* on why he still plays basketball at age 43. He got paid $1,000 for 1,000 words. I kept repeating it: "$1,000 for 1,000 words."

3 The Commissioner surprised everyone by resigning. Suddenly, the air is clear, the bickering is over and the owners can proceed with selecting a successor. A masterful—and necessary—step.

In the wake of his decision many owners are speaking of Kuhn as if he were some kind of god. My own feelings are considerably more mixed.

In the 15-odd years Kuhn has been in office, the major issue confronting him has been labor relations. He has consistently blundered. At the Flood trial he testified on behalf of the reserve clause, warning that baseball couldn't exist without it. Obdurate to the end, he never considered negotiating a modification of the clause that would have been more favorable to the owners than the system they were forced to accept in 1976. I give him credit for ordering spring training camps opened that year—a gesture that may have averted a strike. But prior to the 1981 strike, putative peacemaker Kuhn told union leader Marvin Miller, "The owners need a victory." Bowie's response to the problem of drug addiction, which the

American Medical Association defines as an illness, has been punitive rather than rehabilitative. Arbitrators have quite rightly overruled Kuhn's double-jeopardy suspensions of players who have violated drug statutes and already paid the price in court.

I'll say this for Bowie: At times he stood up to some very difficult owners. In 1976 Oakland's Charlie Finley flouted the game's integrity by attempting to sell off some of his best players. In his most noble gesture Kuhn vetoed the sales. Unlike many baseball executives, Kuhn undoubtedly lay awake at night wondering what was in the best interests of the game. But I feel he too frequently came to the wrong conclusion, supporting as he did the designated-hitter rule, nighttime playoff and Series games and every manner of commercial scheme to promote baseball: a relief award named after an antacid, a playoff award given by a car company, a Series sweepstakes sponsored by a cookie company. Under Kuhn baseball ceased being a pastime and became a product.

Let me use an analogy. Suppose a hot-shot promoter got hold of chess. "Look," he says, "the big problem with chess is that it's too slow. Speed up the game and you'll attract crowds, television coverage and more prize money. My plan is simple: a second queen! Look, the queen is the major offensive piece on the board, and with two queens we'll have twice as much offense!"

He might be right. The game could easily become twice as wide-open; crowds, TV coverage and prize money might increase dramatically. But the essential character and appeal of chess would be altered. It would be a different game.

A question Bowie Kuhn undoubtedly asked upon becoming Commissioner was, How can we better market baseball? He increased offense by pushing the designated hitter. Never mind that a nine-man game became a ten-man game in one league. Forget that the critical late-inning decision on pinch-

august

hitting for the pitcher—the very fulcrum about which so many games turn—would vanish in utter silence. Dismiss the delicious possibility of a half-dozen names entering the box score because a pitcher was pinch-hit for. Example: 1) A left-handed pinch-hitter replaces batting team's pitcher; 2) A left-handed pitcher replaces the righthander on the mound; 3) a righthanded pinch-hitter bats for the lefthander; 4) a righthanded pitcher comes in; 5) when the pinch-hitter bats safely, he's replaced by a pinch-runner, and 6) a new pitcher comes in the following inning. There was more offense, and that was all the Commissioner wanted. Thanks to Bowie, baseball got more TV money for the playoffs and Series by moving weekday games to prime time. So what if baseball was no longer "woven into the fabric of American life"? (I love that metaphor.) You remember the old ritual: kids bringing transistor radios to school and listening surreptitiously during class, adults shirking their jobs and pulling out televisions in the office. Gone forever. And, finally, because of Bowie, baseball reaped all kinds of wealth with his promos. Never mind that the game itself was getting upstaged.

5　　With the able assistance of reporter Ivan Maisel, I got some decent quotes from the owners. None of the editors, however, feels there's a column in Bowie's abdication. Kuhn was doomed, they say, and how he went is basically irrelevant. I wrote a 100-line file for Inside Pitch or Scorecard and flew to St. Louis, where the Phillies are playing, to do a column on new manager Paul Owens.

We now enter into a touchy area of journalism. Bill Giles, the Phillies' owner, had given me a revealing quote about something third baseman Mike Schmidt had said about Owens. I mentioned it to Schmidt, hoping he'd elaborate.

"He told you *that*—on the record?" said Schmidt.

I nodded.

"Do me a favor," he went on. "Don't use it."

I thought for several seconds: "Giles never said it was off the record, but if I use the quote I'll lose Schmidt as a valuable source."

"O.K.," I said. Whereupon Schmidt gave me a juicy quote of his own. Unfortunately, he explicitly labeled it off the record. Wulfie, in town to do a feature on George Hendrick of the Cardinals, was standing nearby.

When Wulfie and I were alone, I asked him, "Should I use the quote and attribute it to an unnamed player?"

"Go back to Schmidt," he said. "If he doesn't want it attributed to a player and you agree with it, use it yourself."

"Tell you what," said Schmidt. "Forget that quote. Here's one you can use on the record." And he gave me a good, if more tactful criticism of Owens' constantly changing lineups: "If [Outfielders] Matthews, Maddox and Hayes were in the lineup, we could win. Matthews struggled and Maddox was hurt, and Dernier and LeFebvre came in and did a good job. At that point the manager has to make a decision. I'm not sure one was ever made. It was a bad decision for [fired manager] Pat Corrales, and I'm not sure it's good now, but if we had an astute guy who wasn't so concerned about making people happy, we might be doing better." A bit convoluted, but the last part plainly identifies Schmidt's unhappiness with Owens.

When a player says "off the record," he's saying, "This is for your knowledge, but don't print it." Sometimes I'll ask the guy if I can use the quote "not for attribution." That means I quote him as an unnamed source. Obviously, it's better to get a quote from someone you can't name than not to get a quote at all. But a quote from a named source has more credibility still.

Actually the OTR-NFA situation is more complicated than that. When people aren't speaking for publication, they usually aren't speaking for *immediate* publication. If a labor or management source gives me off-the-record information during negotiations, for instance, I can often use it during a strike or after a settlement.

Some off-the-record information, however, is just that. Why would people give me information I can't use? Three reasons. First, they like and trust me enough to share a confidence. Ha. Second, they're buttering me up by showing me what regular fellows they are. The goal: More favorable coverage. Third, they're trying to influence my judgment by giving me a point of view they won't have to defend publicly. That's why I'm not always grateful for off-the-record information.

6 The Phillies' manager–general manager, Paul Owens, is the last of a dying breed: the fulltime baseball man. "I don't like people who don't like to talk baseball 24 hours a day," he says.

Owens is so wrapped up in the game that he's had to cut down on activities that traditionally blend with the baseball lifestyle—hunting, golf and drinking. "I'll tell you what it means to be a 24-hour-a-day baseball man," says chief scout Hugh Alexander, whom Owens pointedly introduces as his right-hand man (Alexander lost his left hand in an oil-well accident). "You hate to say this, but you kind of neglect your family. You get up in the morning and you look at every name in every box score. You make phone calls for hours. You go to the park and you aren't through until midnight or one. It's a 16–18 hour day, seven days a week."

"I've been to about 155 games a year for the last 11 years," says Owens. "I never thought you could do the job by seeing half the games, and you have to see the players under adverse conditions, which means before hostile crowds. After the season there's no relaxing until the winter meetings are over, and then it's only for a week. I go to the general man-

agers' meetings, the re-entry draft and the instructional
leagues, do some dinners and signings, and before you know
it, February's around and it's time for spring training. Sure, I
work weekends, but I wouldn't want to be one of those people on the freeways, hating their jobs."

Owens speaks volumes about the appeal of baseball.
Here's an intelligent man who lives in a self-contained universe. Why should he shield himself from other experiences?
Because baseball is so endlessly fascinating that it provides a
lifetime of thrills and insights.

I was discussing baseball's appeal with Ira Berkow the
other night. "Football's too violent," he said. "Hockey's
played by foreigners and is also too violent. Basketball is
angst—all that suffering written on the faces of men playing
in their underwear. But baseball. . . ."

He didn't have to finish: The events of the season speak for
him. Last week the Yankees' Dave Winfield was arrested in
Toronto when one of his warm-up tosses accidentally killed a
seagull. (The charges were subsequently dropped.)

And there's the pine-tar incident, which grows more interesting by the day. In the aftermath of MacPhail's historic decision, New York owner George Steinbrenner declared, "If the
Yankees lose by one game, I wouldn't want to be Lee Mac-
Phail living in New York. Maybe he'd better go house-
hunting in Kansas City." This statement is sure to draw a stiff
fine from the Commissioner. Martin, now as petulant as ever,
has been calling the rule book "meaningless," lashing out at
the umpires, and instigating arguments over obscure and
poorly written regulations. MacPhail has suggested that the
game be resumed on August 18, an off-day for both clubs,
with the Royals leading 5–4 and two outs in the top of the
ninth. "I'd rather forfeit," says Steinbrenner. "Lee has made
enough of a mess of this. I'm not letting him take an off-day
from my players."

Stay tuned.

august

7 Owens' 24-hour approach has me thinking about the subject of managers. The younger skippers aren't as single-minded as Owens and his contemporaries. Tony LaRussa has a law degree. Rene Lachemann, who was baseball's youngest manager before the Mariners fired him recently, goes to museums and theaters. Neither man—both are in their 30's—would say that his other interests limit him as a manager. On the contrary, he'd say they keep him fresh.

A manager has three primary functions: relating to the players, scouting the opposition and planning for a game. Most managers take scouting reports seriously. I think there are some basic differences between older and younger managers in the other two areas.

The younger manager relates, or tries to relate to each player as an individual. He listens sympathetically to a player's concerns. If he's not threatened, he'll even listen to a player's advice. Older managers are generally more authoritarian. Even when they try to relate, there's a certain distance they have to overcome because of the generation gap.

When it comes to strategy, older guys tend to manage by the book. That is to say, they'll invariably bat a lefthanded batter against a righthanded pitcher, or bring in a lefthanded pitcher to face a lefthanded batter. This is seat-of-the-pants managing. A younger manager, who is more likely to use charts of past player performance, won't automatically go by the book. If a certain lefthanded batter is hot against a certain lefthanded pitcher—or is hot, period—he'll go with him.

Not that younger managers are invariably preferable to older managers. Some older men, such as Whitey Herzog, Dick Williams and Earl Weaver, used charts long before the practice was fashionable. Others—Chuck Tanner, Tommy Lasorda and Sparky Anderson come immediately to mind—have the kind of Panglossian or personal or professional approach that seems to work with players of all ages. And all managers need good players. Hall of Fame pitcher Warren

Spahn played for Casey Stengel as a Brave in the 1940s and as a Met in the 1960s. In between, Stengel managed the Yankees. "I played for Casey before and after he was a genius," Spahn used to say.

To me, the overriding factor is "chemistry." You won't find the baseball definition of chemistry in the dictionary, so I'll try to explain it myself. Baseball chemistry is the disparate parts of a team melding harmoniously. It's players from 25 different backgrounds somehow coexisting for 162 games. It's players accepting their roles and performing them well—even if the role is to play utility infielder or bullpen catcher. It's the right combination of pitching, speed, defense and hitting.

The current Yankees are a good example of a team that lacks chemistry. There's actually too much talent—too many guys who should be starting and can't accept lesser roles. And I wonder how long any team playing for George Steinbrenner can maintain personal chemistry. The Orioles appear to have it: a hands-off owner, a low-key manager and players who get along and complement each other's skills. Manager Joe Altobelli's artful platooning in left field, for instance, has created an all-star composite out of several average players.

I can't seem to start a story without using an anecdote. Here's what I tried this week:

"Stranger than truth, stranger than fiction, stranger even than the pine-tar-covered seagull that resigned as Commissioner last week is the 1983 season of the Philadelphia Phillies."

I stuck with this lead until midnight, when I was putting the final touches on the story. Then it hit me:

1) This lead is too free-form for as ordered an editor as Rudeen.

2) I'm taking a long time to get to Owens.

So I substituted an anecdote about Owens, who is trying to wear two pairs of symbolic shoes (manager and G.M.) and was given a real pair in St. Louis that didn't fit. I told myself not to worry, that Ron Fimrite, the best pure writer on the magazine, uses an anecdotal lead in almost every story.

But now that I've filed, I'm having second thoughts. Let's face it, I substituted a pretty straight lead for a pretty funny one. But what really bothers me is not so much my decision as the fact that I made it to suit someone else. This isn't being free and easy and natural, as I was in early June. It's a warning signal.

8   My file on the Commissioner was used as a short Scorecard, and the Owens story was postponed. On Sunday the editors decided to dispatch Wulfie to Hagerstown, Maryland, where the Orioles' Jim Palmer is rehabilitating an arm injury while pitching in Class A. Today was his first start there. Admittedly, an interesting story: a probable Hall-of-Famer returning to the low minors.

9   I'm in Cincinnati doing a story on the Dodgers' troubles, which come in many forms: freak injuries, a pitcher recovering from drug addiction, old players out and new players in, position switches. An interesting story, but the highlight of today's game was something that happened in the pressbox.

Baseball writers have numerous means for avoiding boredom. Tonight Joe Minster of the *Hamilton (O.) Journal-News* and UPI won the pressbox attendance pool. His guess was 14,069. The actual attendance was 14,069. Normally everyone pays $1 apiece, $2 if the winner is within 100 of the actual figure. On the nose? Everyone pays $5. This had never happened before in Cincinnati, and I'm glad I was there to report it for posterity. "Couldn't have happened to a nicer guy," Joe said.

10

Jimmy Potash, a summer intern from Yale, is with me on
this assignment. Eager beaver that he is, Jimmy had lots of
questions. I took him from interview to interview, and before
long he was talking with players on his own. I figured Jimmy
would have some fresh observations, and I asked him to free-
associate. Consider the following a seventh-inning stretch in
this journal. Jimmy's report:

A spanking clean plastic stadium! Located not in some Italian
neighborhood where the smell of pizza permeates the air, nor in a
suburban setting where fields appear naturally—the Cincinnati
stadium lies smack in the middle of downtown. Within this perfectly
round structure are plastic green seats, and plastic blue seats—red
plastic too. Call me a romantic. I still like to mudslide on a rainy
summer day. I still like natural fields. Grass and dirt stains enable
you to tell the hustling players from those who never got in the
game. When a player dives for a sinking liner in the power alley on
this technofield, he gets up with shiny white pants that remain
attractive for the TV cameras.

It's just as well. Dirty pants and cleats might soil the plush carpet
of the Cincinnati clubhouse—and would spoil the look of wealth.
This clubhouse should be a retreat for bank executives, a place
where fat, middle-aged men rolling in dollars go in the late
afternoon to get rubdowns and bake in a sauna. But at those retreats
executives avoid the people who've pestered them all day. For athletes, pestering begins in the clubhouse. I guess being pestered as he
pulls off his jockstrap is the price Johnny Bench pays for the privi-
lege of undressing in luxury. In a plastic carpeted room stocked with
Snickers bars, Cokes, chicken, spaghetti.

I'm slightly ill at ease. Why? Because I'm among important people—to the sportswriter at least—and no one wants to make a fool of
himself in front of important people. Because I'm young and may
look as if I don't know what the hell I'm doing (that would be a false
impression, of course). Because I'm scared to death of asking a
stupid question. To Steve Sax: "Don't a first baseman and a second
baseman have to adjust to each other's timing and style?" It's not a
dumb question but it yields only a stock reply of the "I just go out
there and give 110%" variety. Questions may be too obvious. They

august

may have been asked 4,089 times before—"So, Steve Sax, I guess you've been having some throwing problems?" Or a question may reveal my ignorance, as when I asked Pedro Guerrero to talk about his success at the plate this season. He grumbled something about having been in a slump for ten games and walked away. Then there are the overly sensitive questions. It occurs to me that a guy might not be favorably disposed to revealing his inner-most secrets to a kid he met six minutes ago—a kid who intends to share those secrets with three million *Sports Illustrated* readers across America.

But interviewing is actually more like batting practice than like facing a Nolan Ryan fastball. You approach a player with a friendly smile and begin with some innocuous comments about the nice catch he made the day before, and the guy will probably have something to say. I saw Dan Driessen was chuckling so I approached him. He was friendly and willing to chat. Unfortunately, though, I uncovered no soul-deep secrets.

The athletes seem as confused about how much to divulge to the press as I am about how deeply to pry. They know they have a responsibility to answer questions and they know that the press can make them more popular and help them to the promotional opportunities that accompany success. Yet many players want privacy, to dance naked after a victory without being observed, to sulk after a ninth-inning strikeout without being required to recount their moment of ignominy. Thus, there's a conflict over their status of important person.

Dodger catcher Steve Yeager seems to enjoy toying with the idea of being an important person. I think he knows the importance can be overblown and serious analysis sometimes borders on the absurd. Because of an injury, he had sat in the mezzanine during the game with the task of suggesting defensive adjustments the Dodgers might make. I asked him if he'd arrived at any insights.

"That's top secret information!" Yeager bellows. "That's like asking the Russians if they see any MX missiles." He walks away and I—dutifully taking down anything colorful—begin scribbling away. He comes back, sees me writing, and shouts "Are you writing that down? Don't you write that down about the MX missiles. If you write that I'll sue your ass. *Sports Illustrated*'s got money. I know that. You can't just come in here and start writing things down without asking questions." Oh, no. He's challenging my journalistic method. He's spotted my weakness. Am I doing something wrong? Have I violated THE CODE? Yeager points his finger menacingly at my face. I figure he must be kidding around with the kid. But as he continues, my fear deepens. Is this guy out of his mind? Can he possibly mean it—suing the magazine?

He walks away. As I leave the clubhouse several minutes later, he smiles at me and says "I couldn't let you go without giving you a hard time. I was just kidding."

The shy, sensitive type would not fare well in the baseball clubhouse. Tom Lasorda used "fuck" three times in one sentence. One guy in the Reds' clubhouse let loose a thunderous belch. No problem here. The guy will continue to belch whether or not he's in the public eye. Just as Steve Howe, the Dodger reliever-turned-recovering-coke-abuser, had his drugs despite the seeming restriction of the scrutiny given his private life. He looks maybe a few years older than I. He's a kid with a great left arm, and for it he makes several hundred thousand a year. That's a lot of money to figure out what to do with. If I had so much so young, I'd probably spend some of it on drugs, too.

Being in the Reds' pressbox is a mind-altering experience. It alters a reporter's perception of the game. Now I know how the astronauts felt when they looked out at the earth from the isolation of their space ships. In the glass-enclosed, air-conditioned pressbox, I hear no vendors hawking peanuts and beer, no fans screaming obscenities at umpires, no roar of approval for the hometown hero. At least the astronauts didn't have to look out on an artificial earth.

We flew to Atlanta with the Dodgers. With some free time **12** before a Saturday night game, Jimmy and I visited with one of my college roommates, Jeff Koplan. A medical epidemiologist, Jeff is the assistant director of the Centers for Disease Control. He has traveled widely on the job, touching down in such places as China and Bangladesh. His wife Carol is a child psychiatrist, and their kids, Adam, 10, and Kate, 6, are a delight. We had a relaxed breakfast with the Koplans and a swim at their club. An enjoyable interlude for us; strictly routine for them. Maybe life *is* easier in the South.

14   It was fun having Jimmy Potash along. Fun because I enjoyed his company. Fun because I may have told him a few things he didn't know about sports and sportswriting. Fun because he gave me some good quotes.

One thing that amazes me about the Dodgers is their concern over image. They still contend that Steve Garvey left them, not vice-versa. "We offered him $5 million over four years," says Manager Tom Lasorda. Actually, the Dodgers refused to talk contract seriously until the middle of the 1982 season and tendered the $5 million offer only after Garvey made it clear he was leaving.

More image. According to a beat writer, the Dodgers were afraid Lasorda's expletives would show up on somebody's underground tapes, so they told him to keep a tight rein on his language. He finally let loose this week when he closed the clubhouse doors and blew up at his players.

More image still. As I passed Lasorda on the team bus, he turned to Howe and said of me, "He works for *Sports Illustrated*, you know." Tommy's impressed with glitz, real or imagined. I like him, but I wish, just once, that he'd bring a bricklayer into the clubhouse.

The Dodgers are good interviews when they're going well, uncomfortable when they're going poorly. "These guys are afraid of their shadows," the beat writer told me. "They're always saying, 'Don't get me in trouble.' "

We returned to New York to discover that the Dodger story won't run. They took their second series in ten days from the NL West–leading Braves, so my "What's-wrong-with-the-Dodgers?" approach won't work. No matter. The Phils are still in first, and the Owens story is running instead.

I walked into Larry's office for my weekly assignment. **15**
"What do you throw on a 3-and-2 count, bases loaded in the
ninth?" he asked. "You *challenge* the hitter!"

I didn't get his point. He walked away from his desk and
motioned for me to sit down in his place. "You're editing this
week while I'm on vacation," he said.

A chill went through me. Now I won't be able to rage
blindly at the editors: I'll be one. "I'm going to meet the Devil
himself," I said.

I know this much: Editing at *Sports Illustrated* involves more
than putting paragraph marks on stories. An editor may get a
story at 10 A.M. on Sunday, shudder and have to rewrite. It's
a very creative process. (I don't think I'll have to rewrite this
week. The column will be written by Ed Swift and the lead by
Wulfie. We're talkin' major talent here.)

But story editing is just a small part of the baseball editor's
job. Larry went over some other functions: fitting the stories
to space; reading every Inside Pitch suggestion that comes
from correspondents and going over them with Herm Weiskopf before he writes up the best ones; fitting Inside Pitch on
Sunday night (a job not unlike solving a jigsaw puzzle); writing captions and heads; planning future issues and talking to
writers.

After Larry switched from writing to editing in 1980, I
wrote a "publisher's letter" describing him. Some of his
quotes are worth repeating now:

A writer is like an independent contractor. You know the subject
inside out and write the story, but you have little to do with it after it
gets to the office. An editor, on the other hand, may not be as close
to the subject but handles the story every other step of the way.

I had to adjust to less travel and being desk-bound, but I found
that there were more than adequate compensations. I've been able
to lead a more orderly life with my family, and I've discovered that
editing offers its own creative challenges. Deciding what's to be

covered, for instance, and when and where it will run in the magazine. . . .

I have found that the best thing about editing is its total involvement in the publishing process: helping to choose pictures and layouts, assigning stories, discussing ideas, planning special issues. As a writer, I didn't fully appreciate how much goes into putting out the magazine. Now I do.

What are the qualifications for an editor? Well, let's consider Larry Keith, one of our most respected senior editors. He got ahead the old-fashioned way: He earned it. A professional journalist since he began covering high-school football for the *Charlotte (N.C.) News* at age 16, Larry was the sports editor of the University of North Carolina *Daily Tar Heel* his junior year and the sports director of a Chapel Hill radio station his senior year. After graduation he took a job as an investigative reporter for a Charlotte radio station and won a National Headliner Club award for Public Service (radio broadcasting) as a result of a five-part series on the jailing of indigent mental patients. When he came to Atlantic City to accept the award, he took the bus to New York for an interview with Merv Hyman, the magazine's chief of research. Larry was hired shortly afterwards and went to work a month before I did in 1970.

Five years later Larry became our youngest (27) staff writer at the time. He covered baseball and two college sports, basketball and football, for five years before becoming our youngest senior editor (32) at the time. On the side he was a frequent panelist on a weekly cable TV show, "Sports Probe," which is no longer on the air.

Don't panic, editors-to-be: It's not necessary to duplicate Larry's considerable achievements. I'd say the prerequisites are as follows: the ability to write well (obviously necessary for rewriting); the selflessness to care for copy someone else will receive credit for; the creativity to envision ingenious stories and write clever headlines and captions, and the ability to keep your head while all those about you are losing theirs. "I think it's mainly the responsibility to put into the magazine someone else's story and layout and pictures and research, and bring them all together," Larry says. "In all those roles you're advising, and in some cases you're doing original work yourself. Mainly the position is giving approval. What you like about it is when you see an idea—your own or someone else's—well executed. As far as the public's concerned, you're in the background. At the magazine you have respect commensurate with the responsibility. There are lines of authority, and one person has to oversee the story, just as one person has to oversee the magazine. But I don't see myself as being anybody's boss. The whole notion of the magazine is working together."

A part of me loves the idea of editing: no travel; no agony of writing; no putting myself on the line and getting people mad at me and interviewing players who don't want to talk; no fear of getting a story killed.

But another part of me dreads editing. I'll be in the office five consecutive days starting Thursday, and I'll probably be up all night Sunday. Writing is risky, but there's some freedom attached; editing is safer, but the style of life is more predictable. What I keep telling myself is that editing will help me as a writer: Know that Devil.

I got a taste of editing when Larry led me through some steps of a typical Monday. The editors had already decided that Wulfie would do the lead on the Yankees. Larry wanted to do the column on the half-dozen rookie pitchers the A's are using. He called in Swiftie, and we went over the idea. Larry told Swiftie to emphasize the "Gee-ain't-it-great-to-be-in-the-majors" angle, and I pointed out that *The New Yorker* had just run a Roger Angell story on A's president Roy Eisenhardt, who figures to be a good source. Larry and I walked over to the office of the picture editor, Barbara Henckel, and suggested that we get group pictures of the six rookies and the four of them in the rotation, as well as individual shots.

Late in the afternoon acting managing editor Ken Rudeen

and assistant managing editor Mark Mulvoy decided that a column on Mets reliever Jesse Orosco would be more timely, since Orosco hasn't allowed a run since the last Ice Age. (This creates a situation Larry wanted to avoid: two stories on New York teams.) Still thinking like a writer, I was relieved for Swiftie; it's much easier to write about one player than six. Swiftie was amenable to the change, although he'd already made reservations for a flight to Oakland and looked through the A's file. "My head is spinning," he said. Par for a Monday afternoon.

At 6 P.M.—closing time—I realized I had forgotten to give Barbara Henckel some details about the new picture assignment. I streaked around and finally tracked her down at a cocktail party for summer interns on the eighth floor.

My head was spinning, too.

18 The first full day in the life of an *SI* editor:

10 A.M. The Yankee cover originally assigned to Wulfie may not fly, Ken Rudeen tells me, because the Yankees have lost three straight and putative cover subject Dave Winfield hasn't hit. I tell Wulfie to hang loose.

11 A.M. I go to a color showing. When rolls of photos arrive at the Time-Life Building, picture researchers choose a few dozen favored "selects" and make slides of them. Then the slides are shown at a meeting attended by the M.E., representatives of the photo and art (layout and drawings) departments, the editor in charge of the story (me), the story's fact-checker and, if available, the writer. They're showing pictures of both the Yankees and Alan Trammell–Lou Whitaker, the Tigers' double-play combination story that Wulfie was putting the finishing touches on. "Take *that*," Rudeen keeps saying. I finally realize that he is ordering removal of a slide from the carrousel for further consideration.

Everyone agrees that the pictures aren't very good. Whitaker has a dazzling smile that doesn't show up and

Trammell has a bad complexion that does. So the Tigers have to be reshot. Alas, they're playing in the Minnydome, where the lighting is terrible.

Noon. A meeting in Rudeen's office to plan the issue. They're talking about the cover. It would be nice to shoot Greg Louganis at the Pan-Am Games, but divers don't photograph very well, especially for covers. How about football? Well, a name team, Dallas, is an obvious choice, but the Cowboys don't play until 9 P.M. Saturday. Pretty late to shoot, and that stadium with the hole on top isn't very promising for pictures at any hour. "What about Miami-Washington—the Super Bowl revisited?" asks pro football editor Joe Marshall. "And it's Friday, so we'll know where we stand Saturday." Mulvoy thinks Dallas is a better story, what with its drug troubles and generally declining image. Baseball still looks grim photowise: Maybe we can shoot Trammell-Whitaker outside the Minnydome. As for the Yankees, we're considering reducing the lead to a column on the conclusion of the Pine-Tar Game—if they decide to play it tonight. The Yankees and their fans just got an injunction, but the American League is appealing, with six hours to gametime.

After the meeting I speak with Swiftie about the Orosco column; with Ron Fimrite about the Cecil Cooper feature he's writing; and with Bill Nack about a story Mark Mulvoy thinks he should write on the final days of Johnny Bench and Carl Yastrzemski. People keep asking me to do things. If I don't write them down immediately, I'll forget. My head's spinning.

2 P.M. The photo department needs to know if we're doing a studio shot of Trammell-Whitaker. I see Rudeen in the hallway and ask him. "Why don't we wait until people get back from lunch to discuss what kind of picture we need—three or three-fifteenish," he says.

I'm thinking, "What does he mean by 'three or three-fifteenish'—some term for picture-size?" So I say, "I don't know what that means."

august

"The time of day—when people get back from lunch."

3 P.M. We have another cover meeting. When to shoot Trammell-Whitaker? "Let's go outside," says Mulvoy. "Maybe we can shoot them at the University of Minnesota. Of course, they don't like us over there." I assume he's referring to a celebrated story we wrote blasting Minnesota's basketball program.

Rudeen: "One thing we've got to be careful of is how we shoot it. If it's on a sandlot somewhere, we'll have to shoot straight down on them to retain the major-league look."

I put in that maybe we should shoot them around a base— the old DP combination, remember. It looks as though we'll shoot them both as a posed shot and in action, and on both Friday and Saturday. I'm amazed that everyone is interested in my opinion; they're treating me as if I've been editing for years.

5 P.M. Things change very quickly around here. Lane Stewart, the photographer assigned to do the next round of Trammell-Whitaker shots, argues convincingly for a studio pose. "Shooting down on people is very difficult to bring off," he says, "and the subjects look foreshortened."

A few minutes later Rudeen calls me into his office for perhaps the sixth time today ("Why don't you come around?"). He's decided that the Pine-Tar Game, now scheduled to be completed in an hour with the AL having won its appeal, will be this week's column. I call Wulfie to tell him to write it. Orosco can run later, as will the A's pitchers.

I feel, unsurprisingly, like a man after his first day at a new job: trying to keep up without looking too stupid. The good part: I didn't have to panic and wonder how to bring off the Pine-Tar Game as a story. The bad part: I don't like getting up early and spending an entire day at the office. I never denied I was spoiled.

I'm also getting a useful insight. Based on what happened today, I'm starting to doubt the existence of a draconian conspiracy against me or any other writer: There just isn't time. In thinking about what works best for a given issue, the editors may understandably forget that a writer has been on the road for ten consecutive weeks or hasn't published in awhile. I suppose we writers would have fewer complaints if there were a fulltime editor whose only duty was to puff up our pillows. Barring that pipe dream, I better start thinking more about the magazine and less about myself.

The Pine-Tar Game concluded last night with the greatest **19** moment of the season. Let's pick up from Wulfie's story:

As the game resumed, George Frazier, the Yankee pitcher, threw to first base on an appeal play; the Yankees were claiming that Brett had failed to touch first on his home-run trot 25 days earlier. Umpire Tim Welke signaled safe. Frazier threw to second on another appeal, and Umpire Dave Phillips signaled safe, at which point Yankee Manager Billy Martin strode out of the dugout to argue. How could Phillips have known that Brett had touched first and second if he was working in Seattle on that long-ago day?

Phillips then produced a notarized letter from the original umpiring crew saying that both Brett and U. L. Washington, who was on base at the time of the homer, had touched all the sacks. It was a stroke of genius on the part of the American League. "Whoever thought of that should be the next commissioner," said [reliever Dan] Quisenberry.

Actually, MacPhail and his assistant, Bob Fishel, thought of it after having lunch with some Yankee officials a few weeks ago. Fishel had suggested that the Yankees promote the suspended game in a big way—little pine-tar bats and such—but the Yankees reacted in such negative fashion that Fishel and MacPhail realized that the Yankees had not yet begun to fight. So they anticipated the appeal and subsequently requested that Umpire Joe Brinkman's crew notarize a letter.

Here were two of the nicest men in baseball—MacPhail and Fishel—totally squelching George Steinbrenner and Billy Martin. As Wulfie wrote, the Yankees had blown a chance to make the most of their misfortune. Wulfie spelled out some ideas for spectacular promotions: Brett and Gossage playing Wiffle Ball before the game; minor-league teams being flown in to play a pre-game game; the little pine-tar bats. The game was played despite efforts by the Yankees (featuring their attorney, Roy Cohn of McCarthy-era fame), to postpone it. Behaving no better than their employers, Yankee players considered staging a combination forfeit and pool party at Gossage's house. The Royals, whose next game was scheduled to be played in Baltimore, were literally left up in the air while the case went to court. At 3:35 P.M. Justice Joseph P. Sullivan ordered the game completed. "As far as the stay," he said, "I can state it best in two words: 'Play ball.'"

What a scene it was! George Brett, long since booted from the original game, watched the resumption at the Spanish Tavern in Newark with Larry Ameche—a TWA rep and, yes, Don Ameche's son. The Yankees, spiteful to the end, had pitcher Ron Guidry in center and lefthanded Don Mattingly at second. Two fans, Jack and Dot Gunnells, drove 3½ hours from Atlantic City, where they were vacationing, to watch the game with 1,243 others. "The last time we were here was in 1956 when we saw Don Larsen pitch in the World Series," Jack told Wulfie. "So we've gone from a perfect game to a very imperfect game." The Royals won 5–4.

But back to the job at hand. For the first time, I attended the meeting held every Friday at 11:30 A.M. to plan the next six weeks' issues. For years the meeting was presided over by the now-retired Jeremiah Tax. Gabbing away, lingering over every detail, he could prolong the session for an hour and a half. "Jerry loved it," one senior editor told me. "He was in his element." Mark Mulvoy used to time the meeting, injecting quips every now and then, and that just egged Jerry on. Today Mark was in charge, and the meeting was over in half and hour.

First, we updated where we stood on this week's issue—possible columns, features, news stories, covers—with everything subject to change. We were given the week's fourth "mock-up," a sheet showing each page of the current issue and what's running on it. Early in the week a mock-up will show only the kind of story on a page—column, lead, etc.; later it will name the story by sport or subject. For any given issue, we'll get eight or more different mock-ups.

Then we went over the next six weeks' prospective issues. A six-week projection list comes out every weekend, with fewer and fewer stories listed for the later weeks. Nonetheless, Mark asked editors what they had in mind for their sports over the next six weeks. Fortunately, Larry had notified me what he had planned.

After the meeting my day didn't slacken. Fimrite called, Nack arrived to discuss the Yaz-Bench story, and Herm Weiskopf put an economic decision in my hands. It seems that Seymour Siwoff, the obstreperous boss of the Elias Sports Bureau, wanted $400 for some statistical research his computers could produce in a few hours. I had to decide whether to give in or drop the project. "Offer him $100," I said, Solomonlike. He accepted!

Having spent some time watching the Elias Bureau in action, Herm was more sympathetic to Siwoff than I. "Our guys should go over there to understand how complicated the process is." Herm said. He's undoubtedly right.

I've reached a similar conclusion: that all our writers should edit for a week, the better to understand what's being done to their stories.

I was so busy all day that I never got around to editing copy. I had to take home the stories that arrived today—Swiftie's Orosco column (which can be processed a week early to lighten next week's load), Wulfie's monster job on Trammell-Whitaker, and Herm's first few Inside Pitch items. Editing them was fun—a game. And it was satisfying when I could see that my changes had improved the stories. But I'm exhausted.

20   I had lunch with Audrey, Wulfie and California pitcher John Curtis, one of the brightest people in the game, and one of the most universal players. He has worked off-seasons as everything from a sportswriter for the *San Francisco Examiner* to a substitute teacher to a shoe salesman. He reads heavy novels, seeks out foreign movies and likes Billy Joel. Plainly, a man worth questioning on a variety of subjects.

Audrey asked him whether today's ballplayers are better prepared for life after baseball than previous generations. "With long-term contracts, you have time to think about the future," Curtis said. "Before, you played a year at a time. Suddenly, you were out of baseball, wondering what you'd do next."

How tough is it to stay in shape from year to year? "When I was young," said Curtis, now 35, "I'd relax all winter and get in shape in spring training. Now I have to keep in shape all year." I asked him to name the best manager he ever played for. "Joe Altobelli," he said unhesitatingly, citing the man's thoughtfulness and consideration. Altobelli, who managed Curtis in San Francisco, is now the Baltimore skipper.

"Baseball's something you pass through," John concluded. "I have to keep telling myself that how I play has nothing to do with what kind of person I am. Sometimes I find myself saying, 'I just gave up seven runs—am I that bad a guy?' You can't take it personally."

The day went surprisingly well. Part of the reason is that I wasn't working under much pressure. Because of the poor natural lighting in Minnesota, the second batch of Trammell-Whitaker action photos wasn't much better than the others. The story won't run this week; instead, the players will be shot in daylight next week. Meanwhile, I find that I've edited almost everything—the column and 90 percent of Inside Pitch—that will run this week.

On a normal Sunday an editor may be working on three or **21** four current or future stories. By all odds, I should have had an easy closing day. All I had to do was watch for Inside Pitch items and write some headlines and captions. Then why wasn't I out of the building until 4:30 A.M.? Well, because of vacations and leaves, there's a dearth of editors, and those in the building had to close the special football issue as well as the current one. But people kept telling me, "It's always like this."

One problem is that technological improvements have facilitated last-minute closings. The upshot is that the guy in charge can wait and wait and wait before deciding what to put in the issue and where. But I still can't understand why it took more than ten hours to close my captions. And I'm worried about how spending 18½ hours in this air-conditioned tomb called the Time-Life Building must affect people who do it almost every week.

To isolate my own case, I had about four hours of legitimate work. The rest of my time? Well, there was the usual fair fare in the cafeteria at lunchtime and the usual excellent catered meal for dinner. Otherwise, I must have watched eight or nine hours of movies and sports on the TV in Larry's office (all editors' offices have TV's). Fatigue came and passed, with waves of nausea and stomach pains. I had to wind down for an hour after leaving the building and still be up in time to make the 11 o'clock Monday meeting. "After a night like this, you're blown out all day Monday, and you don't really re-cover on Tuesday," an editor told me. On Wednesdays the editors receive a special delivery copy of the issue they just closed, and on Thursday they return to work. Everybody acknowledges that late closings have become a human problem. I think it's also a professional one. How creative can our editors be when they're practicing survival journalism? When I see Gil, I'll pass along these thoughts.

Meanwhile, I got another insight about the editing process. Sometime around 8 P.M. Sunday Ken Rudeen called me into his office. "Is the Orosco piece ready to run?" he asked.

"Well, sure," I said, "but what's wrong with the pine-tar story?"

"It doesn't make sense to me," Ken said.

As it happened, there were only a couple of sentences that needed to be clarified. I can understand Ken's problem, though. He'd been working hard all day, and he was tired. The technical aspects of the story no doubt confused and irritated him. Because I was rested and familiar with the subject, it was easy for me to enlighten Ken. But there's a lesson here: Many of us writers feel there are times when senior editors should be more aggressive in speaking on behalf of our stories. How many stories have been killed because M.E.'s were tired and senior editors were hesitant?

For all my complaints, I'm still glad I edited. My name won't be on the stories, but my touch—a word change here, a headline there—will. In the future I'll be more sympathetic toward editors (though I still think they overedit) and more helpful with photographers (I can see now that I should have given our man more players to shoot at the College World Series).

All week people kept asking me, "How do you like editing?" No one was surprised when I answered, "It was useful, instructive and enlightening. And I was happy to do it—once."

22   As I write, Audrey and I are flying to Amsterdam for the last week of my vacation. We're going to Baarn, a small city outside of Amsterdam, because Audrey has friends there.

What a country! Our first contact was with the pleasant KLM flight attendants and the pilot, who talked like the Swedish Chef on "The Muppet Show." As the plane was landing, I looked out the window and though I saw the face of the moon with a few horses thrown in. I quickly realized I was being introduced to a thick Dutch fog.

O.K., let's get to the wooden shoes. "We are more than wooden shoes," says our host's sister, Agnes, who picked us up at the airport. But there's a reason some people still wear wooden shoes: Much of Holland is below sea level (hence, the Netherlands).

Unsurprisingly, vegetation is lush in this watery climate. Driving to Baarn, we saw fields criss-crossed by canals; cows and sheep grazing everywhere; just one windmill, and, thankfully, no mountains. My arbiter of taste, George Orwell, didn't like mountains.

Getting now to the people. Our host is Wil Nieuwenhuis, the foreign editor of *NRC Handelsblad,* one of the country's leading newspapers. Audrey met him when he was a TV news correspondent in New York. Wil lives in a striking modern house with his children Maartje, 16, and Dirk Jan, 13 (his wife, Annelies, died two years ago). They're spirited, engaging and international people. And organized: Wil has his days planned to the minute.

Before dinner Agnes and her friend Ad took us on another drive. We headed first to a polder, or reclaimed land from the sea. Whole cities are springing up on them.

The next stop was Breukelen, as in Brooklyn. What a lovely town is my borough's forebear! It has a nifty square, ancient houses lining narrow streets, mansions and cupolas on the river. The Breukelen Bridge is about twenty feet long. Naturally, I bought postcards.

Back at Wil's we had dinner consisting of a herring appetizer and excellent pan-fried sole, then drove to a lake for coffee at sunset.

august

I'm already in love with Holland. It's one of the most densely populated countries in the world, yet one of the most livable. Every house seems to have a garden. Nothing looks garish. No one appears to be poor or sick. Even old people ride bikes. Hell, the doughty little kingdom once went to the finals of the World Cup in soccer.

Is Holland too good to be true?

23 We spent the day in Amsterdam, where we took a canal ride, visited the Anne Frank House and wound up at the Van Gogh Museum. Impressions: Beautiful city, mostly medieval, Venetian in parts, with many narrow houses (rent was once charged by width), few of more than four stories.

24 If it's Thursday, it must be Belgium. Wil drove us to his office in Rotterdam and we took his Alfa-Romeo to Brugge, a Medieval city in Flemish Belgium known for its history and French-fried potatoes. We found a local cafe and had a lunch consisting of pommes frites and steak. A very American meal, yes-non? But also a very Belgian one.

Once a commercial center, Brugge was surpassed by Ghent and Antwerp and Brussels. While the others grew and changed and were bombed in wars, Brugge maintained its character: the town square and central marketplace, the guild halls, the old buildings, the narrow streets, the canals.

Flemish (Dutch) Belgium is more French than Dutch in character. Among other things, there's the two-hour lunch break, and people don't speak English.

25 Wil got a friend to lend me some clubs, and I played nine holes at the Hilversum Golf Club. It was as impressive and attractive as many a private U.S. course, with intelligently planned, challenging holes and undulating fairways lined by purple heather. I played as I usually do on an unfamiliar course with unfamiliar clubs: butchering the first two holes and playing the last seven in maybe six over par.

In the afternoon we visited a Dutch TV studio and saw a documentary Wil did on the 1972 U.S. elections. Audrey, then an elementary-school teacher in East Harlem, was featured. Typically, foreigners often see us more clearly than we do. Wil caught the mood of America by asking simple, open-ended questions and letting the interviewee do the talking. He asked a drug dealer why heroin proliferated in America. "Profits," the guy said. A conservative Texan told Wil he was voting for Nixon because he didn't want to wreck the free-enterprise system and destroy incentive. East Harlem, meet Texas.

6   It could have been a kids' soccer league in Greenwich, Connecticut: tow-headed kids chasing a ball toward a goal. Only it was the Baarn mixed field-hockey league, and Dirk Jan was trying out for the olde town team. Depending on his performance, he would either make the A, B or C team.

He did well and scored a goal, but I was surprised that neither he nor his teammates celebrated. "We were playing against our friends," he said. "It would have been different in another town." But American kids would have been celebrating with high-fives.

In the afternoon Audrey and I visited the Kroller-Moeller Museum. It's set in the middle of a national park, and it blends in perfectly. Indeed, with its glass walls and outdoor sculptures, one becomes confused: Where does indoor end and outdoor begin?

At night we took the train—they're all on-time—to Amsterdam, had a splendid Indonesian dinner and heard some good jazz at Cab Kaye's Piano Bar.

august

27   If it's Sunday, it must be Great Britain. We had decided to spend the whole day traveling. Wil drove us to Utrecht, and we took a train to the Hook of Holland for a 6½-hour trip to Harwich. Ah, the Hook of Holland! All week we'd been having fun with the name, playing on it, expanding on it. The red-light district in Amsterdam houses the Hookers of Holland. The Netherlands are flat; that's the Look of Holland. A scandal in the royal family suggests the Crook of Holland. And the Bible is—what else—the Book of Holland. Journalist's humor.

   We had first-class seats on the boat, and we saw "Superman III" and some British television. But mainly we thought about Holland. The real appeal, I think, is that it's so peaceful. I want challenge and excitement in my life, and I'll accept dislocation at times, but I'm sick of the arguing and fighting and bickering. Maybe there's no other choice in a pluralistic society. Holland isn't perfect. Dutch artists are heavily subsidized, and as far as I can see they don't accomplish much unless they leave the country (have you ever seen a Dutch movie?). And when the unemployed aren't required to take work unless it pays as well as their last job, some incentive is lost. (On the other hand, Holland 's so tension-free precisely because people are taken care of.) But my unrest is apolitical. I'm just sick of constant competition and confrontation—in every phase of life. I'd rather see—and write about—people working together.

29   Audrey's friend Trevor Taylor met us at Harwich and drove us four hours to Stone, Staffordshire. I thought I knew a great deal about Great Britain. I knew only about London. For openers, I had no idea how many canals there are. "The Dutch use them for irrigation, we use them for travel," says Trevor, who teaches international relations at a polytechnic institute. "When they were built, the cost of transportation dropped from 10 to 1½ pence a mile. People forget that in the old days it was much easier to travel by water than land, what with muddy roads and highwaymen."

In the new days the reverse is true. Canals are narrow and interspersed with locks. A favorite British vacation is to take a "long boat" up the canals. These narrow wooden boats aren't permitted to travel at speeds in excess of four miles per hour, and much time is spent lifting and lowering them through the locks. No matter. People travel leisurely, stopping at pubs by the bank.

Then there's British sport. Or perhaps I should say, British-American sport. The fact is, almost every sport we play was either derived from a British sport, or was invented or popularized by the British. I was happy to hear this because I was raised to be an extreme anglophile. On the links or at the billiard table, my parents and I were always saying "*Shot,* suh." (I don't know if that's a British expression, but it sounds British.)

Trevor gave me some background. The British have been sporting sorts ever since the Middle Ages, when games became the focal points of village celebrations and religious holidays. As intervillage competitions began, governing bodies were set up to formalize rules. The result was two important features of British sport: friendly competition followed by a pint in the pub, and rigorous organization. The following international sports are headquartered in Great Britain: badminton; cricket; billiards; snooker; darts; curling; croquet; European horseracing; tennis; rugby; sailing and table tennis. Several other headquarters were transferred from Britain to neutral countries in times of war.

British sport, I was sorry to hear, owes its grov th largely to unappetizing aspects of British civilization: imperialism and the class system. The British exported sport as well as the tea hour. If the French saw their colonies' captive soldiers as mere mercenaries, the British viewed their own as part of a "regi-

august

mented family," according to Tony Clayton, a graduate student at the University of London who published a paper Trevor showed me called "Sport and African Soldiers." Like other family members, British colonials underwent athletic training to learn such virtues as fitness, discipline and esprit de corps. To this day polo is played in Nigeria—by Nigerians. Sports was an important feature of racial reconciliation when Rhodesia became Zimbabwe. Australians used sport to build their national identity.

As for the class system, the gentry had always been physically active. During the Industrial Revolution, the lower classes were encouraged to take up sport, although not always for the most benevolent of reasons. "Some of the first working-class teams were founded by churches, chapels and footballing philanthropists who believed that football [soccer] could also be used to moralize the lower orders and weaken the attachment to the demon drink," Christopher Andrew wrote in the May, 1982, issue of another publication Trevor showed me, *History Today.* And between 1880 and 1914 the middle classes took to sports, especially golf.

Every British male seems to play cricket or rugby, or at least darts or dominoes at the pub. The Taylors—Trevor, his smashing, German-born wife Petra Schlupp, and their children Eleanor, Jessica and Edward—took us to a village cricket game. The sport is even more leisurely than canal-riding. I can't get into the rules, which I barely understand, but some basics will suffice. The batter doesn't have to swing at a pitch, unless he's afraid it'll hit the wicket behind him for an out. And once he's hit the ball, he doesn't have to run to the next wicket unless he's sure he'll make it. How is he retired? Most often, as far as I can tell, by hitting a ball that's caught on the fly. The British wonder when we'll score in baseball; we wonder when they'll make an out in cricket.

Dressed in long white pants and sweaters, cricket players conduct their games for five and six hours at a time, breaking for drinks, lunch and tea (yes, how civilized). Like baseball, the sport features little action and much reflection. I also learned the meaning of "sticky wicket." The wicket is not only the hard wooden object behind the batter, but the hard grassy strip between him and the pitcher, or bowler. With a straight-armed motion, the bowler throws the ball to the batter on a bounce off the grass. A firm wicket will produce a relatively uniform bounce, while a sticky wicket creates a high or low one.

A major difference between baseball and cricket, I think, has to be the level of fear. A baseball batter may be hit by a pitch, but a cricket batter is certain to be. Guarding the wicket, he takes a terrible pounding, face mask and shin guards notwithstanding.

The next day I played my first round of British golf and lost four balls. Usually I don't lose any. On a British course the rough is everywhere, including the middle of the fairway, and is very heavy. Hit a ball in and wave good-bye.

After dinner one night, we stopped at a local pub for drinks and dominoes. Two surprises: shandies, which are a nifty mixture of lemonade and beer; and the many wonders of dominoes. In England it's a spirited and competitive game. Each piece has from zero to six dots on each end. The idea of the British-version game is to place a piece on the board so that the outside dots in the line of dominoes add up to multiples of three and five. People usually play with partners, and there's much signaling and jockeying. Petra and I beat Audrey and Trevor, and I grew loud and cheery and generally obnoxious in victory. Most un-British. "The British view of sport is that if you lose, you lose," Trevor said.

Some random nonsporting observations. The Taylors threw a dinner party and invited three other couples. Everyone was chatty and cheery. At one point a woman remarked that the weather had grown so hot people were wearing shorts to shop. Ah, the cheeriness of it all! "Here we are!" the

august

captain said as my Manchester-London plane landed today. "Why don't you pop over to the next counter?" said a British Airways rep. There's no skimping on food. I became bloated on three squares a day (not counting tea). In a small town like Stone, everyone has a garden. British TV is wonderful. I watched maybe four hours of sports and saw no commercials, little chitchat and much action.

The British countryside is as placid as Holland. I'm plenty familiar with the troubles of Great Britain, but only with the greatest trepidation do I return to the colonies. What do I fear? Chaos, corruption, cynicism, competition.

september

I figured the cheeriest way to face the U.S. of A. was to **2** think of nothing but baseball. On the plane I buried myself in box scores and standings and stats.

More updates, through games of September 1. In the AL: Randy Moffitt (6–2, 9 saves, 3.93 ERA); Buddy Bell (.279, 12 HR, 58 RBI); Bob Stanley (8–9, 26 saves, 3.03 ERA). In the NL: Dickie Thon (.298, 17 HR, 70 RBI, 17 game-winning RBI); Nolan Ryan (13–6, 145 K, 160⅓ IP, 2.36 ERA); Rose (131 G, 110 H, .248); Carlton (12–14, 229 K's in 240⅓ IP, 2.92 ERA).

Conclusions: Moffitt has tailed off badly. He'll be a free agent at season's end, but I'm not sure anyone will draft him (no one did). Stanley, overworked by the pathetic Bosox, has also tailed off. Thon, Ryan and Bell are continuing in form. Rose, after surging through July, has fallen back and probably won't be used in the final days of the division race or kept on the roster next season. O tempora, O mores.

Getting now to some of my main men. Since the All-Star break, Ron Kittle's power stats have dropped off precipitously, and Greg Walker's average has been plummeting. Kittle is a streaky hitter, so I'm pretty sure he'll recover. Walker lost his momentum during the All-Star break. He never really had a chance to get it back because Tom Paciorek has been on a tear. Greg will end the year as he played most of the first six weeks: as a deluxe pinch-hitter.

The best news is that Doug DeCinces has had fewer than 50 at-bats since the All-Star Game. I consider this good news because it means that he went on the disabled list and properly rested his aching body. If he can return, rested and repaired, to play well in September he'll be set for the free-agent sweepstakes.

4 My faith in America was somewhat restored in my first week back. The cab scene at Kennedy was as crazy as ever, but I wound up with a nice driver who took me on as a second customer and told me to name a price. And then I heard that Ken Moffett, executive director of the baseball players association, and American League president Lee MacPhail, soon to become chief owners' negotiator, are doing a joint study on the drug problem. Cooperation!

To my dismay, the office had no assignment for me. Fimrite and Wulf are doing an Atlanta-L.A. news package and a new staffer named Jaime Diaz is writing the column. I did speak daily with Ted Beitchman, the baseball editor during Larry's vacation, about doing a story for next week. I wanted to do Montreal centerfielder Andre Dawson, who is in contention for the Triple Crown. Mark Mulvoy, the managing editor during the last three months of Gil's absence, prefers next weekend's Pittsburgh-Philadelphia series. Since there will be a feature on Cecil Cooper next week, Mark wants to avoid another personality piece in the column area. Some writers feel we should be basing our decisions on news, not balance. Editors can't be purists, though. There are pictures, esthetics and advertising as well as content to contend with. To become an editor is to realize that life isn't simple.

5 My 13-year-old son Matthew L. Kaplan returned from a six-week trip to Spain, where he stayed with a family and picked up some Spanish. He's bigger, his voice has deepened and he's got a little mustache and a red streak in his hair. All in six weeks.

Plainly, it's time for a rite of passage. There's an architect with precisely the same name—Matthew L. Kaplan—who has an office in my neighborhood. For some time the boys have been joking about how we ought to introduce the two Matthew L. Kaplans. Today I called up Matthew L. Kaplan, architect. "I've got a son by the same name," I said.

"Are you kidding?" said Matthew L. Kaplan, architect. We immediately agreed to get together soon.

That, friends, was a good move.

7 I went to Shea Stadium, where the Mets and Phillies are playing, to get some background on the Philadelphia-Pittsburgh rivalry. Tug McGraw and Tim McCarver gave me some good information. I also found the Phillies in disarray. Third baseman Mike Schmidt and shortstop Ivan DeJesus are the only regulars. Yesterday Schmidt told an AP writer that the club was in a state of chaos. Today manager Paul Owens answered him through the press. This may prove to be a tempest in a teapot, but it raises some fundamental questions. Can a team win without the continuity of a consistent lineup? And is the NL East so weak that these mediocre Phillies can finish first? One of the problems with divisional play is that a team could win a division with a sub-.500 record. In 1973 the Mets, who were 82–79, won the NL East and went to the seventh game of the World Series.

9 The office staff took yesterday off to attend to U.S. Open tennis tournament. I declined to go and spent some time poring through the Phillie and Pirate files.

So what happened this morning? Minutes before I was scheduled to catch a cab for the airport, Larry called with a change of plans. "Go to Chicago and do the Cardinals," he said. "If they finish the weekend in first, the defending world champions are back. If they lose, they're in big trouble. If they don't drop back or go into first, they're hanging in. Anyway you look at it, you've got a story."

I was a little skeptical. The Cardinals as a team aren't very interesting. Even if the story is worth doing, which I doubt, I didn't figure to reach Wrigley Field until the last few innings of today's game. As it happened, Travel got me right on a plane, it reached Chicago early and I made it to Wrigley for the fifth inning. There followed a game perfectly illustrative of the Cardinal season—one replete with good plays from unexpected players, bad play from good players, freak injury and good and bad luck. The Cardinals won in extra innings. At least I'll have a lead.

If I can write it. As I was coming down the escalator at O'Hare, the Portabubble popped out of the luggage carrier, bounced down the steps and whacked some lady on the back of her leg. The good news is, she wasn't hurt and didn't sue. The bad news is, the computer doesn't work properly. I called the regional maintenance director of the Teleram company, and he said he would either have the thing fixed by Saturday night or leave me one of his. What surprised me was that during this crisis I didn't panic. Could it be that writing is no longer a life-or-death matter to me?

At night I dined with another college roommate, Chicago lawyer Ed Mogul. He brought along a University of Chicago professor named Allan Bloom, who had some probing questions about sports: Why are tennis players so badly behaved? And why are there so few blacks at baseball games? The easiest way to describe tennis behavior is to compare the sport with golf. In golf, parents raise kids to behave. There are tough rules to punish misbehavior, the players understand that the game is bigger than they are, and the role models are exemplary. In tennis, parents not only permit poor behavior but encourage it. The sport is poorly governed, with piddling punishments for poor sportsmanship, and the very players on whom kids model themselves feel they're bigger than the game. There's another important factor. In tennis, the players often come of age as athletes before they come of age as people: They have no time to mature.

The baseball question is much tougher, and I've never heard a satisfactory answer. Older blacks, who remember the Negro Leagues and Jackie Robinson, follow the game closely. Younger blacks are understandably more attracted to basketball because it has a larger percentage of black players than baseball. The pride in authorship has passed from Jackie Robinson to Dr. J. But that's just an educated guess.

The Cardinals lost, and I wrote about both the problems **10** they've had this year and why they're still in the race.

I kept asking myself if I had a proper focus. It helped me to think, "What title would I use?" I finally settled on a neat little *SI* pun, "Stranger than Friction." Once I had the concept, the writing came more easily. But I still don't think we should be doing the Cards; the Pirates and Phillies are having a bang-up series.

The story was killed. Mark wanted to get Wulfie's story on **11** the Cardinals' George Hendrick in the magazine. Since Wulfie and I had written on the same team, we couldn't very well publish both stories at once. Then why was I sent to Chicago? Apparently they didn't read Wulfie's story until to-day. Another late-breaking decision, like the Owens-Palmer business. But I'm only guessing. Neither Larry nor I have been told exactly why I'm dead this week.

In order to print the Hendrick story, they're going to have to increase the column area. But since Wulfie had written a full-length feature, they're also going to have to cut his story 200–300 lines, I'm told. That won't make Wulfie happy.

september

They're going to jack around the Inside Pitch space, which won't make Herm Weiskopf or the checker happy. And, of course, I'm miserable, not only because my piece isn't running but because I haven't been told why. But I understand how things work: the product first, the people second.

As is my wont at times like this, I begin questioning: my choice of career, my competence, my security. I know the futility of brooding or complaining to friends. I have to speak with an editor. If I remain silent, they're going to get the message—we can do anything we want to this guy.

I had a 7 P.M. flight out of O'Hare, but I wanted no part of Chicago or Wrigley Field, so I switched to 2 P.M. In the morning Mogul drove me around Graceland Cemetery. The place has some spectacular monuments and crypts, but mainly it has bodies.

12   In ten years as a checker I learned a lot about how to vent frustration and how not to. I used to walk into editors' offices and bitch. That got their backs up. Or I'd write nasty memos. That was better for the simple reason that I had vented my anger by the time I finished writing and could tear up the memo and not send it. I've learned three things. First, if I have a grievance, I have to state it or get run over again. Second, I can't go around getting people's backs up. Third, I have to come in with something to offer.

At 5 P.M. I spoke with Peter Carry, the editor in charge of writers' problems. "I've been back from vacation for two weeks," I said, "and I'm a little frustrated. The first week I didn't get an assignment. The second I got an iffy story that you quite properly dumped when something better came along." Note that I'm not being antagonistic. "I think there are better ways I could be used during the last three weeks of the season." I gave him some ideas and we had a general discussion about covering the divisional races.

In all, I was trying to be the Good Soldier Schweik: a hard worker eager to contribute. At the same time I hope he understood that I expected to be used more.

Meanwhile, the Phillies and Pirates had a rip-roaring weekend. Here's what I could have written:

"What's the greatest rivalry in baseball? In their wisdom, the people who run the game have put most natural rivals— the White Sox and Cubs, Cardinals and Royals, Mets and Yankees, Giants and A's, Dodgers and Angels, Astros and Rangers—in separate leagues.

"The Dodgers and Giants? Not since they left New York City. As Southern and Northern California teams, they're too far apart geographically, and most of the time they're too far apart in the standings. The White Sox and Brewers? A natural geographical rivalry, but, incredibly, they're in separate divisions! The Cubs and Cardinals? Not bad, but the Cubs rarely contend. The Yankees and Red Sox, or Yankees and Orioles? That's the problem: not a clear enough two-team rivalry in the AL East.

"The runaway winners are the Phillies and Pirates. For one thing, they're in the same state. 'We play for bragging rights,' says Phillies pitcher Tug McGraw, 'to see who's the baddest team in Pennsylvania.'

"They've long had disparate identities—the raucous Pirate 'family,' presided over by benevolent manager Chuck Turner, and those brooding existentialists in the city of brotherly discord, managed by . . . whom?

"But the main reason to link the Phillies and Pirates is the kind of competition they've had. Since the start of divisional play in 1969, the Phillies or Pirates have won the NL East 10 of 14 times. Other twosomes have dominated divisions—the Dodgers and Reds, Yankees and Orioles, A's and Royals—but none has gone head-to-head year-in, year-out as often in recent years. 'That's what makes this the rivalry it is,' says Phillie manager Paul Owens. 'We've been fighting for first place the last eight or nine years.' Indeed, this weekend the Pirate and Phillies played three rock-'em, sock-'em extra-inning games in Pittsburgh. The first-place Phils took two of three and left town feeling like winners for the first time all season. It would be esthetically pleasing if this turned out to be the turning point of the NL East season, etc."

13   I flew to Houston to do a story on the Astros. They've been playing superbly, but because of their 0–9 start they probably won't win the NL West. Normally, I'd be reading xeroxes from the team files and preparing questions. This time I'm going to concentrate less on information and more on atmosphere, ambience, humor, pathos.

Somewhere between New York and Houston I started to get mad. This is the year I would take on greater and greater challenges, but since spring training I've published eight columns and only two news stories. The columns (Bell, Stanley, Righetti, Thon, Rose, Owens, Lynn, Moffitt), in my view, were good. In the Rose story—my own idea, by the way—I broke the news that Phillies owner Bill Giles was thinking of canning Rose after the season. I felt very good about the Moffitt, Lynn and Stanley stories, and the others, to my mind, were more than acceptable. For the news stories (Ryan's record, Cardinal defense) I got nothing but rave reviews. Then why haven't I been given more big assignments? Larry told me recently that my timing has been unfortunate, that I've missed assignments I would have received if he or I hadn't been on vacation.

14   I find that I'm recognized by many of the Astros—Harry Spilman, Dickie Thon, Bob Knepper, Dave Smith, Nolan Ryan. I've been around the team so often I'm practically a beat man.

I was also recognized by a reporter from Dallas. He invited

me out for a drink, and the whole time I was trying to remember his name (this happens a lot to *SI* people). Finally, I asked to look at a story he'd written; I was too embarrassed to come right out and say, "I've forgotten your name."

Doing a story on the Astros is another silly idea. Sure, they've played well, but not, I've discovered, *that* well. Every chance they've had to get in the race they've blown. At least, that's what the players say, and ballplayers aren't known for downgrading their accomplishments. When I speak with Larry tomorrow, I'll plead for a column on leftfielder Jose Cruz, who is bidding to become the oldest NL batting champion in several decades. Now *that's* a story.

They bought the Cruz idea! I interviewed him this **15** afternoon and wrote the story during and after a game with the Dodgers. I will be very, very surprised if the story doesn't run, unless Cruz goes bottoms-up at the plate this weekend. I've done everything possible to make the story work—gone on assignment an extra day early, napped before going to the park to stay fresh, interviewed everyone under the Astrodome and, yes, picked up atmosphere and personality. What's more, Cruz himself is an interesting character. He takes a high, Mel Ott-like step with his front foot when he's batting, he has a large collection of antique cars, and he's always doing or saying something unpredictable. When I first saw him the other day, he was impishly slamming his bat against a table in the clubhouse. "The sound of his bat has been echoing ever louder through the National League," I wrote.

I had a long conversation with John Lowe, the walking Baseball Encyclopedia from L.A.'s *Daily News.** I approached him and suggested he do some "Hot Stove" baseball stories

*He moved to the *Philadelphia Inquirer* in 1984.

september

for us. "Take some established notion and destroy it," I said.

Our subsequent conversation convinced me I was right. "The most overrated concept in baseball is batting average, and offense in general," he said. "Look at the Red Sox: They could win the Triple Crown and finish sixth. I never buy it when managers say, 'Wait til our batting comes around.' The pitcher's the guy who puts the ball in play. He, to a large extent, determines whether your batting comes around." We agreed that the Dodgers, Orioles and White Sox are winning divisions because of their pitching. "It's still pitching, defense and speed," said Lowe.

16 Larry told me that I could take until tomorrow to write the story. "It's important that you do the best job possible, based on what's happened the last two weeks," he said. Well, I did my best, but when I checked out of the hotel this morning, I couldn't find any way to improve the story. So I sent it in.

When I got home late this afternoon, I hoped against hope that I wouldn't hear from the office. The boys were coming over for a relaxed evening, and I had bought a nice birthday cake for Benjamin, who turned 15 yesterday.

At 4:30 Larry called. "Two things," he said. I was immediately relieved. It's when he says, "We've got a problem" that I know a story is in trouble. Mulvoy had two minor questions about the piece, and Larry wanted to pass them on. Then he was going to send the copy to the typists. Go Jose!

17 I've now been assigned four columns on teams. Two (Cardinals and Dodgers) didn't run and the other two (Phils and Astros) wouldn't have run if I hadn't convinced the editors to let me write on individuals instead. I find that team stories are only assigned to the column area if they're iffy, and that a team angle rarely works in 180–220 lines, the standard column length. If a team's important er..ough to be written about, it should be in the news area.

Cruz went 4-for-4 last night. There's no question he'll still be in contention by week's end. I feel as confident of publishing as I'm capable of feeling these days.

18 For the first time since 1980 I'm not going to cover the playoffs. A usual playoff writer, Ron Fimrite, and an unusual one, Frank Deford, got the assignment. Deford, who wrote a two-part series on White Sox pitching, will cover the AL playoffs. Frank was originally going to write a third installment and be through with the team, but he was too tired after covering the U.S. Open tennis tournament. If Chicago wins, he'll have some bonanza or other to write.

Don't ask me how I feel.

19 I went to the Chemical Bank money machine—and was refused. The machine claims I'm $395 overdrawn. I'm sure there was a clerical error, but the only way to get proof is to have snapshots taken of every check I've written since the last statement. That takes several days. Meanwhile, I can't even cash a check. With 70 cents in my pocket, I had a candy bar for lunch. A colleague, Connie Tubbs, saw me at the adjustment window and asked what had happened. When I explained, she said, "The next step will be thievery." I think I've just discovered the root cause of crime.

Things improved after lunch. I was able to pick up $275 by doing my expense account and collecting what the company owed me. Then I had a very satisfactory talk with Gil Rogin.

His temporary office is on the 34th floor, where the top Time Inc. bosses hang out. I passed by a guard, a portrait of Hedley Donovan and a row of spectacular photographs. Gil's office looks north over Central Park.

september

I got right to the point, which was not my current dissatis-faction (no talking out of school). "I think every writer should edit. We tend to rage blindly when something happens to our copy. Better to know what we're raging at. I found that I was much more sympathetic to the editing process after a week in Larry's chair. I know it will help my writing.

"The week I was editing I had only Inside Pitch and the baseball column to edit. Most of my work was done by Sunday morning, but I didn't leave the building until 4:30 A.M. Monday. I realize they were also closing the special football issue, but the lateness was a bit mystifying. I've thought about it since, and I've concluded that the whole process—staying up Sunday, being blown out all day Monday, still tired Tuesday—has to sap morale. And somewhere down the line, the product suffers, too.

"My other point is that the whole process of putting out the magazine is so byzantine that it needs to be explained to people who don't understand. Perhaps if you held some lunches or meetings. . . ."

Gil thanked me for my concerns. "I especially like the idea of having writers edit," he said. "So many things can hap-pen—the film can be bad, the story may not work, or some-thing important can bump it. I'd like to see writers be a little more sympathetic." He added that the Company is trying to deal with the late closing/morale problem. A consulting firm has been interviewing employees, and Gil will be speaking with writers and editors when he returns in December.

23 The Cruz story turned out fine. He made it timely by going on a tear and ending the week tied for the lead with Bill Madlock of the Pirates. Today I was sent to Atlanta to cover a three-game series with the Dodgers. The catch: I won't be writing unless the Braves win every game.

The Dodgers won the first game, and I was on the next **25** plane home. Soon after I returned, Larry asked me to write a preview that could run as a box with Wulfie's story. Normally a playoff preview involves wires to correspondents and exhaustive analysis of statistics: a week's work. Getting only a few hours to research the piece, I spoke with Wulfie, Fimrite, reporter Ivan Maisel, the Elias Sports Bureau and the redoubtable John Lowe, and put together what Larry later described as the best possible story under these late-breaking circumstances.

It didn't run. "It was mostly a matter of space," said senior editor Joe Marshall, who handled the story when Larry got overbooked. "They had to cut Wulf's story 100 lines, and if they'd used your sidebar they'd have had to cut Wulf even more. Mark also told me that your story didn't tell him much he didn't already know."

"How much could I do under such a deadline?" I said.

"That's true. You shouldn't feel bad about this in terms of your writing. It was one of those things."

I had a talk with Mark Mulvoy, the latest interim managing **26** editor. As usual, I tried to come in with something to offer. "I want to talk with you about the World Series," I said. "Most years, I think, there's a good sidebar subject. It gets written and then killed because of space. I don't know whether I'm arguing for more space or the idea of a sidebar, but I wanted to call your attention to the subject."

He said he agreed that sidebars usually worked with the Series coverage, and that he hoped to get as much space as possible.

"Of course, I'm not totally disinterested in the subject," I went on. "I hope to write the sidebar."

My concern shifts to how I can get in the magazine be-

september

tween now and the next baseball season. I met with one of the regionals editors, Linda Verigan, and got her approval on three story ideas: British sport, Trivial Pursuit and the priorities for the next baseball commissioner. She also gave me a fourth assignment: the art exhibit that will be running at the Winter Olympics. In fact, there's a preview of it tomorrow at the Spectrum Gallery.

28   Audrey and I attended the preview of the "Art and Sport" exhibit. If there's one thing I've learned form Audrey, it's that there's an esthetic to everything: how you walk, how you talk, how you dress, how you prepare food, how you display it on a plate. Breakfast with her is like a state dinner at the White House. I mean, orange juice in wine glasses?

This story shouldn't be particularly difficult to write. As soon as I said I was with the magazine, the gallery director and other principals descended on us. The next morning I had breakfast with the Yugoslavian art dealer responsible for the show. And a great show it is, featuring Glazer, Rosenquist and other notables I've actually heard of. It was also fun writing the review. If you can't free-associate about art, what can you free-associate about?

october

Here are the final stats of the players I've been following **3**
closely:

Hitting

AL	AVE.	AB	R	H	2B	3B	HR	RBI	BB	SO	SB
Bell	.277	618	75	171	35	3	14	66	50	48	3
DeCinces	.281	370	49	104	19	3	18	65	32	56	2
Kittle	.254	520	75	132	19	3	35	100	39	150	8
Lynn	.272	437	56	119	20	3	22	74	55	83	2
Walker	.270	307	32	83	16	3	10	55	28	57	2
NL											
Cruz	.318	594	85	189	28	8	14	92	65	86	30
Rose	.245	493	52	121	14	3	0	45	52	28	7
Thon	.286	619	81	177	28	9	20	79	54	73	34

Pitching

AL	W	L	PCT.	ERA	G	SV	IP	H	BB	SO
Moffitt	6	2	.750	3.77	45	10	57.1	52	24	38
Righetti	14	8	.636	3.44	31	0	217	194	67	169
Stanley	8	10	.444	2.85	64	33	145.1	145	38	65
NL										
Carlton	15	16	.484	3.11	37	0	283.2	277	84	275
Ryan	14	9	.609	2.98	29	0	196.1	134	101	183

Carlton leads Ryan in career strikeouts 3,709–3,677. Kittle is
almost certain to be named American League Rookie of the
Year. Rose, still 201 hits short of Cobb's record, is almost
certain to be released by the Phillies. "I think someone will

pick him up," says Wulfie. "The club that should do it is Montreal. He could give them the chemistry they need to win."

4   Although I won't be writing a story, I'm attending the play-offs to do clubhouse interviews and see the games.

You think it's glamorous work? Read on.

The day did start well. My plane arrived in Los Angeles ten minutes early, at 11:30 A.M., and my fourth college roommate, Jeff McGrath, came with his wife Ann Wolken to meet me. Jeff's a freelance animator and Ann's a freelance artist, so they were able to take the day off.

They drove me to *SI* headquarters at the Beverly Hills Hotel, where press credentials for me and tickets for them were supposed to be waiting. Nothing.

I checked in and we had a swim and lunch, all the while making futile calls to *SI* people. At 3 we left the hotel and headed to Dodger Stadium for a 5:20 TV start. We reached the press gate around 4:20. No tickets, no credentials.

I called the P.R. office and was told Larry had all the goodies. I didn't know if he was at the park or not, so I told the P.R. people to have him meet me at the gate. I also stopped a writer I knew and asked him to send Larry over if he saw him inside. I, of course, was stuck outside. Before gametime I found Fimrite and Wulf, and they were just as much in the dark as I.

Larry arrived with everything two minutes before gametime. Here's what happened: 1) Ivan, not Larry, originally had the credentials and tickets. He left to play golf and dropped them in Larry's name at the hotel desk. He thought he had told Larry of his plans, but Larry thought tickets would be left individually in each staffer's box. 2) Larry returned from lunch to discover himself in charge of everything. He called the rest of us, but we'd all left for the park, ticketless. 3) Larry arrived in the nick of time with credentials for the staffers and seats in the stands for Jeff and Ann. It was really nobody's fault. The point is, this scenario or something like it happens almost every year at playoff time.

The fabulous *SI* seats, courtesy of the Baseball Writers' Association, were in a temporary press area constructed in the stands somewhere around the 14th deck. I exaggerate slightly. The "press section" where we were seated consisted of boards built over seats, with a few TV monitors sprinkled in. We were so far up we couldn't tell whether a fly ball would be caught by the shortstop or a fan in the centerfield stands.

The Phils won, 1–0. It was my kind of game: short, sweet, good pitching, low-scoring. The lowlight: Bob Wirz, the Commissioner's P.R. man, came up to our section and sat down. "Good to see you, Ron," he told Fimrite. "Hi, Steve," he said to Wulf. Then he looked at me. "I don't know if I'm glad to see you or not," he said. I spread my arms and looked skyward. Wirz is still mad about the strike stories I wrote two years ago. "Just kidding," he said.

Afterwards, we divvied up the assignments: Fimrite roaming; Wulfie to the interview room; Ivan to the winners' clubhouse, Kaplan to the losers'. What the hell—it had been that kind of day.

I got good quotes from the Dodgers, who were unusually expansive in defeat. Indeed, I took notes for so long that when I finished, all our staffers had gone and I had no ride. Taking a crowded elevator to the press bus, I overheard the Dodgers' Dusty Baker make an interesting comment about winning pitcher Steve Carlton, who got him to pop up in a key situation: "He held off on that pitch until he needed it." Then Dusty looked over to me and said, "Oh, oh, someone's taking that down." I pretended to scribble furiously, and everyone cracked up. Of course, I *did* take mental notes.

It had started raining. With cardboard boxes over our heads, a bunch of us ran to the press bus. On the way to the press headquarters, some writers were talking about how slowly baseball changes. "It took ten years to get the sacrifice bunt approved and twenty to get them to even consider the concept of a team error," said Jack Lang of the *New York Daily News*. It will take 100 years before Jack lets magazine people in the Baseball Writers' Association.

Some things never change. The playoff headquarters is at a dingy downtown hotel. Downtown is not the place to be in L.A. The cocktail party there was depressing—a couple dozen writers and a mariachi band. I had a drink and took a cab back to the Beverly Hills. Somewhere along the way I lost my press pass.

5 Before playing tennis with Larry on the hotel courts, I had breakfast in the hotel coffee shop. Gordon Parks, the photographer, author and cinematographer, was a few seats away. Heading for the court, I passed Mike Wallace. Larry and I were given a court by host pro Alex (The Chief) Olmedo, the former Davis Cupper. Celebrities are so numerous here as to be commonplace.

Fimrite drove me out to Dodger Stadium. The magazine's best pure writer, he's a raconteur, bon vivant, movie buff, trivia expert and alltime San Francisco booster. Expansive and generous, he treats everyone the same—even people he doesn't like. The only time he seems tense is when he's driving. "I hate freeways," he said. "It's not so bad in San Francisco, where you can drive the city streets." We passed what passes for downtown L.A. "What distinguishes Los Angeles from New York or San Francisco is that people here entertain at home instead of going out," he said. "San Francisco has more restaurants per capita than any city in the world." And Ron has been to all of the good ones.

The Dodgers won a dull, poorly played game, 4–1. Larry discovered that Dodger pitching has allowed 17 runs in 14 games with the Phillies this year. An angle, should the Dodgers win the best-of-5 series.

Defense, I'm happy to say, has been pivotal in the first two games. The Phils won the first game in part because Sixto Lezcano ran down a liner with the bases loaded. And they lost the second when shortstop Ivan DeJesus and center-fielder Garry Maddox made errors, and a bad hop turned a single into a triple past Lezcano. Alas, the best defensive work passed all but unnoticed because it didn't figure in the outcome. Quite simply, 40-year-old Joe Morgan had one of the finest innings in the history of second base. With the second game tied 1–1 in the fourth and L.A.'s Ken Landreaux on first, Mike Marshall hit a hard grounder up the middle. Morgan ran it down and forced the speedy Landreaux by diving and tagging second. "It was the only play I had," Morgan said later.

Bill Russell then singled Marshall to third, and on the first pitch to catcher Jack Fimple, Russell headed for second. Philadelphia catcher Bo Diaz threw to Morgan in plenty of time, but Russell deliberately stopped midway between the bags.

Now Morgan was in a position second basemen dread. "This is the way the play works," he said deliberately. "I come in to take the throw from the catcher. If the base stealer continues running, I tag him. Otherwise my job is to run him down without letting the runner score."

Like a vaudeville dancer crossing the stage, Morgan ran toward first with his head cocked at right-angles toward the third-base line. Marshall made a few feints and charged home. By waiting to throw to Diaz until the right moment, Morgan set up the rundown that got Marshall out.

Ah, but Russell had taken second on the play. And when Fimple sent a liner toward right-center, the Dodgers had surely taken the lead. But Morgan, who holds the record for most consecutive errorless games (91) by a second baseman over two seasons, leaped high to spear the ball and end the inning.

How often does it happen: a guy makes three great plays and then bats third the next inning! With a runner on second and one out Morgan had to settle for a walk (no one in baseball history has more) and the Phillies didn't score. The rest is history. But so was Morgan's little-noted nor long-remembered fourth in the field.

Rose had one hit in the two games. He's playing only because his heir-apparent at first, Len Matuszek, was brought up from the minors too late to be eligible for postseason play.

6 Before flying to Chicago for the end of the AL playoffs, I spent the day with Jeff and Ann. Jeff cooked up some nifty yeast pancakes and the two of us later drove around Beverly Hills to buy some birthday presents for Ann. I never once called the office, nor anyone else. With Larry on the plane to New York, I had no professional obligations. It was nice to spend one slow, unplanned day.

It was also nice to take a flight that included the radio broadcast of the second Chicago-Baltimore game, courtesy of United. But every once in a while I looked at the button on my lapel and got depressed. On it was a picture of a batting parrot, with the inscription, "Los Angeles 1984 Olympics." So far so good. Teams put out their own buttons for the playoffs and Series; why shouldn't the Olympic Committee?

My problem was with the little inscription at the bottom: Coca-Cola. I immediately thought of an article Norman Mailer wrote in a recent *Esquire.* Mailer was covering the British elections. After describing the Conservative and Labour positions, he asked himself whom he favored. And he concluded: What difference does it make when the quality of life is so diminished? If I remember correctly, Mailer used the analogy of an otherwise exemplary cocktail party in which the drinks are served in plastic cups. Already, he lamented, our enjoyment is reduced by 10 percent. I have nothing in particular against plastic cups, but I have everything against a sponsor meddling in athletic events. Commercialism is interfering with everything, even our simple pleasures.

Before the third Chicago-Baltimore game, I asked Tony **7**
LaRussa if Kittle and Walker had changed over the course of
the season. "Kittle hasn't changed one iota," Tony said. "No
matter how much success he's had, he won't change. Walker
is more confident now about being a major-leaguer. He knew
he made his contributions by being here. To give him his
proper due, half-serious and half-joking, we voted him
unofficial rookie of the year during the final series. His only
difficulty is that he won't get as much playing time as he
wants and probably deserves. I get to play two of three guys
[Kittle, Walker and Tom Paciorek]. No matter which one sits,
he deserves to play." During the first two playoff games,
which the White Sox and Orioles split, Kittle and Paciorek
have started. Kittle is 1-for-6; Walker struck out as a pinch-
hitter in the second game.

Later I was speaking with *Times* men Ira Berkow, Murray
Chass and columnist George Vecsey. "Did you read Mike
Royko's column in today's *Sun-Times*?" Ira asked. "He used
the term 'bat envy,' and he was plainly referring to penis
envy. He also did it tastefully. But it never would have made
The Times—they'd have found it vulgar."

"I quoted Pedro Guerrero as saying 'No more bleeping interviews,' " said Vecsey, "and the guy on the desk made it,
'No more interviews.' But 'No more interviews' wasn't the
point; the figure of speech was."

"And it's gotten worse," said Chass. "You used to be able to
use 'Damn' or 'Hell.' No more."

Times-style is incredibly conservative. A writer can't say
"shortstop Cal Ripken, Jr." He must say, "the shortstop," or
"Cal Ripken, Jr.," the "Baltimore shortstop," or some other
method that doesn't use "shortstop" as part of a title. "They
won't let us use 'unique,' except in quotes," Vecsey added,
"because who is a writer to say what's unique? I love to use
'unique' in quotes."

october

8   The Phillies and Orioles advanced to the World Series, each winning their playoffs three games to one. I saw four of the eight games. I don't know if they were the best four, but I certainly saw the best one. That was the Chicago-Baltimore finale, which the Orioles won 3–0 in the 10th. It was a wonderful spectacle, all those goose-eggs stretching out on the scoreboard, all that excellent pitching and fielding prolonging the drama into overtime. The spectators and benchwarmers grew tenser and tenser. As the players kept saying afterwards, the most relaxing place to be was on the field, too wrapped up in the play to get nervous.

There will be endless second-guessing in the aftermath of the game. Should LaRussa have left in starter Britt Burns, who was pounded in the 10th? And what would have happened if Jerry Dybzinski hadn't made a baserunning error that may have cost Chicago a run in regulation? A Sox victory would have set up a fifth game between their Cy Young Award winner LaMarr Hoyt and crafty Scott McGregor.

Kittle went 2-for-7, with a single and a double, but all those off-speed pitches had him struggling. Walker had a single in three at-bats. In the National League Rose rebounded to go 3-for-4 in the third game and 2-for-5 in the fourth. "The man has incredible spirit," said Philadelphia leftfielder Gary Matthews, himself the NL playoff MVP.

9   Maybe it was just as well that I didn't get the assignment. For two days I sat next to Frank Deford, the best known writer on the staff.

I don't consider Frank *SI*'s best pure writer; as I've said, I think Ron Fimrite is. In fact, Frank's mind is so fertile and bubbling that his writing sometimes gets ahead of his readers and needs clarification. Frank isn't the best journalist on the staff; for my money, Jerry Kirshenbaum is. And though Frank's a riot, he isn't necessarily the funniest writer we have;

Steve Wulf and Curry Kirkpatrick are certainly on a par with him. But there's no one I'd rather read than Frank Deford.

The reason, I think, is the quality of his insights and observations. He writes with such assurance that even his most outrageous opinions seem plausible. Watching the last two games of the Baltimore-Chicago series, Frank had little interest in play-by-play, why someone got caught off base, etc. "The morning papers will have that," he kept saying. Frank was looking for information that the morning papers didn't have and, preferably, would describe or symbolize the whole series. Some of his observations about the White Sox:

- They stranded 36 runners, including 19 from the seventh inning on.

- Chicago got only four extra-base hits in the last three games.

- Chicago's frustration culminated in the last game, when the White Sox reached base all ten innings without scoring.

- In the first game LaMarr Hoyt threw first-pitch strikes 26 out of a possible 31 times.

- Chicago hadn't played a .500 team since mid-August.

His Orioles observations weren't so statistical:

- They teased the White Sox sluggers with fastballs, then got them out on breaking balls and off-speed stuff.

- Oriole heroes are guys who stand and wait—a 21-year-old "player to be named later," a rookie brought up when a starter was hurt.

- Lots on the Oriole "character." General manager Hank Peters is quoted as describing "an Oriole type" as, "He knows how to win, he does several things and he's willing to accept a role." Even if that role is pinch-hitter or utility infielder.

In avoiding play-by-play and chronological reportage, Frank opened with something I can rarely bring off: a "thought lead." He contrasted the old Oriole spirit—"scuffling, beer-swilling scoundrels, full of spit and tricks, with squeeze plays, high spikes, Baltimore chops (of course) and whatever else it would take to beat you"—to the "new, improved Oriole spirit" of "inspired moderation." Actually that was the only part of his story I questioned—the "new" Oriole approach is quite a few years old.

I have Frank's copy in hand, and I think I might be able to learn something by outlining it:

- Thought lead (27 lines).
- What effect Oriole system had on White Sox (stranding runners, etc.), concluding with a last-game stat (13).
- First-game description that isn't belabored; he quickly relates it to denouement (41).
- Why Chicago was in trouble even after winning first game—most notably, because of poor competition in AL West (19).
- Last game! How does he tie it in with first? Because the Sox had another problem—never having faced "the stranger who would ultimately beat them." Description of final-game hero Tito Landrum and what he did (71).
- Second game, concentrating not on play-by-play but hero and series MVP Mike Boddicker (32).
- Oriole homers (13).
- Third game, featuring hitting star Eddie Murray (21).
- Description of the series brushback controversy, an amusing sidelight the papers played up. Deford draws interesting conclusion that the controversy distracted White Sox from business at hand: getting to struggling Oriole starter Mike Flanagan (70).
- Conclusion on Oriole character and its relationship to the city of Baltimore (25).

Basically, Frank went from thought to thought rather than game to game. His rhetorical flourishes were natural rather than forced—"milling and cooing" to describe the emptying of the benches after one alleged brushback. The overall effect: a thoughtful, entertaining story.

(In covering the National League playoffs, Ron Fimrite took

a simpler but equally effective approach. He began by describing the series' critical moment—a key homer by Gary
Matthews—and moved on naturally from there. There wasn't
a word of overstatement. What over-reaching sports writers
described as revelation and truth and brotherhood and suffering, Fimrite's humor and wit and irony reduced to reality.
He covered what he saw before him: a bunch of ballgames.)

The genius of the Baltimore system is role-playing. Every **10**
player knows his role, performs it well and is satisfied. While
flying from Chicago to New York, I mulled over the Orioles'
success and was amazed at its relevance to myself and the
magazine.

I've been unhappy of late because I haven't been assigned
any news stories. Naturally, I expect to write many more in
the future, but when I started to think like an Oriole I realized
I've been performing a valuable role anyway. Sure, the Cardinal infield feature was the highlight of the year, but wasn't I
just as valuable suggesting stories to Larry; writing all those
regionals, including the best one (Brooklyn Bridge) I've ever
done; contributing to Inside Pitch and doing a slew of columns? Of course! Once I start seeing my role and stop counting my credits on the contents page, I can be happy.

I think the office—and every other company I'm familiar
with—suffers from the *People* magazine complex: Unless
you're somebody, you're nobody. But we don't put out the
magazine with star writers and editors alone: We need support troops. A play can't be produced without technicians
and understudies; that's why the stars are so generous in
their praise.

The magazine would profit if people better understood and
appreciated their roles. They should be content, in the words
of the Army commercial, to be all they can be. No more, no
less.

october

But role-playing cuts both ways. Checkers complain that they never hear from anyone until they make mistakes; they deserve praise for doing good work on tough assignments. The little-noted support troops—secretaries, copy editors, proofreaders, production, wire room, picture editors and artists—must be long-remembered. Meanwhile, the designated bigshots must rein in their egos. A writer has to realize that there's going to be more to his Monday marching orders than, "Write 400 lines anyway you want and we'll take care of all complications." And editors should understand that a writer will lose confidence if too many stories are killed or drastically cut because of space problems, poor pictures and other forces beyond his control.

If there's a sense of teamwork and shared respect, people will be satisfied. The best contribution I made during the playoffs was not my assigned job of doing clubhouse interviews for Fimrite and Deford. It was secretarial work. Secretarial work! My finest hour began at 7 A.M. Sunday. Deford hadn't been able to find a Sports Com person to run his typewritten copy through a telecopier to New York. How could he file? "Just give me your copy," I said Saturday night, "and I'll type it into my computer and send it along." Frank slipped it under my door in the dead of night and I started typing at 7. The words fairly flew off my fingers; never have I written so well. I was done at 9, and the office was spared a Western Union mishmash or a late closer running into the Columbus Day holiday. I had played my role well.

11   The World Series is not an especially pleasant event for sportswriters. For one thing, there are so many of us that it's difficult to get a player alone. For another, most games are played on cold October nights. And the Series has lost some of its importance because of the playoffs. That's where the real pressure is. After surviving those tense, 3-of-5 championship series, players are happy just to be in the World Series.

Being there is the goal; winning the Series has become secondary. What makes the event worthwhile is the spectacle, and that began today with my favorite form of travel.

Larry, Ron, Roger Angell of *The New Yorker* and I took the Metroliner to Baltimore for the first game. A description from E. M. Forster's *Howards End* seems fitting:

> Like many others who have lived long in a great capital, she had strong feelings about the various railway termini. They are our gates to the glorious and the unknown. Through them we pass out into adventure and sunshine, to them, alas! we return. . . . . Italians realize this, as is natural; some of them who are so unfortunate as to serve as waiters in Berlin call the Anhalt Bahnhof the Stazione d'Italia, because by it they must return to their homes. And he is a chilly Londoner who does not endow his stations with some personality, and extend to them, however shyly, the emotions of fear and love.

We took the two-hour and 18-minute journey to Baltimore in the first-class Club Car, which costs $30.50 more than coach. For the $30.50 I got a free chicken kiev lunch, with wild rice, and apple pie for dessert. I also got a small bottle of wine for $1.50. Larry, who has contracted the jogging obsession—it will cost him his job and his wife and his life—made the mistake of ordering a salad for lunch. When he asked if he could also have a piece of apple pie, the waiter told him it came only with a full meal.

"Are there any pieces of apple pie left?" Larry asked.

"Yes, but we won't give you any."

"Well, what do you expect?" Larry said. "This is the Club Car."

We took cabs from the Baltimore station to the Cross Keys Inn, an elegant hotel-cum-mall in a semirural part of the city. Normally, I'd rather be downtown, but the Series headquarters at the Hilton is, yes, another dingy place. And an inefficient one. Despite reservations at the Hilton, Wulfie, Bruce and Ivan were exiled to Columbia, Maryland.

october

Having already thrown a splendid party last night at the aquarium, the Orioles now laid out a fine pregame buffet of crabcakes, oysters on the half-shell and roast beef. In a light drizzle, the *SI* team sat under the eaves in right field and watched a quick 2–1 Phillie victory. I elbowed my way around the Phillie clubhouse tracking down information on reliever Al Holland, who could make an interesting sidebar should the Phils win the Series. A fearsome performer, he's nicknamed Mr. T. His college coach at North Carolina A & T told me that after a bad practice Holland once called a meeting and read out the entire squad; the next day the team won. Holland hired a Lincoln Town Car limo to chauffeur him and his wife to Series games. Yet his driver says, "I can't believe how different he is from his image. He's a quiet family man who just happens to go first-class."

There were postgame cocktails in a makeshift room down the left-field line, after which we caught the press bus to the Hilton and took cabs to the Cross Keys. A quick game, yes, but also a night Series game that didn't start until 8:30 P.M. I'm finishing this entry at 2:30 A.M.

12   All I know about the second Series game is that I'm 0–2 in wearing the proper clothes. Last night I neglected to bring a sweater and had to warm myself with newspapers, like some derelict. Tonight I wore a sweatshirt, shirt and jacket. It was 72 degrees at gametime.

The big news to some may have been the Oriole victory. To others it may have been the imminent benching of Pete Rose, who has one hit in two games. To me it was Jim Kaat, the 44-year-old pitcher and Hall of Fame candidate, asking me if I'd like to collaborate on a fitness-and-nutrition book. Kaat pitched more years (25) than anyone in baseball history and still hopes to catch on with a team in 1984. Unfortunately, he isn't the household name he should be. But we can have some fun with a book project, and we already agree on the important point: We won't proceed without a good advance.

How many projects have I envisioned this year? The chess column, the DeCinces book, the defense book, this journal, and now the Kaat book. Sooner or later, I'm going to publish.

With the Series tied at one game apiece, it was travel time. I **13** got up late; transferred some scribblings onto the computer; had lunch with my aunt, Sara Azrael, a lively widow back from a barge trip in France—and missed the Metroliner to Philadelphia by one minute. I caught a regular train, which was so shaky I couldn't read or write.

I took a cab from 30th St. Station to Adam's Mark, a hotel on the outskirts of the city; the Bellevue Stratford (Series headquarters) had lost our reservations. After a swim and a run, I felt much better. Then the office called. Reporter Armen Keteyian told me Scorecard was interested in Commissioner Kuhn's future plans. I didn't know them but said I'd check. Then I asked Armen to switch me over to Linda Verigan, and she informed me . . . that my Olympic arts column is running! (Why do I use exclamation points every time I hear that something of mine will appear in the magazine?)

"Oh, well," I said, "accidents do happen."

"Your story was very well received around here," she said. Think positively, Jim.

At 7 P.M. the *SI* party took the press bus to a high-rise building at 1818 Market St., where the Phillies were throwing a party to honor both the Series and their own 100th anniversary. There was a cake shaped like Veterans Stadium; waitresses dressed in period costumes; oysters, Philadelphia-style cheese steaks—and even some retired greats. I shook the hand of Vic Power, one of the best-fielding righthanded first basemen ever (for my money, the Mets' Keith Hernandez is the best lefty).

october

Off-day jottings:

"The second-day pitchers showed the difference between the leagues," said Peter Gammons of *The Boston Globe*, baseball's most respected beat writer. The Phillie pitcher was Charles Hudson, who throws almost exclusively fastballs. The Oriole pitcher was Mike Boddicker, who throws off-speed breaking balls.

Kaat on his chances for the Hall of Fame: "You never know how they'll vote. I know a writer who said he'd never vote for Harmon Killebrew because Harmon had a .256 lifetime average."

"But he hit more homers [573] than any righthanded hitter in the history of the American League," I said.

"Right. And nothing against Rod Carew, who will make the Hall with all those batting titles, but as a clutch hitter he couldn't hold a candle to Killebrew." (In his fourth year on the ballot, Killebrew finally made the Hall in January, 1984. Maybe there's hope for Kaat.)

Kaat and I were chatting with Tim McCarver, who had been pushing the Pirates' chances all year because of their appreciative manager Chuck Tanner. "Players need a pat on the back when they win as well as when they lose," McCarver said, "and Chuck gives it to them. Ballplayers need affirmation."

"Tanner saved my career in 1973 when we were both with the White Sox," Kaat added. "I had started out at 4–1. Then I lost six straight and everybody was after me. I felt awful. Tanner called me into his office and said there was nothing wrong with the way I was throwing, and that he'd put me in the bullpen a week and then start me. I wound up 21–13 and won 20 the next year."

I asked Kaat if there's anything to the sophomore jinx. He said there is. "When you're a rookie, no one expects anything of you. If you've had a good season, though, you start setting goals for the next year and people watch you more carefully. The pressure is really on."

Before being released by the Cardinals last summer, Kaat had become close friends with reliever Bruce Sutter. The word around the league late in the season was that Sutter had lost his stuff. "I don't think so," said Kaat. "The problem was, there were long periods when he didn't get to pitch because there were no save situations. He lost his rhythm, not his stuff. Of course, that can happen to any pitcher early in the season, when there are so many days off and rainouts. One possibility would be to use three pitchers a game, each for three innings. But managers won't do that because what will people say if they take out a guy who's going well and the next pitcher gets bombed? The manager won't look good, so he won't do it. So much of baseball is covering yourself."

Wulfie, Ivan and I left the party before the 10 P.M. fireworks. On the way back to Adam's Mark, we heard on the radio that KC's Willie Wilson and Willie Mays Aikens have been arraigned for allegedly attempting to possess cocaine. A couple of guys who, at their best, can behave like teddy bears.

"Why would they do it?" the cab driver asked. "They've got so much going for them."

Maybe too much: too much money, too much leisure time, too much temptation, too much pressure, too much publicity. Baltimore physician Torrey Brown, a medical consultant for the National Basketball Association, points out another factor. "I think most athletes believe, 'I can beat anything,'" he once told me. "That's a necessary attitude to become a winner in sport, but they extend the attitude to drugs."

Susie Kamb, the regionals editor in charge of my arts story, **14** called this morning and said Ken Rudeen wants a rewrite. I had led with a description of a poster. He felt I should have been more to the point; how many artists, how they were brought together, etc. I called Ken to confirm his criticisms— no sense in losing anything in translation. Fortunately, I had a *october*

copy of the story with me, and I was able to rewrite in about 90 minutes. But it was a bit sobering, considering how high I'd felt about it last night. Ken is no longer the interim M.E., but, as I've said, an assistant managing editor can often get a story killed if he feels strongly enough. That's one reason I'd rather do news stories; many of them are so important they just have to run, all editors' reservations notwithstanding.

Roger Angell had a beer with me while I was lunching at the hotel. We got into a discussion about how schlocky the Series has become. In Baltimore the P.A. announcer was hawking a contest sponsored by a cookie company. If I got my facts right—I wasn't exactly glued to the announcer's words—the contest winner was named honorary bat girl, and her parents got free tickets to the second game. And, I mean, they were announcing the results during the game! This in addition to the relief award named after an antacid and the playoff MVP given by a car company. A high priority of the new Commissioner, Roger and I agreed, must be ridding baseball of spreading schlock.

Alas, nothing is sacred any more—not even *The New Yorker.* In last week's issue there was a men's cologne spread, complete with a scent that permeated the magazine. "The intent of the writers and artists was disrupted," said Roger, "and the writing and art are the very reasons the subscriber bought the magazine." Yes, *The New Yorker.*

15 The Orioles won again and lead the Series three games to one. Sidebarwise, it's been a complete bust for me: I can't do Al Holland because the Phillies are losing. If the Orioles win, Fimrite will do the sidebar because he's been assigned to their clubhouse. This time, however, I'm not crushed. The Holland story, which I've partially written, will make a decent column next spring. And I've collected plenty of stuff for my Viewpoint on the next Commissioner's priorities.

It's all over now. The pressbox is littered with postgame **16** quote sheets. The field is remarkably uncluttered. Not what I'd expected. In 1980, when the Phillies won their first world championship here, a huge contingent of police—some mounted, some holding attack dogs, all in riot gear—lined the field. The fans were predictably respectful. In the press bus a Canadian writer began carping about a "police state," and I responded at my jingoistic worst:

"At least we don't have a President who suspends the Constitution, as Trudeau did, eh? How aboot that?"

Today I thought the mood was growing ugly as it became more and more apparent that the Orioles would win the Series. It didn't help that the Phils were carrying on at their slapdash worst: Joe Morgan, slipping as he left third on what should have been a Pete Rose sac fly (Rose went 0-for-1 as a pinch-hitter in the third game but rebounded to get two hits in each of the last two games. Wulfie's right: someone will sign him); catcher Bo Diaz, forgetting the count and rolling the ball to the mound after the second strike. This time there were no cops near the field, though I detected a few behind the rightfield fence.

The game ended—and nothing happened. Oh, a few fans ran onto the field. Cops and security guards led them back to their seats—and released them.

I'd been covering the Phillie clubhouse, and I wasn't going to shirk my responsibility now. I stood in a pack of reporters and got some quotes from Schmidt, Rose, Morgan and Hudson, who lost both of his starts. I thought the Phillies were remarkably dignified and restrained. Later I got more quotes in the Oriole clubhouse. Series winners always disappoint me. For one thing, they're spraying each other with champagne; they should be drinking the stuff. For another, some of the players invariably say of their championship, "This is one thing no one can ever take away from us." A curious, but somehow balancing end to the season: The losers dignified in defeat, the winners silly and defensive in victory, the ritual continuing.

But I felt terribly depressed. At first I thought it was because another season had ended. It wasn't until I attended the postgame party and had a meal of hot dogs, french fries, ice cream and beer that I realized the depression came from hunger and sugar lust. I can't even get depressed properly.

17   I got 4½ hours sleep last night in Philadelphia. The choice was to turn in or have a drink with Ron Fimrite and Herm Weiskopf (Ivan, Bruce and Larry had returned to New York, and Wulfie was writing the main World Series story). It didn't seem right to go our separate ways without celebrating the season, so I opted for the drink. Inevitably, it turned out to be more than one. It was a nice end to an up-and-down season.

After being on the road for 12 of the last 14 weeks, I expected to spend this week in the city. Maybe not. Pro football editor Joe Marshall called me into his office and reluctantly told me I might go to the Seahawk-Steeler game in Seattle. My fate apparently hangs on Franz Lidz' jury duty. If his case is dismissed or settled, he'll cover the game. If it isn't, well, I don't mind. I can't very well bitch and moan about being inactive, and then gripe about getting an assignment.

18   Franz' case was settled, but he has to hang around two weeks for possible recall. So I'm going to Seattle. Or am I? "Our lead story is Baltimore-Miami," Marshall told me, "and I just realized that the winner will be in second place behind the Bills, whom we've just done. I'll call Mark tomorrow. If we decide that's not a story, we might send Paul Zimmerman [the main pro football writer] to Seattle and make that the lead. Trouble is, the lighting's so bad in the Kingdome that Mark's reluctant to do anything more than a column with one picture." I assumed they wouldn't waste Zim on a column, so I might go after all.

I spoke with my agent, Dominick Abel, about the Kaat book. This is at least the fourth subject I've discussed with Dom this year, and he's still receptive. "It might work," he said, "but it needs a good title and a gimmick, since Kaat isn't that well known to the general public. He must have an exercise and diet program you can spell out: Do this, do that. Ordinary people have to be able to do it, unless you want to gear the book to special people, such as athletes. Check out the Fonda book and other health–stress reduction books for their formats." Dom saw my book as a trade paperback and mentioned $20,000 as a top advance. But he added that if it sells well, it could make good money. I'll call Kaat tomorrow.

I got up very early to play golf. That, on top of yesterday's zombie routine, left me totally wiped out. But the round was worth losing sleep for. The leaves were turning and some purple flowers had come out. The course's new owners have vastly improved the place in only three weeks. At one point Marty Rosenmertz put his fingers to his lips, motioning for silence. Except for a far-off plane, we could hear nothing. "And you know," Marty said, "I've noticed the same thing at 86th and Lex."

I couldn't putt and shot a 91, but after a minor adjustment, I hit booming drives on the last six holes. That's what golf is about for most of us—getting in trouble and adjusting—so I count the round a success.

9 No story. "We're already doing one story on the coast this week," Marshall told me, "and we want to avoid two late closings." So barring complications, I've got this week to work on my regionals and this journal.

I started the Viewpoint on the new Commissioner's priorities. In addition to detailing the issues I've been harping

october

on (scoring, the beanball, commercialism), I mentioned preventing a strike as his number one priority; nothing else will matter, after all, if there's no season in 1985. The Viewpoint came across at first as a bit too strident, so I rewrote it as an open letter. The style change seemed to soften the tone.

I'm starting to concede the importance of style. A story like this won't work without the right approach. it needs to be chatty and informal—helpful rather than stern. Funny how many of our writers use that approach.

20   Marshall called me at 4 P.M., just as I was about to leave the apartment. He wants me to do Mike Quick, the not-so-quick wide receiver for the Philadelphia Eagles. Well, I've already got the makings of a lead.

I called Ed Wisneski, the club P.R. man. He not only alerted Quick that I was coming but got his O.K. for dinner tomorrow. The NFL's high-powered P.R. machine swinging into action.

I'll drive down tomorrow. Tonight I attended parents' night at the Collegiate School, where Benjamin is a sophomore. I like the school, and I like even more what Benjamin's doing there. After completing freshman biology, he took the college achievement test—and got a 700.

21   Up at 6. Drove 2½ hours to Philadelphia. Looked through clippings Wisneski had collected for me and got phone numbers of some good sources who could be helpful on the story. Stood in cold during practice, caught a couple of Eagles for interviews—no time for more because football players don't linger in locker room—and had two-hour dinner with Quick. They said I wouldn't get much from him. Ha! With tape on during dinner, he was expansive. Then I transcribed tape and made phone calls well into night. Thus does glamorous sportswriter spend Friday evening on road.

All's well that ends well. On phone Audrey referred me to story about Doug DeCinces, who signed three-year, $3 million (including incentive clauses) contract the day before he would have become a free agent. I called but couldn't reach him.

Welcome to a curious phenomenon called "death of a champion." A team wins a title and is through before it gets off the blocks again. By "through" I mean that the club either self-destructs as a competitive entity or suddenly loses face with its fans.

After Boston's miracle pennant in 1967, Jim Lonborg broke a leg skiing; exeunt Red Sox. The Mets released the beloved Ed Charles the week after they won the 1969 Series; they were never again the people's cherce. The Reds traded Tony Perez after winning the 1976 Series; their decline began that moment.

And now we have the Phillies. Less than a week after the Series, they've released Pete Rose; retained manager Paul Owens, who was supposed to return to general managing; fired popular coach Bobby Wine and promoted a minor-league coach named Jim Balmer, apparently as Owens' heir apparent. The local press is portraying Owens as a backstabber, owner Bill Giles as Owens' dupe, and Wine as a blameless individual. The club seems to have promoted Balmer because he'll be tougher on the players. But who will deal with the angry fans and media? The Phillies' home attendance actually dropped this championship season. Wait til next year.

Now that I know what can make or break a story, I'm a **22** willing prisoner of pictures. so when I met with photographer George Tiedemann, I was prepared. I suggested he shoot Quick with Harold Carmichael—his good buddy and fellow pass-catcher—and with Quick's girlfriend, Teresa Har-

rington. For the first shots, Tiedemann got a wire trash bas-
ket, upended it and stood on top of it, all the better to shoot
the guys while an assistant P.R. man threw them passes.
Later George and I drove out to Quick's suburban town-
house, and George shot Mike and Teresa playing catch with a
football, posing on a car and sitting in front of the house. The
two sessions took more than an hour apiece. Story-telling,
bantering, suggesting new poses, George never let things
bog down.

And yet, he said sports photography is less creative than
news photography. "They'll only let you shoot from certain
angles at games," he said, "and most angles have been done
before."

Some of his other comments that I found interesting:

• "The biggest thrill I get is when someone I've shot likes the
pictures."

• "I like working with writers and word editors. A writer may be
the first one to know if there's a change in the way he and I are being
asked to approach a story. A word editor may have a better idea than
I do which of my pictures goes best with a story. When I was working on a piece about Philadelphia gays for the *Courier-Post* in Cam-
den, New Jersey, my editor, John Schaffner, picked out a picture of a
guy walking against the flow of pedestrian traffic. I hadn't noticed
how symbolic it was."

• "Going to Vietnam as a Marine was one of the best things that
ever happened to me. It taught me discipline and patience, which I
never would have learned in college."

What's frustrating for an *SI* photographer?

• To take a great picture that isn't used. Tiedemann got one of
Mike Schmidt standing at home plate after his last strikeout at the
World Series. A picture researcher missed it and it was never shown
to the editors.

• To spend weeks on a story that isn't used. I think that's tougher
on a photographer than a writer. The subject talks to a writer, but

may have to pose hours on end for a photographer; the photographer loses more credibility, I think, if his work isn't used. Of course, it's the magazine that suffers in the end. "I know it wasn't your fault," a subject may say to a writer or photographer, "but I'll never put out again for *SI.*" And just try to explain to athletes the myriad of reasons a story gets killed. Half the time *I* don't understand them.

Joe Marshall called a little after 10 A.M. "What did you **23** think of your story?" he asked.

Oh, oh, I could see it coming. I'd say, "I liked it," and he'd say, "I did, too, but Mark/Peter/Ken thought. . . ."

"I liked it," I said.

"Well, I thought it was excellent," Joe said, "and Peter thought it was the best story you'd written in some time. I was just wondering, because I never know what a writer thinks of his own work."

"Don't scare me like that."

Well, it *was* a great story. I opened with the schtick about how Quick isn't very quick, progressed through what makes him successful, hit on his relationship with Carmichael, and included a funny quote from Teresa that works perfectly with the conclusion. It was a good story not only because of the information but the writing. The column held up even after Quick had a rare bad day—two catches for 37 yards in a 7–6 upset loss to the Bears.

Driving home, I reminded myself of what I'd done. With one story I reversed the tide of non-stories and criticized stories and did it in an area where I wasn't a specialist—a sport other than baseball. The experience was more than reassuring to me; it was the essence of professionalism. For the last two months I haven't complained openly or despaired privately. I've hung tough, made suggestions and waited for an opening. In other words, I've matured. And when I got the opening, I made the most of it. A good journalist should be able to cover any story. If he's unfamiliar with a subject, he should be willing to ask basic, even naive questions in order to background himself. That's what I did. Marshall tells me that my column was one of the best to arrive today and was welcomed joyously. There won't be any more talk about Kaplan being in a "slump" (at least not for another week). Moreover, a good story is a good story is a good story. I should relish it for its own merit, beyond any benefit that accrues to my standing at the magazine.

While having these self-congratulatory thoughts, I missed the turnoff to the Walt Whitman Bridge and struggled along a boring road in the rain. I finally stopped at a restaurant outside Princeton. I ordered a steak and watched the Pittsburgh-Seattle game at the bar. Afterwards the bartender turned to a video show of the week's top 10 recordings, maybe one of which I'd heard of. The show was a living advertisement for those "Disco Sucks" T-shirts. I looked around the room. There were some fine old posters—Bogie, Bette, the Marx Brothers. I could hear an old Sinatra record in another room. Then I returned to the horror show on TV. It was a bad way to end a good day.

24   "Your story was as fluid as Quick himself," Senior Reporter Angel (Sting) Reyes told me. I fairly wafted about the office. It was nice to feel good about myself for a change.

Now I'm going to hit 'em again, harder. By Thursday I'll have finished the Commissioner story and rewritten Bryn Mawr.

25   I'm thinking seriously about taking the boys to the Hall of Fame this weekend. There can be no more appropriate climax to the baseball season.

Ira Berkow called and mentioned a friend of his at Rodale Press, a publisher of health-oriented books. Rodale Press is located in Pennsylvania, not far from Kaat's farm. Sounds almost too good to be true.

Now I'm definitely taking the boys to the Hall. We're going **26** Sunday and returning Monday, which the kids have off for teachers' conferences. I haven't yet decided how to get there. Flying costs $138 a head and driving takes five hours. Tomorrow I'll ask Travel about trains and buses and stagecoaches.

Before putting the final touches on the Commissioner's story, I called Ken Moffett, the head of the players association. Moffett's predecessor, Marvin Miller, fought pitched battles with management, as was necessary in that time of strife. Moffett is more conciliatory and would like to work with management. I'm all for that if both sides have baseball's best interests in mind. Unfortunately, Ken admitted that the next set of negotiations could be tough. There's every indication the owners will seek givebacks on pensions, arbitrations and other economic matters. Takeaways invariably produce strikes.

Oh, goody. The only thing worse than covering a strike is being on one. When the players went out in 1981, I sat around for weeks at a time trying to reach owners who wouldn't speak with me and waiting for non-news meetings to end. I wrote some stories criticizing the owners and got predictable responses from them. Taking everything too personally, I suffered.

I sent in the Commissioner and Bryn Mawr stories. When I **27** reached the office at 4 P.M. Larry hadn't had time to read the Commissioner story and regionals editor Linda Verigan was home sick. I did discuss with Larry the idea of sending Gil the October 10 entry from this journal. Larry said to go ahead. The entry so nice you have to read it twice.

october

Audrey and I had a Japanese dinner and saw "Rear Window," each for the second time. It was exquisite: what dialogue, what interplay between Kelly and Stewart, what a period piece on the '50s.

28   Larry wasn't wild about my Commissioner story. He said he disagrees with some of my arguments (which is no problem in a Viewpoint) and that some of my points seem contradictory. Verigan's still sick, so I doubt there will be any action on either story for a while.

At Ira Berkow's suggestion I spoke with Rich Huttner, the books-division publisher at Rodale Press. Rodale puts out *Prevention*, a health magazine, and Huttner said the Kaat book could interest him, as long as Jim doesn't train on cigarettes or beer. No problem there. Huttner said Jim and I should send him a statement of purpose and an outline. Looks promising.

29   Moments of revelation:

Samantha (Sam) Catz, perched on a window sill, her exquisite cat's face outlined against the morning sun in Audrey's apartment. James Joyce called these moments "epiphanies." Virginia Woolf called them "moments of being." In the reduced language of the 1980's they're known as "good bits."

Later I'm cleaning my apartment, really cleaning it for the first time in months. I clear junk out of closets and corners, creating my own space like Mies van der Rohe. I find long-forgotten clothes, utilize places lost in memory and experience.

We see "Never Cry Wolf." A man spends six months in the Yukon studying wolves. He looks at the frozen tundra and feels wonder for the first time since childhood. Where has my wonder gone?

We dine at Gino's, an excellent East Side Italian restaurant where prices are low because no credit cards are accepted. A find. A good bit. A moment of revelation.

30

For once I made the right plans—or rather, my man in Travel, Ralph Spielman, did. Ben, Matt and I took a train up the Hudson to Schenectady, then rented a car and drove to Cooperstown. Much better than a five-hour bus or auto trip. The scenery by the Hudson—autumn leaves, bluffs, West Point—makes the whole trip worthwhile. The Cherry Valley scenery on the ensuing 1½-hour drive is even better. So enchanted was I that I had no idea we were going 70 up a grade. A couple of state troopers did. I can either appear at the Cherry Valley Barn November 9 or pay my fine by mail. Despite the scenery, I'll fly by mail.

31

My baseball Odyssey could only end at the Hall of Fame, in Cooperstown, New York.

I had heard nothing but praise for Cooperstown. Even so, I was overwhelmed. Cooperstown was created explicitly as a historical artifact by James Fenimore Cooper's father and the New York Historical Society. In addition to the Hall of Fame, there's a Farmers Museum and the Cooper House of New York memorabilia. Awash in Halloween colors, Cooperstown is a picture postcard of a town, its ancient wooden and brick houses overlooking evocative Lake Otsego. Listen for awhile and you can hear the distant sound of old Indian tom-toms. Look out over the water—isn't that Rip Van Winkle in yon hollow? Was that Ichabod Crane disappearing over the ridge?

But the Hall is what I came for, and the Hall is what I got. The kids and I went right downstairs to the Hall of Fame Gallery housing the 184 brass plaques, one for each inductee. It's awe-inspiring. On one end of the rectangular room is the trophy for the winner of the Hall of Fame exhibition game played annually between two major-league teams, and on the other a striking obelisk honoring ballplayers who served in the armed forces. Lining the sides are tall marble columns. And set back in alcoves behind the columns are the plaques themselves.

The yappiest child grows instantly reverential at the sight of them. I found myself reading every word on every plaque, and I noticed immediately that the tone doesn't change from one era's immortals to the next. Grover Cleveland Alexander struck out Tony Lazzeri with the bases loaded in the final "crisis" at the 1926 World Series. Hank Aaron led all baseball in "long" (extra-base) hits. "I've tried to keep the same style," said the Hall's publicity director, Bill Guilfoile, who has been writing the inscriptions on new plaques for the past few years. "The only change I've been making is to cut down on wordage because some of the plaques seemed too crowded." Guilfoile should make an addition, though, on a plaque he inherited. That one, honoring Jackie Robinson, doesn't mention that he integrated baseball. Branch Rickey's plaque says he brought Jackie Robinson to the majors.

I had few objections to other exhibits. My passion for defense was whetted when I looked at old gloves, some of them as small as golf gloves. No wonder Harry Hooper, a major-leaguer from 1909 to 1925 and one of the best rightfielders of all time, had a lifetime fielding percentage of .966, a figure any mediocre modern can top. We moved on to the Hall of Fame Library, probably the last word on baseball history, and I picked up enough new material on defense to write a new proposal. The kids toured the Ballparks Room and got a whiff of what ballparks were like when ballparks were really ballparks. "Dad, Dad!" Benjamin said, running up breathlessly. "Did you know that the Polo Grounds were 475 to center and 258 down the rightfield line?" Even Guilfoile, who must maintain professional impartiality, admits he misses the old parks.

october

But what permeates the Hall is the aura of the Babe. The Babe photographed at his induction ceremony—tieless, socks falling around his ankles. The Babe, smiling, pictured with his favorite companions—kids and women. The Babe in old film footage, taking a shuffle step in the batter's box before homering. I mused over a ridiculous old debate: Was the Babe the game's greatest player? Of course he was. No one ever approached his double play—a record-setting pitcher and the greatest slugger of his time. And the special Ruth exhibits establish something every bit as important: that he was the game's best drawing card. Says so right on his plaque.

The more I thought about the Hall on the ride home, the happier I felt. Here was the best of baseball, frozen in time and space. The owners and entrepreneurs can tinker with rules and rituals, but not with history.

november

A New York story. At 7 A.M. I boarded the IRT's Broad- **1**
way–Seventh Ave. express at 72nd St. As usual, I had to
stand until the train let out at Times Square. As usual, I got to
sit afterwards. A good thing, because the train came to a dead
halt after the Penn Station stop. And stood there for more
than an hour. Fortunately, the air conditioner was working,
and everyone stayed cool in every sense of the word, except
the guy in front of me, who kept swearing.

Eventually we were herded out the back of the train,
through a "rescue" train and onto the Penn Station platform.
The explanation for the delay: a brake failure. We whipped
over to the local tracks, where all trains were now traveling.
The first express came along and I couldn't get on: too
crowded. I hopped onto the next train, only to discover that it
was a local. At 14th St. I got off and caught an express to
Borough Hall in Brooklyn. There I hoped to transfer immediately to the RR. Not my day: two M's came before my
RR. I finally reached the course at 10 A.M., only to see my
three regular partners teeing off. The starter had paired them
with a fourth person, and I had to play with strangers. Some
days it's tough to be a New Yorker.

At night Audrey and I attended a Yale Alumni Association
meeting at which Ken Moffett was the featured speaker. My
role at the function was to make some introductory remarks.
Normally I'd have carefully prepared something and rattled it
off. This time, for some reason, I wasn't worried enough to

prep myself. Five minutes before the program, I went into the men's room and scribbled some notes on a piece of paper. The introduction went fine.

Later Audrey and I were talking about creativity and accomplishment. We agreed that sometimes success doesn't come from careful planning. Even scientists make great discoveries through sudden inspiration. Sometimes you just have to wing it.

That's what I'm going to do, more or less, with this week's story. It's Brown at Penn State—one of the college football season's more glaring mismatches. Oh, I'll get the necessary background, but the story will hinge on observations, humor and irony.

2   This morning I took a U.S. Air commuter plane to Harrisburg. It required a full five minutes to get the Portabubble under my small seat and a full hour before the plane left LaGuardia. I rented a car at Harrisburg and began the 90-minute drive to State College. Unfortunately, I missed the turn off 81 South to 322 West. A state trooper put me on a side-road shortcut back to 322 and I saw some spectacular rolling hills and ramshackle towns. I finally reached Penn State around 3 P.M. Sports Information Director Dave Baker took me to practice, where I spoke with Coach Joe Paterno and several players. Penn State has had such a bad season that they're taking Brown seriously. Later I had a nice dinner with Baker and his wife and bought a winter hat and scarf. There's a golf course right on campus, but it's too cold to play.

4   A productive day. I walked around campus, got a possible lead from the field hockey game (Penn State won 2–1) and more good information from the Brown coach and one of his co-captains. At night I attended a symposium at which

Paterno and Brown President Howard Swearer made some quotable remarks. Tomorrow's game is going to have to be awfully interesting to merit more than a few paragraphs in the story.

I was pretty tired from all the activity. Unfortunately, a loud band at the Sheraton kept me up until 2 A.M. I hope the football teams slept better.

The game was more interesting than I thought it would be.   **5**
In fact, Brown trailed by only 17–7 at the half and led in total offense. Penn State went on to win 38–21, but I couldn't kiss off the game. Out went a long lead on Brown hanging tough—in field hockey. I had planned on using that as a lead-in to my description of a blow-out in football. For the longest time I couldn't think of any lead at all. I did the only thing possible under the circumstances: finish the rest of the story. Finally, I wrote the simplest lead possible, stating that Penn State had beaten Brown in the most controversial mismatch of the college season (first paragraph) but that the score didn't tell the whole story (second). From there I went into a general description of the game and how it came to be scheduled, adding some game details and the mood of the teams afterwards. I had a great deal of trouble developing a focus. As I reconsider the assignment, it doesn't seem like a worthwhile project. If Penn State is so lousy this year, who cares if they were scheduled to play Brown?

As I feared, the story isn't running (although they're using   **6**
parts of it in the Football's Week roundup). "Nothing to do with your writing," said John Papanek, who edited the piece, "it just wasn't very interesting material." I spoke with several editors, and no one knows whose idea the story was.

november

9   The ratman cameth. A friendly exterminator, he always spreads good cheer while spreading rodent poison. Upon learning that we're both 39, we exchanged state-of-the-health news. I remarked that I'm losing my memory. "That's an old wives' tale," said the ratman. "If we forget something when we're young, people say it's because we're absent-minded. Now we say we're losing our memory. Actually, we forget things at this age because we have so much more to do."

Hey, I remembered everything he said! Feeling energized, I transcribed the diary from the end of June to August 20.

12   I was at a party the other night during the Duran-Haglar fight. "Who's going to win?" a guy asked me.

"I don't know," I said, "but at 3½-to-1 odds, you take the underdog. There's no telling what will happen when two guys get in the ring. History is full of upsets. Why, Liston was something like 7-to-1 against some kid named Cassius Clay. Foreman was never going to lose."

Well, the favored Hagler won, but barely. I think I made my point.

Ivy League football's the same way. A couple of weeks ago last-place Yale almost beat first-place Dartmouth. Today I took the boys and a friend of theirs, Filip Rensky, to the Yale-Princeton game, and previously winless Yale won 28–21. My feeling is, any football player good enough to make the varsity—even an Ivy League varsity—is an excellent athlete. Put a bunch of excellent athletes on the field, add a program that's smalltime enough to be volatile and fun, and there's no telling what will happen.

13   The days are growing shorter. And so are these entries.

I met an old friend, Chris Swindells, in the subway. He has **14**
left Chemical Bank and formed his own company. He now
commutes regularly to Saudi Arabia, selling computers to the
government. I can't imagine anything as bold as starting my
own company. That's why, reputation to the contrary, the
business world may be more creative than journalism. Most
of the time we're just jimmying around with existing for-
mulas.

My philosophy for the week is hardly original: I may die
tomorrow. It only sounds morbid. By acknowledging death, I
realize that life is finite. There's only so much time to accomplish my goals. So today I called Jim Kaat, after having delayed two weeks for no particular reason. We're going to get
together and write a book proposal during baseball's winter
meetings next month.

I took the train to Darien, Connecticut, and was met there **15**
by Gordon L. Hough and Germain G. Glidden, who drove
me to the National Art Museum of Sport (NAMOS) in New
Haven for my latest regional. NAMOS is a worthy institution,
but it's buried in the University of New Haven library and
loses many works to the glitzier halls of fame. Nonetheless, I
won't be accenting the negative. As I've learned time and
again, we don't introduce the readers to something or somebody only to derogate them—remember Dickie Thon? As
long as the museum has something to offer—and it does—
I'm providing a service by pointing it out.

After writing the regional and getting in 14 holes of hands- **18**
freezing golf the last two days, I drove back to New Haven.
I'm going to the Harvard-Yale game tomorrow. Today I had
lunch with Kevin Rooney, the Brooklyn schools coordinator
at the Yale admissions office. The office is located in New

november

Haven's oldest building, a little white frame structure that must seem comforting to visiting high school seniors. "The same questions keep coming up," said Rooney, a young Notre Dame graduate. "At Princeton it's about the eating clubs and whether the school is too preppy. At Harvard it's whether the university really cares about the undergraduate school. And at Yale it's New Haven."

I lived in New Haven as an eighth grader, and I can testify that it's underrated. There's considerable open space—East Rock, West Rock and the Sleeping Giant parks in particular—good theater and, of course, Yale. The school has so much culture that students rarely need to leave the campus. In four years there all I missed was women and pro sports. And Yale is now coed.

One of my reasons for speaking with Kevin was to point out that Brooklyn, a city of 2½ million people, sends about a dozen students to Yale each year. Kevin pointed out that many Brooklyn kids go to school in Manhattan, and he's right. But alumni volunteers come across many attractive candidates that Yale turns down. In a sense, it's a tug-of-war: We want to get Brooklyn kids into Yale and the admissions people want tougher interview reports, the better to reduce the field to the lucky few who get in.

After lunch I brought my luggage to the home of Jim Fesler's parents (his father, also Jim, is a retired Yale political science professor). I was going to drop my stuff and head back to the campus, but when I called the office, I found I had work to do. Ken Rudeen felt my approach to the sports museum was too flip. I'd started out by saying that NAMOS was just the kind of place for people who have hang-ups about art; Ken said I shouldn't have assumed our readers are anti-art. So I spent the rest of the afternoon rewriting.

Later Audrey and Fesler the Younger arrived and Jim's mother Frances "threw together" a little dinner—salad, scallop casserole, french bread and a meringue with ice cream and raspberries. I should throw together such dinners on my best nights.

In the morning we visited the remodeled *Yale Daily News* **19** building, where I spent at least half my waking hours in college. The remodeling had been ballyhooed, and I expected to see some old *YDN* editors—Bill Buckley, Kingman Brewster and the like. They weren't around. We did run into Jimmy Potash, the summer intern I took on the road. He doesn't want to be a sportswriter any more. He says he was soured by the clubhouse scene in which grown men ask overgrown boys questions like "It must have been great making the play that won the game?" I know how Jimmy feels.

We sat through the 100th Harvard-Yale Game, which Harvard won 16–7. The Game wasn't too exciting. Nor were the anniversary festivities, though the tickets carried Walter Scott poetry and some 32 old football captains were on hand for the coin toss. What I'll remember longest was a parachuting competition and the incredibly high prices for anniversary paraphernalia. Nothing is immune from hype—not even the Harvard-Yale game.

Ken Moffett was fired by the baseball players association. **23** His critics say he wasn't hardworking. Possibly, but I think the players couldn't handle his conciliatory approach to labor relations. Will next year's negotiations be shades of 1981?

Overheard at the supermarket checkout line: "Abandoned in the woods by a pack of wolves, he was raised by his parents."

Thanksgiving dinner at Audrey's cousins. Very relaxing. **24** Nice dinner, following by ten games of table tennis (suddenly, I'm spectacular!) and HBO. Even watching "Rocky III" was fun.

25   At 11 A.M. John Papanek called from the office. He wants me to do the college basketball column. Once again, I'm not about to turn down a story. Once again, it's a story in which facts are less important than feelings. Basketball is back at NYU after 12 years. Go for it: Free-associate!

Audrey and I attended a 3 P.M. press conference and met some NYU old-timers, including Dolph Schayes, the greatest Jewish basketball player of all time. Then we watched varsity practice, which didn't end until 8 P.M. "Hangout," Jimmy Breslin is always saying. That's what so much of journalism is about: hanging out.

26   I woke up feeling incredibly energized. I did 50 situps, ran for about ten minutes with a minimum of discomfort and downed two bowls of 40% Bran Flakes with banana slices. The fear that sometimes inhibits free-and-easy writing had disappeared overnight. I cranked out a Scorecard on Moffett's firing and sent it in. "Great job," said Bob Creamer, this week's Scorecard editor. "Comes to the point without being preachy or overbearing." He's going to make a box of it and give me an interior by-line ("Steve Rogers told *SI*'s Jim Kaplan").

Then I started writing the NYU story. Why not? Tonight's game may be worth only a few paragraphs, I reasoned, and I can insert them later.

Actually, the evening was worth a little more than that. There was an old-timers' exhibition of two-handed set shots, followed by an exhibition game between NYU and CCNY alums, followed by NYU's first varsity game in 12 years—a win.

november

I finished writing at 3 A.M., slept until 8, put some **27**
finishing touches on the story and sent it in. Then I had
breakfast and went out to play paddle tennis with Matthew
and his friend Noah. When some good Brooklyn players
showed up, I played especially well and began thinking of
competing in tournaments again.

Both the Scorecard and NYU story worked well, although
the basketball column lost a lot of color when it was cut from
about 250 lines to 150 to accommodate four pictures. (I think
Mark likes pictures even more than Gil does.) When my copy
undergoes drastic surgery, I never read the final version wondering what has been cut. Too painful. I read it as if for the
first time, like the reader. Despite the surgery, the patient
survived. Margaret Sieck, who took on the story when
Papanek got overloaded, did an excellent cutting job.

I figure I've now had 21 by-lines, counting the interior one
in Scorecard. Since 20 was my goal, I think I've had a productive year, the September-October drought notwithstanding.
And I also think the quality of writing has been good in part
because of the nonbaseball stuff.

Mr. Games Goes to the Dentist. I used to enjoy trips to my **28**
dentist, Bobby Fischer (I told you I like chess). I even took a
kind of macho pride in refusing novocaine. After today my
pain threshold is lower than ever. Fischer poked around and
drew a lot of blood. It was all I could do to concentrate on
anagramming the word CASTLE that appeared on the light
fixture.

When I got to the office, they were closing my Scorecard
item. I'm amazed at how imprecise my writing can be. I had
written, on the drug question, that the clubs had enacted
noxious penalties. The editors changed "clubs" to "baseball
officials," since both clubs and the Commissioner can act; and
changed "penalties" to "fines and suspensions" to be

november

specific. Was it fair for us to refer to the new-old union chief, Marvin Miller, as "intransigent"? I decided "firm" was better. So many things to consider, and any little change can affect the tone. To think that some people write on sensitive topics every day.

In the afternoon I learned that my office is being given to a researcher. Most of the writers will eventually be moved to the 19th floor. For the next month I'll be sharing an office with Bob Creamer, the distinguished author of *Babe* and *Stengel*, the ultimate biographies of Babe Ruth and Casey Stengel. The senior writer of our senior writers, Bob scurried about the office, trying different desk-and-table arrangements, creating space, carving out an esthetic. His enthusiasm was fascinating and catching.

I had hoped to remain in my old office forever. In three years there I had turned the place into a discomfiting mess. The move will force me to ask myself what I really need and what I should discard. I didn't come close today. The movers will come tomorrow and I'll be there to direct them and start adjusting and self-examining. Here, in the most literal sense, is dislocation opening up new areas of experience.

december

I was looking forward to a nice sporting weekend—golf on **1**
Friday, paddle tennis on Saturday and Sunday—when Bill
Colson called shortly before lunch. He wants me to go to
King's Island, Ohio, for the Division III college football play-
off between Union and Augustana.

I was supposed to have dinner with Audrey but I canceled.
Dinner would have meant leaving early tomorrow and arriving frazzled. Instead, I bustled over to the office and picked
up money, tickets and what little information was available
on the two schools. Then I caught the 7:50 to Cincinnati. I
now have a full day to prepare for a win by either team.

I had breakfast with the tournament P.R. man, watched an **2**
Augustana film with the coach and some ABC-TV people,
went to a press lunch and interviewed players on both teams.
One oddity: After doing much taping, I took written notes on
my last interview of the day. I found I was paying closer
attention than I would have when taping. Score one for note-
taking.

At night I couldn't sleep. I used a technique I learned five
years ago in est training. First, I lay flat on my back, arms at
my sides. That seems to be the most restful position for me:
No body part supports another and each one is equally supported by the mattress. Then I started going through the
body parts, intoning to myself, as the est instructor had, "Let

your consciousness and awareness go into the little toe on your left foot." I thought of the little toe, wiggled it a little, introduced myself to it. "Fine. Now let your consciousness and awareness go into the little toe on your right foot. Good, now. . . ."

I was asleep before I reached my waist.

4   Before the noon game, I drove over to the College Football Hall of Fame, which has a nice time tunnel but otherwise falls short of the baseball Hall. I immediately got an angle in my head about football reverting to its roots in this low-pressure, no-scholarships, small-college bowl. The angle stuck in my head all through the game—an excellent contest won by Augustana, 21–17. The writing was only fair. After filing at 8 A.M. Sunday, I realized that the game provided a better opening angle: the winning coach passing up a short field goal that would have sent the game into overtime, and instead going for the winning touchdown. I batted out another version, burying the historical angle deeper in the story, liked it and sent it in. Bill Colson, who edited the story, also preferred the later version.

5   Here we go again, again. Just when I thought I'd run the editorial gauntlet, the story was scrapped. I'm talking about getting the bad news at noon Monday.

First, I learned, my story had been in competition with the New Orleans–New England football game. If New Orleans won, I was out. New Orleans lost. Then the editors were waiting for pictures from a marathon in Tokyo. They were fine and that story ran, apparently bumping mine. Even so, I was still breathing until a hockey story was expanded from four to six pages. That ate up the two-page spread I was supposed to get. I've now had half a dozen stories killed this year, and only once was I told that the problem was the writing. This time I'm not so much mad as numb.

I didn't have time to whine about my misfortune. No sooner had I learned about my story than Larry told me to beat feet to Nashville for the baseball winter meetings. Before leaving, however, I sent agent Abel my revised proposal for the book on defense. It now has four chapters: an all-time defensive all-star team, planning a defense, the history of defense in baseball, and the importance of defense.

Larry and I caught the 11:45 A.M. flight to Nashville. On **6** the way he gave me the game plan. If the meetings are a bust, there probably won't be a story. If there are a lot of juicy tidbits, Herm Weiskopf will write an Inside Pitch. If there's a big story—probably a new Commissioner—I'll do a column or lead and Herm may still do an Inside Pitch.

This is the fifth consecutive week I've had an assignment, and I'm exhausted. Too much travel, too much uncertainty. I'd like nothing better than to collect quotes for Herm's story.

We're staying at the Opryland Hotel, which is as large as a small city. Whole football fields could be placed in some of the lobbies. I'm not impressed. The place is all style, no substance. The room phones have receivers with square ends that don't fit in the computers. All transmissions must be sent from the press room, which has ordinary phones. The hotel employees are friendly—too friendly. They treat people like long-lost buddies, which I find phony and condescending. I bumped into a guy in the coffee shop. "Sorry," he said. "Please excuse me. My fault. All due apologies. I'm the lowest swine there is." Well, practically.

Covering the meetings is bewildering. There are 26 teams, two leagues and one lame-duck Commissioner to keep track of. Major developments are announced in press briefings, but that's useful only for the daily press. We have to buttonhole

december

execs in the lobbies and find out where the clubs brief their beat men.

My potential book mate, Jim Kaat, here doing radio work for two Chicago and one Philadelphia stations, took me to the Phillies' briefing. They were happy to have me. And why not? If I wasn't an Astro beat man, I was virtually a Phillie beat man this year.

7 I met Kaat in the press room at 9 A.M. and we went back to my room and taped for an hour. Good stuff. Basically, Kaat avoids red meat and sugar, which is not unusual, but consumes a fair amount of pasta and beer, which is unusual. He also walks rather than runs and stretches a lot instead of using the popular Nautilus equipment. He quotes Phillie fitness guru Gus Hoefling as saying, "Flexibility permits motion and strength creates it." Motion is very important for a pitcher, who must be able to move his arm in a variety of ways without discomfort.

I think the best part of a Kaat book would be his observations on stress control. When Kaat pitches against a very good team, he pretends it's no big deal. When he pitches against a very poor team, he cranks himself up, as if for the World Series. Money for money's sake doesn't interest him. A butcher friend of his created a meat product and sold it to Heinz for millions. Now the guy's rich, idle—and unsatisfied. Kaat believes in keeping busy. When he isn't pitching, he's breeding harness-racing horses or working on his broadcasting career. But I get the impression that he won't be satisfied unless he catches on next year with another team—at age 45. A remarkable man.

8 Having read my diary through August 20, Larry said he liked it and added that the discipline of keeping it will be good for my writing.

Larry and I had an interesting conversation with Roy Eisenhardt, the A's president. He said that the next Commissioner must lead the owners, rather than vice-versa. I couldn't agree more. Eisenhardt thinks the game may one day be run by the "macro-rich," whose major income will be from businesses other than baseball. With all costs increasing geometrically, he sees teams surviving primarily in major TV markets, and most of the income coming not from gate receipts but from TV. If baseball becomes the "software," in Eisenhardt's scenario, for a TV station, an individual game becomes potentially a substitute for a rerun of "Hogan's Heroes." Eisenhardt wonders whether that situation would be desirable. So do I.

A bunch of cities are giving presentations to sell themselves as expansion sites. They're actually recommending their dome stadiums. Hasn't baseball already been sufficiently diluted? Will more teams mean another round of playoffs? Eisenhardt said that he was "esthetically" opposed to expansion, but that it was hard to resist a city that is equipped to handle a team. He seemed resigned to the imminence of expansion.

Eisenhardt is widely considered the brightest new executive in the game. He's a decent, considerate, intelligent man. But I don't think he should be viewed as the savior of the game: By necessity he's too preoccupied with his own team and with baseball's business side. Many of the other owners have demonstrated they know only about themselves. The game's remaining special interests—the players, umpires and networks—have their own gardens to cultivate. The Commissioner is hired—and fired—by the owners, but he also possesses considerable power to be used on behalf of "the game's best interests." That's why I'm interested in the identity of Bowie's successor: He's the only person charged with looking out for the game. I said "game," not business.

december

9   I had an interesting day, featuring breakfast with Phillie scouts Hugh Alexander and Ray Shore and pitching coach Claude Osteen. At some point during all the activity, I began to understand the meaning of the winter meetings.

This is how the game renews itself at the end of every year. Oh sure, the meetings have become depressing on a certain level. The threat of a strike in a couple of years is in the back of everyone's mind. The owners are having trouble selecting a new Commissioner. It's more difficult than ever to make trades because of contractual problems. But even in this, the worst of times, the meetings teem with fascinating talk and speculation and, damn it, action. Today alone I've thought about six different topics that have interested me this week:

(1) The Red Sox traded lefthanded pitcher John Tudor to Pittsburgh for lefthanded-hitting outfielder–first baseman Mike Easler. Everybody's got an opinion on this one.

Jim Kaat's thoughts: "Easler's going to a league where there are more lefthanded pitchers and fewer fastball pitchers. He'll have to make an adjustment. Tudor's going to a much larger park. He's been pitching outside a lot at Fenway. Now he can be more aggressive."

Alexander's thoughts: "The Pirates now have three lefthanded pitchers [Candelaria, McWilliams, Tudor] they can throw at you. And Tudor has a good curve to go with his fastball."

Sox writers are disappointed Boston didn't wait longer and get a better player—no one knows if Easler can play every day because he's generally been used part-time. Red Sox P.R. man Dick Bresciani says the Sox were 19 games under .500 against righthanded pitchers, and that Tudor didn't pitch very well in Fenway Park.

2) The Phillies, one of baseball's big traders, didn't make any major moves. "Last year we had two needs and we got them with [pitcher] Al Holland and [outfielder] Von Hayes," says vice president for baseball operations Tony Siegle. "This

year we feel we're a pretty good club. We've got excellent depth in the outfield and infield."

Alexander says, however, that they have looked into trades. "The Yankees are looking for a righthanded hitter, but if they give up a pitcher, they want one back. We asked about Shane Rawley and they said, 'You'll have to give us your number three pitcher [Charles Hudson].'" The Phils weren't interested. They'd like to unload Garry Maddox and his $750,000 salary. Some people are speculating that Alexander and Co. will wait until late in the extended spring-training trading period to make some deals.

3) The Expos got lefthanded pitcher Gary Lucas in a three-way trade with the Cubs and Padres. The trade brought up the subject of Montreal's annual failure to win despite superior talent. "I think the media overrates us and under-rates some other clubs," says Montreal special assignment scout Whitey Lockman. "With the stars we have, there's the tendency toward hype. We don't have much depth. There's no one like Andre Dawson to run in if he's not playing. Leadership? Maybe we've got it by example, but we don't have a Pete Rose." Not yet.

4) In the winter meetings' most unusual event, the Reds signed Pittsburgh free agent Dave Parker. Here's a conservative club, previously opposed to spending big money on free agents, landing one of baseball's all-time free spirits.

Parker stood at the podium, clean-shaven as per Cincy rules, with the Reds' new manager, discipline-conscious Vern Rapp, and club president Bob Howsam, another hard-liner. Parker was wearing gray slacks, white shirt, blue blazer and tie and red carnation "to show my jubilation going back home [he's from Cincinnati]."

"I feel younger and the wind feels brisker against my face," said Parker, rubbing his chin. "I feel I'm capable of hitting .300 with 20–25 homers. The key is, I'm healthy." His litany of injuries includes torn ligaments in his thumb, strained ligaments in a wrist and a knee, and a persevering Achilles problem.

"I lost 10 pounds last night when I shaved my beard," he said. "Rules are made to be abided by. There's no substitute for discipline." Asked about his effect on teammates, he said, "I think it's going to be a jubilant clubhouse. Dave Concepcion and Dan Driessen are motivators, too. Outspokenness? I can't anticipate having anything to speak out about. It's going to be nice to be in a new environment and home among friends. I've mellowed out over the last five years."

Rapp: "He's my man [has Rapp ever said this before?]. Anyone who has won two batting championships and three Gold Gloves can make us a contender. . . . I've changed for the simple reason that I have more experience and more knowledge. If I don't capitalize on it, I'm my own worst enemy. Dave said, 'Hey, Skip, I got a fresh start.' I said, 'Dave, so do I.' We're going to start out together and do whatever is necessary to make this club a contender."

5) Milwaukee owner Bud Selig has been coordinating the search for a new Commissioner. It's been a frustrating task, with many names being mentioned in the papers, and no one apparently being interested. "This job has been offered to no one," Selig insisted. "No one has withdrawn. There wasn't a scintilla of impatience [over no new Commissioner being named when he reported to the owners this week]." But then he added, "If anyone wants this God-damned job [running the search committee] they can have it. This is a job without precedent. It's a job without any framework of reference. I never believed we'd have this [no Commissioner] 12 months after we started. There was never any way of judging how long we would take. We're just doing it [the search] very well, that's all. There are a lot of logistical problems: the interviewing, all the members of the committee seeing the candidates, the committee members and candidates being busy."

6) K.C. chairman of the board Ewing Kauffman says the

Royals can neither trade nor sign free agents. The free agent class is weak, he says, and the team has little to trade with. George Brett and Frank White, he insists, are untouchables.

The team that puts the lie to the no-trade talk is Oakland. Easily the busiest club here, they've made seven deals since the end of last season and landed a good first baseman (Bruce Bochte) and reliever (Bill Caudill). At the meetings they got reliever Tim Stoddard from the Orioles in exchange for third baseman Wayne Gross. Stoddard pitched better the second half of last season than the first; Gross will platoon at third for the O's. "Our biggest needs were the bullpen and a right-handed hitter," says manager Steve Boros, who is on his way to San Diego to speak with Dodger outfielder Dusty Baker about accepting a trade to Oakland (Baker has the option to refuse one). "Since we've also picked up [pitcher] Ray Burris, we can use a pitcher to get a righthanded hitter [if they don't get Baker]. It just takes a lot of work. We've got a young, aggressive organization that's not afraid to make a decision."

The A's Wally Haas approached the White Sox' Jerry Reinsdorf in the lobby.

"You did all you could do," said Reinsdorf.

"We had to catch up to your pitching," said Haas.

"I think you did," said Reinsdorf.

6) Bobby Brown, a surgeon and former Yankee third baseman, has been appointed the new president of the American League. The press is impressed with his intelligence and candor. "This looks like a very irrational act [switching from surgery to baseball]," Brown says. "I've been in practice 26 years in a tough specialty [cardiology]. You deal with the worst types of catastrophic medical emergencies. I reached the point in my life where I had to decide how much longer I could effectively do this. I felt another five years. I began to make plans as to how I could lighten the load. When this came along, it offered me an unusual opportunity.

"Most doctors don't have the opportunity to move laterally.

december

This accelerated my plans and allowed me to stay in something I'm very interested in. I'm not trying to get into a tension-free atmosphere, because there's no such thing. I'm trying to decrease the life-and-death situations that we run into all the time."

On baseball's problems: "I have to comment as a fan. If you list them, you'd have to look at the economic structure. I'm concerned when most of the teams are losing money [he admits he hasn't seen the books]. Drugs are a problem in every area of society.

"My highest salary as a player? It was $19,500. My present contract? Five years. [Asked about his expertise] I could help somebody if they had a pain in the arm. I certainly know how the game is played. I was president of the Rangers for six months in 1974, and I've been going to 15–30 games a year. I don't think I'm totally ignorant about decision-making."

Now get this: "The designated hitter? As a baseball purist, I'd prefer that they had the original nine guys playing. I always liked it when the pitcher was in the lineup and they had to maneuver the pinch-hitters. But that doesn't mean I'm advocating a disenfranchisement of the DH. Please don't say that."

Handsome, well-dressed, intelligent and forceful, Brown's a notable contrast to the embarrassing sloppiness of so many people in the game. He says he was interviewed twice by Selig's search committee. What I'm asking myself is, Why wasn't he named Commissioner?

Since I was having such a good day, I decided to do something really productive: cut down on sugar, as per Kaat's recommendation. I'm a sugar junkie who needs a fix three times a day. Or so I thought. For dinner all I had was a salad and a beer, and I haven't gone into withdrawal pains.

Henry Hecht, one of the few reasons I read the *New York Post*, said something the other day that deserves mention. "The problem with the designated hitter is much the same as the problem with society. Part of growing up is making decisions. We make lots of them—some are trivial, some are important—but this ties in with the decline of standards and the era of permissiveness. We're getting away with not having to make them. Look at the DH. The manager doesn't have to decide whether to take out the pitcher for a pinch-hitter or leave him in. The general manager doesn't have to decide whether to get rid of the DH. If he had to play in the field, he could bat .300 and hit 30 homers and knock in 90 runs and lose 10 games with his glove: Do you keep him or trade him? And with the DH, a guy can put off quitting because he can't field anymore. I'm sorry, but I don't want a Willie Stargell or a Rusty Staub hanging around as a DH if he can't field. I'd like to see Reggie Jackson play til he's 40 but if he becomes a liability in the field, then someone should be forced to make a decision."

Bob Klapisch, another reason I read the *Post*, is a heavily muscled young baseball writer who pitches in a semipro summer league. "How'd you do this year?" I asked him on the plane back to New York.

"Great," he said. "I made the all-star team."

"What minor league does your league correspond to?"

"Double-A."

"Hell," I said, "you should consider trying out for the majors."

He seemed surprised. "Aren't I a little old at 25?"

"Not at all. Some major league club drafted a 30-year-old pitcher out of the minors."

One of the saddest stories in baseball is that of the talented kid who opts for a career outside of sports, usually at his parents' urging, and never finds out how far he could have gone as an athlete. He spends the rest of his life wondering,

december

living vicariously by throwing batting practice, coaching kids or playing semipro ball. "Things worked out for the best," he'll say, privately doubting himself.

"Go for it," I told Klapisch. "Don't let the dream die."

11　We heard Audrey's friend Howard Rodstein read from his novel last night. It was not unlike *Catcher in the Rye*. I would never have the chutzpah to read aloud something I'd written; you can always tell when the audience doesn't like it. Howard could tell that his audience did.

I've now adopted Kaat's entire diet. I've cut down on sugar, eaten only one dessert in three days and, most important, eaten little. It's a great feeling to wake up with an empty stomach.

We saw "Terms of Endearment" last night. I know the movie's supposed to be great, but I can't think past the cheap shots taken at New York City. When a cashier at a Des Moines checkout counter is rude, someone says, "You must be from New York." Later the young Midwestern mother goes to New York and meets a bunch of career women who seem to have had nothing but bad marriages and abortions. The Midwesterner, meanwhile, spends much of the movie barefoot and pregnant. When I see something like this, it's difficult to appreciate whatever is good about the movie.

12　"It was a good proposal," agent Abel said when I called about the defense book. But then he outlined some vexing problems:

1) People don't pay much attention to defense. How commercial can this be?

2) Four chapters aren't enough.

3) I never really got into the unappreciated aspects of strategy.

4) The idea won't sell without a sample chapter.
He says that I would have to write a book of about 70,000 words. I can feel the project slipping.

If one project doesn't work, go on to another. I spoke again **13** with Rich Huttner at Rodale Press, and he's very interested in the Kaat book. He agreed with my suggestion that we gear it to middle-aged businessmen, and he asked me to send him a sample chapter and outline.

I spent the day working on the Kaat proposal and printing **14** up entries from this diary. I'm now up to October 1. Sometime in the next few weeks I'm going to excerpt 2,000 lines or so of baseball material and give it to Larry for an off-season story.

I spoke with Ira Berkow, who has written half a dozen books. He gave me some useful tips for the proposal. "Touch on all the main points of the book in your sample chapter," he said. "You might start with a dramatic moment—say, his appearance at age 43 in the 1982 World Series. What was a 43-year-old man doing out there? How did he feel pitching in front of millions of people? How did he get in such good condition? Mention the uncommon stuff, like his aversion to running. Make people identify with him. Has he spoken with nutritionists? What about all the times people said he was finished? How has being a maverick thinker affected him? Flesh out his personality."

Kaat called. I told him about my conversations with Dom, **15** Ira and Rich, and we decided to do the outline soon. In fact, next Wednesday the boys and I will spend the night at Kaat's farm outside of Philadelphia. While we're there I'll ask him the final questions for the outline and Matthew will take pictures of him doing his exercises.

22 We spent a splendid day at Kaat's place, which is called Sweetwater Farm. Established in 1734, it sits on 38 acres and consists of five buildings, 19 horses and 30 sheep, not to mention the Kaat family and some tenants. He breeds his harness horses when he isn't playing ball or golf or broadcasting. As he says, keeping busy keeps him young.

Kaat lives on the farm with his charming wife, Linda, and his kids by a previous marriage, Jim Jr., 23, and Jill, 18 (when they aren't away at school). He walked us around the place— a workout in itself—before taping with me and doing his exercises for Matthew's camera. Later we took Jim and Linda to dinner at a country inn and watched "Mad Max" on the VHS.

The Kaats restored the main house without altering its character. I slept in a colonial-style bed cum canopy. They've got all manner of old furniture, a wood-burning stove, a vintage chess board, three Christmas trees and I-don't-know-how-many fireplaces.

23 My experience at Kaat's historic farm has me thinking about baseball history, and specifically about the Hall of Fame. Let's get right down to it: Does Kaat belong there?

No one has ever been elected unanimously, and some voters won't go for Kaat. They'll point out that, while he pitched 25 years in the big leagues, he averaged only 11.32 wins a year. They'll say he allowed more hits than innings pitched (4,620–4,527.2). And they'll scoff at his lifetime earned run average of 3.45.

Happily, a stronger case can be made on behalf of Kaat. Any 300-game winner is a surefire bet to be elected. Kaat won 283 games: close enough. The 11.32 wins-per-season figure is misleading; Kaat only pitched briefly in two early and one late-career seasons, and he was used primarily as a reliever in his final five years. During the 18 seasons when he started regularly, he averaged a solid 14.4 wins a year. And let's hear it for longevity: The guy pitched an unmatched 25 years over four decades. His hits-per-inning and ERA figures are high because he insisted on throwing strikes, a practice much in vogue of late. Kaat averaged fewer than one walk every four innings. And he won an unprecedented 16 Gold Gloves for his fielding. In short, he was a modern pitching coach's dream.

Justly or not, players also are elected to the Hall for reasons other than their statistics.* Johnny Evers, Joe Tinker and Frank Chance were elected in part because they belonged to a storied double-play combination. Rabbit Maranville's name didn't hurt him. Jackie Robinson was elected more justifiably as the first black player and one of the three greatest heroes in baseball history.** Statistics can only tell so much about a player. They don't tell about his character or competitiveness,

*Herewith a plea on behalf of two players whose stats will never enshrine them: Curt Flood and Jim Bouton. Flood, a Cardinal outfielder of near-Hall statistical stature, issued the courageous and historic challenge to the reserve clause that presaged the modern economic and legal order. Bouton, a pitcher who neither won nor lost 100 games, wrote the autobiographical *Ball Four* that forever changed the way baseball would be perceived and covered. His book was also a stirring defense of the game because he found that he loved baseball in spite of its abuses.

**The other two, in my opinion, were Babe Ruth and Joe DiMaggio. Di-Mag is the weakest of these choices, and I will happily entertain arguments for Hank Aaron, Lou Gehrig, Ted Williams and others. But while I'm on the subject, I should point out that a revisionist argument could be made for enshrining Jackie Robinson on the basis of his playing ability alone. Though he wasn't promoted to the majors until age 28, he had a .311 lifetime average. He played three different infield positions for a season or more and was primarily an outfielder in two others. And as any old-timer will tell you, Robinson was arguably the most exciting baserunner in baseball history— one who could steal home, escape from a rundown or advance from first to third on a bunt.

and they don't tell much at all about his defensive skill. Errors and fielding percentage? A good fielder will reach more balls than a poor fielder, and as a result may commit more errors. Assists? Often a terrible measure of an outfielder's ability because runners are more likely to try for the extra base against a weak fielder than a good one. Total chances are a fairly good statistic, but pitchers, infield surfaces and overall team skill can unduly affect them. Total Gold Gloves may go to players like Kaat who deserve them, but may also go to players with reputations, rather than fielders who have just had good years. Overall, fielding stats aren't very catchy. That's why the positions that are the most demanding or physically punishing—third base (7), catcher (8), second base (8) and shortstop (12)—have the fewest players in the Hall. It's necessary to watch a player day-in, day-out to truly understand his defensive skill.

As luck has it, Kaat's case improves further still with his nonstatistical accomplishments. He helped to revolutionize baseball thinking by challenging the assumption that pitchers should rest their arms between starts: They throw a lot more on off days now. In fact, Kaat's whole training regimen is exemplary (Kaplan said impartially). Kaat was a great clutch pitcher, a great team man and your basic "great guy in the clubhouse." He's also a fine person and interview—two factors that shouldn't affect the voting but routinely do.

I went on thinking for some time about Jim Kaat and the Hall. Baseball's hitting and pitching statistics, at least, are meaningful and catchy enough (20 wins, a .300 average, 30 homers, 100 runs batted in) to provide a standard of excellence that spans generations. And the Hall represents not only tradition but continuity. As I picture Boston's Jim Rice, I look right through him and see his famous predecessor in left field, Carl Yastrzemski. As I picture Yaz, I look right through *him* and see Ted Williams (one does not look through Jack Kennedy and see Abe Lincoln). In other sports the action is

december

too fast or the players too anonymous or the statistics too meaningless to permit such reflection. Ah, but baseball. The positions and players and teams and eras and accomplishments stood alone the day we visited Cooperstown, outlined against the blue-gray October sky (sock it to 'em, Grantland baby). Yet they're also woven into the wonderful fabric of baseball. These thoughts will carry me right through the hot-stove league.

Merry Christmas! Audrey gave me a traveling alarm clock, **25** a Brooklyn Bridge monogramed money clip, a terrycloth robe, a fingernail brush and face cloth, and a multitude of socks. Her brother Jim gave me David Halberstam's basketball book and a scarf. Her parents gave me a box of 15 golf balls. And the boys gave me a kitchen clock.

For once I gave as good as I got: digital traveling alarm clocks that play Mozart, dop kits with school colors and books to each of the boys; a membership in a health club to Benjamin and a flash attachment to Matthew; another slew of presents to Matthew, who turned 14 yesterday; Kareem's autobiography to Jim McGinn; Persian plates, a robe, room freshener, a wallet and eight tall glasses to Audrey.

We were speaking with Mel Bourne, a movie production designer, at a Christmas party. Last summer he was doing the sets for a movie based on Bernard Malamud's *The Natural*. In order to locate a stadium that was in use in 1939, they had to go to Buffalo. "We used California production people" said Mel. "It took twice as long to do as it would have in New York."

What they were trying to do was recreate baseball as it existed in 1939—complete with old uniforms, coaches' and batters' boxes, and that extinct path between the mound and the plate. As bad as the West Coast people were, Mel was

december

nevertheless glad to be recreating baseball when it still had "dignity," as he put it. That word stuck with me: dignity. I guess that's what I've been harping on all year. Baseball may have more teams and crowds and money than ever before, but it also has unprecedented hucksterism. The dignity is endangered.

28   I decided to take People's Express to Boston because the fare is $20 less each way than on the shuttle. I made a terrible mistake. First, the cab ride to Newark cost $40, or precisely $20 more than to LaGuardia. Then they jacked up the ticket price $6 when I checked two bags, including one full of presents that had to be marked FRAGILE. Furthermore, I had to wait an extra hour for takeoff and walk an extra half-mile or so just to reach the gate. Some things money can't buy.

The boys had flown up to Boston yesterday. When I arrived they were in my parents' living room with my parents, my sister, Nancy Mansbach, and her children Adam, 7, and David, 4. Nancy's husband Charlie arrived later. I had presents for everyone and Nancy gave me some kitchen implements. Later my friend Ed Droge, the new admissions director at the Cambridge School of Weston, came over. The two of us eventually headed over to Peg and Roy Lamson's for a cocktail party. The Lamsons, old friends of my parents, live in an apartment on Memorial Drive that was built for retired people, and retirees were at the party in force. They all looked great. Even my pediatrician, Dorothea Moore, who must be close to 90. Just as Jim Kaat says: Age is an arbitrary limitation others place on you; it need not mean so much.

29   My mother examined this journal for several hours. "I've never learned so much about you," she said. It's true. I'm usually very private and very closed. Indeed, not even on

december

these pages have I disclosed some of my worst worries and fears, mainly because they involve other people who would be embarrassed. But I did open the door a crack. More than anything, I'm amazed at how insecure I am. Each time a story is killed, I react as if the editors were saying, "We knew it all along—you're no good." Plainly, the magazine is my security blanket. Just as plainly, security must come from within.

I asked Mom to consider the possibility of the magazine publishing some of the journal's baseball entries. After much thought, she isolated some themes: the players talking about baseball, the commercialization of the game, how baseball has changed over the years. I'm inclined simply to go with a bunch of off-the-field items, which are basically what I've been recording anyway. Nonetheless, her suggestion was useful. I sat down and reviewed some of the themes that have come up:

• Commercialization. Baseball is *not* a business; it's a game that has been abducted by businessmen. I once told Bowie Kuhn that commercializing baseball was analogous to plastering advertisements all over St. Patrick's Cathedral. I don't think he understood. Dammit, Bowie, baseball is a secular religion, and it's being defiled. Those of us who attend games to worship at the altar of the sacrifice bunt and the stolen base and the blessed ambience of the ballpark are being distracted by pagan music and mascots and messages. The game is losing its soul.

• The players. Sure, many of them are spoiled and money-conscious, self-centered and insecure, poorly prepared for life after baseball. Yet in speaking with ballplayers, I've come to believe that they're the best hope for the game. They love to play and they love to win, and by and large, they act in the game's best interests. I wish I could say the same about the owners.

• Defense. Quite simply, the most fascinating aspect of the game—and the least appreciated. I hope I've opened a few eyes.

• The pine-tar incident. More than anything, I think it's alerted people to the humor, variety and complexity of baseball. Just re-

december

cently I learned that the Cardozo Law Review will run two or three articles on the pine-tar incident in its issue that comes out in March. The pieces will touch upon many legal subjects including free speech; rules interpretation; the spirit vs. the letter of the law; commercial law; sports and the law; the appellate system; and statutory vs. common law. "For anyone interested in a legal career," says my father, "this could be the place to start."

• Baseball as a way of life. I won't go as far as Paul Owens: I'm not a 24-hour-a-day baseball man, but I could easily spend 16 hours a day on it. My bias aside, baseball has become a respectable profession. In the old days the game may have been more pristine, but it was also considered less desirable. The players received neither the money nor the status they deserved. If modern baseball has too much clash and commercialization, it also has infinite respect. Inevitably, that respect extends to those of us on the game's periphery. Despite my occasional discomfort at being something of a public figure, I can revel in my profession. There are no Rodney Dangerfields in baseball.

30 While in Boston I had dinner with an old friend, Charlie Wyzanski. He and his Turkish wife, Nilgün Gökgür, have just had a baby girl, Talya. An attorney, Charlie works for the Middlesex County D.A. and teaches a course in legal writing. "My job's completely different from yours," he says. "I have to be at my office every day, and I'm always busy."

31 Well, what did 1983 mean to me? As I review my New Year's Resolutions, I realize I haven't succeeded in every respect. I didn't read enough or become significantly more relaxed. I did begin to get in shape, thanks to Jim Kaat; I haven't cranked or cramped or seen a specialist in some time. I learned to change directions on assignments without being asked: Witness the Pete Rose and Jose Cruz stories. Though I didn't receive enough big assignments and suffered a painful fallow stretch, I did achieve my annual goal of 20 by-lines and wrote three of my best stories ever (Brooklyn Bridge, Nolan Ryan, Cardinal defense). I found by year's end that I didn't need compliments as much: I can survive without that verbal bag of oats. I better appreciate my role with *Sports Illustrated.* I saw a lot of the kids, and all the time I was worrying about getting a book contract, I did write a book: this.

Europe and Toronto were great trips. I felt less comfortable than ever with American commercialism—God knows, I've babbled about that—but I love this country's freedom and energy more than ever, too. The best movie I saw was "Diva." The best books I read were *Growing Up, The Color Purple* and *Dinner at the Homesick Restaurant.* I shot a 38 for nine holes in golf (how did I leave this out of the journal?) and I'm playing paddle tennis well enough to consider returning to tournaments.

There's much unfinished business. The Bryn Mawr and Commissioner stories are sitting on an editor's desk somewhere. I realize the importance of friends: I need more. As I review the journal, I perceive that one of my prime problems is being preachy. I'd better watch that tendency; people who scold usually aren't happy with themselves.

The highlight of the year was unquestionably keeping this diary. It's been a great place to record odd thoughts and events that otherwise would have been lost to memory. Surprisingly few modern Pepyses have kept diaries: I recommend the practice to one and all. Whatever 1983 lacked, I experienced the year more vividly than any other simply by writing things down. Turmoil? Confusion? Worry? At least I know I was alive.